FOR

H. S. M.
M. E. M.
H. P. M.

# Matthew Flinders

*Captain Matthew Flinders, R.N.*

JAMES D. MACK

# Matthew Flinders

1774 – 1814

NELSON

1966

THOMAS NELSON (AUSTRALIA) LIMITED
597 Little Collins Street, Melbourne, C1

THOMAS NELSON AND SONS LTD
Parkside Works Edinburgh
36 Park Street, London W1

THOMAS NELSON AND SONS (AFRICA) (PTY) LTD
P.O. Box 9881 Johannesburg

THOMAS NELSON AND SONS (CANADA) LTD
81 Curlew Drive, Don Mills, Ontario

THOMAS NELSON AND SONS
Copewood and Davis Streets, Camden, N.J.

———

First published 1966
© James D. Mack 1966

Registered in Australia for transmission by post as a book
Printed at The Griffin Press, Adelaide

# Preface

A century and a half has passed since the death of Matthew Flinders in 1814. Quite apart from his published narrative, *A Voyage to Terra Australis*, there exists a fairly substantial documentary corpus available to his biographer. Family letters, logbooks of ships, records of Admiralty administration, perhaps two thousand documents in all, have survived the years. Careful work by archivists around the world, a just pride in ancestry in Flinders's descendants, and a vast amount of good fortune have combined to preserve these papers for posterity. With the present volume modern studies have now appeared on Cook and his three principal followers, Bligh, Vancouver, and Flinders. None of them would have been written or even possible without the same happy circumstances.

To a large extent Flinders's misfortunes and early death have been allowed to overshadow his record as scientist. His personality has often failed to come through. And too frequently he has been lifted out of the context of his times. His career has evoked sympathy and regret, but to date little more. The result has been an undeserved obscurity. But the question arises : Why ? For few if any men have been remembered in so many place-names on the map of the earth as he.

To begin with, Flinders made his career in Australia; and Australia, however closely allied culturally with Britain (and the United States), is still a far-away land. Only with the advent of telecommunications and jet aircraft has she begun to takē her rightful place. Again, with her relatively small population, Australia could not be expected to produce the sheer numbers of historians necessary to a thorough, systematic study of her past.

But the practice of surveying *per se* is not particularly dramatic. It lacks both the excitement of battle, and the adventure of discovery. It can, in fact, be downright monotonous, although in the present case it was not. Just here another difficulty arises. Not since Queen Elizabeth's 'men of Devon' rode the seas had England produced a naval figure of the very first rank. Then, within the space of two generations she produced two, James Cook and Horatio Nelson. Thus the biographer of Flinders quickly realises that invidious comparisons will be made, and that there is nothing he can do about them. In Flinders's chosen profession Cook was, and still is, the model. He is *sui generis*. And in the public esteem even Cook himself is overtopped by the memory of Nelson.

Finally, it must in good conscience be pointed out that Flinders's mission failed. Whatever the reasons, and there were several sufficient ones, he did not complete the task he had been set. As a result he is not an object of instant, unequivocal admiration.

In order to put the reader on his guard, an author is morally bound to disclose whatever bias he is aware of in the subject at hand. His views may then be fairly discounted to whatever extent seems necessary. Apart from a love of the sea common to most men, I will confess to two predilections. First, I admire the breed of men who, in the name of the British Crown, flung their hats into the air and conquered the world. There is little doubt today that this affinity is *déclassé*—but then so is their *joie de vivre*. Second, I am for the disinterested scholar wherever I find him; and Flinders was one of these. I happen to enjoy the lucidity and precision of a mind like his.

If I have made a contribution here, it lies, I feel, in the fundamental approach I have consciously introduced in presenting the voyage as a case-study in government-sponsored scientific research. With all the defects of its virtues, the Flinders case remains a classic of its kind. I trust the concept does not obscure the human drama.

I have been greatly blessed by the number of people who have shown an interest in this book. No author can ever name all who have helped him. On the other hand, no author has a right to neglect his friends :

A handsome grant from the American Philosophical Society enabled me to go to London in 1960 to gather materials. I owe a special debt to the several directors of the Institute of Research of Lehigh University, for continuing financial support of my work. Among those who have given permission to publish manuscripts in their archives I must express my thanks to the

Keeper of the Public Records (London); to the Royal Society
of London; to the Trustees of the Mitchell Library (Sydney);
to the National Maritime Museum, and especially to Miss A. F.
Petrie and J. F. Petrie, Esq., owners of sixteen Banks letters
on deposit there. Other libraries have generously permitted me
to use their collections: The British Museum; the British
Museum (Natural History) (South Kensington); the India
Office; the Hydrographic Office (London); the British Admiralty (London); the Royal Commonwealth Society (London);
the State Library of Victoria (Melbourne); the Library of
Congress; the New York Public Library; and the Sutro Library
(California). The staff of the Lehigh University Library have
been both patient and helpful. Two in particular have assisted
me far above and beyond the call of duty: my Secretary, Mrs
Paul J. Abel, who typed the manuscript, and Mrs Glenn M.
Flannery, Assistant Librarian, who provided the index.

William Westall, A.R.A., accompanied Flinders on board
the *Investigator* as 'landscape and figure painter.' Much of the
work of this gifted artist now belongs to the Royal Commonwealth Society. In 1962 a beautiful volume, *Drawings by
William Westall*, appeared over the Society's imprimatur. By
its quality and authenticity it has truly become a landmark in
the historiography of Australia. I am therefore deeply grate-
ful to the Council for permission to reproduce a number of
illustrations from this brilliant collection.

Others who gave help and wished me well include: Bern
Anderson, Rear-Admiral, U.S.N. (Ret.); Mr N. Atherton,
Hydrographic Office (London); Professor J. C. Beaglehole;
Mr Harold Moore Cooper, South Australian Museum (Ade-
laide); Dr Joseph N. Corriere, M.D.; Mr Warren R. Dawson,
Editor of the Banks Correspondence; Sir Gavin de Beer,
Science Editor of Thomas Nelson and Sons; Professor Maurice
Ewing, of the Lamont Geological Observatory; Miss Susanna
Fisher, National Maritime Museum; Professor L. H. Gipson;
Mr and Mrs R. B. Honeyman; Miss Phyllis Mander Jones; Mr
I. Kaye, Royal Society of London; Commander P. K. Kemp, R.N.,
Admiralty Library (London); Mrs Jere B. Knight; Mr W. S.
Mack, M.B., F.R.C.S., Edinburgh; Miss Mavis Mackinnon;
Mr Frank Maggs; Professor C. Northcote Parkinson; Mr A.

W. H. Pearsall, National Maritime Museum; Dr Vernon D. Tate, U.S. Naval Academy; Mr E. K. Timings, Public Record Office (London); and Lieut.-Commander David W. Waters, National Maritime Museum.

Finally, I should be ungrateful if I failed to thank my family for protecting the time I needed to write this book.

JAMES D. MACK

*7 October 1963*

# Contents

# List of Illustrations

*Captain Matthew Flinders, R.N.*

# Maps

# Abbreviations

Repositories whose documents have been cited in references are indicated by the following abbreviations, and include:

| | |
|---|---|
| B.M. | British Museum |
| B.M. (N.H.) | British Museum (Natural History), South Kensington |
| I.O. | India Office (Commonwealth Relations Office), London |
| M.L. | Mitchell Library, Sydney |
| N.M.M. | National Maritime Museum, Greenwich |
| P.R.O. | Public Record Office, London* |
| S.L.V. | State Library of Victoria, Melbourne |

* Unpublished Crown Copyright material in the Public Record Office, London, has been reproduced by permission of the Controller of H.M. Stationery Office.

# PART I

# The Early Years

## 1774-1800

# CHAPTER ONE

# The Great Wide World

## 1774-1795

1

On 31 March 1774 the British Parliament closed down the port of Boston, Massachusetts. The Boston Port Bill has long been recognised as one of the injudicious acts of ministerial pique whose principal consequence was that it helped to precipitate the American Revolution. Almost exactly forty years later, on 11 April 1814, Napoleon Bonaparte signed his deed of abdication and retired to Elba. Across the four decades separating these two events, Europe lay wracked by a series of convulsions which, as they rolled round the world, altered decisively the social, economic, and political structure of civilisation.

It so happens that these same two events, forty years apart, measure almost precisely the life span of Matthew Flinders, Captain in the Royal Navy, and circumnavigator of Australia. Moreover, the vast drama in which they occurred quite literally dictated the course of his career. In the birth of the United States of America the First British Empire collapsed, to be succeeded by the Second, of which the Australian penal colony became a significant part. In France the established monarchy gave way to a revisionist rabble, who were in due course peremptorily set aside by the Corsican adventurer. In later years it was one of Napoleon's generals who brought about the ruin of Matthew Flinders.

Into these troubled times, then, Matthew Flinders was born at Donington, in Lincolnshire, on 16 March 1774, the fourteenth year of the reign of His Majesty George III.

Lincolnshire lies on the east coast of England, facing the North Sea. It is drained by the Humber, and at its southern end is

3                                                                 2

deeply indented by The Wash, a long bay whose shore begins where the clearing of the fens for new farmlands had left off in the seventeenth century. Although Flinders became a sailor, except for Sir John Franklin the county has never had a great reputation for the breed, that distinction having been left to Devon and Cornwall, where young boys could watch the sun drop into the Atlantic off Land's End. Rather the men of Lincolnshire usually turned to agriculture for a livelihood, their principal business being in wheat and barley. The town of Donington, since passed by, is about ten miles south-west of Boston, and ten miles from The Wash. At the turn of the nineteenth century, its population stood just above 1,300. There Matthew's father, also Matthew, surgeon-apothecary, served the local inhabitants and the families of the surrounding farms. He was evidently a sober, intelligent man, able, after raising his family, to leave an estate of both land and securities appraised at upwards of £6,000.

Matthew, the navigator—to distinguish him from his father —was the eldest of seven children. He, his sisters Elizabeth and Susanna, and his brother Samuel, were born to their father's first wife. There were also two half-sisters, Hannah and Henrietta. Besides these six, there was a third boy, called in the father's Will, 'my unfortunate son, John,' who was presumably the victim of a congenital mental defect. Of him nothing further is known.

Apart from the occurrence of his mother's death, Matthew's childhood appears to have been quite happy and normal: no serious illness, no neurotic behaviour, not even a scrape of consequence. Even as a boy, he had a stern appearance. His dark, piercing eyes, thin lips, and aquiline nose forecast a serious, thoughtful man. And if his stature was below the average—as an adult he stood only five feet six—he carried himself easily, lightly.

His formal education, providing him with Greek, Latin, and mathematics, continued to his fifteenth year. No evidence of his standing in school has survived, but we may suppose at the very least that he was an average pupil. Judging by both his later ability as a navigator and his skill at writing solid prose, he was probably bright enough to please any teacher. However that may be, by the time the boy finished his schooling his father had reason to hope he would follow him into the practice of medicine. As the eldest son, Matthew would have taken his father's place at Donington. At least he might have begun there. But these parental hopes were soon upset, and in a most unexpected way.

It seems that around his fifteenth birthday, young Matthew came across a copy of Defoe's *Robinson Crusoe*. That he devoured it would not in itself have been thought unusual, or even bookish. *Crusoe* had been a best-seller since the day it was published in 1719. What was unusual was his reaction to it, for he forthwith flatly determined upon a naval career. Quite naturally his father opposed him. Whether there was a scene does not really matter; but most likely the boy was admonished to get over these romantic notions and begin thinking seriously about his medical studies. But Matthew would not be put off. Later in life he acknowledged that he had been 'induced to go to sea against the wish of friends, from reading *Robinson Crusoe*.'[1] He talked the question over with his Uncle John, his father's brother, whose career as a lieutenant in the navy was not exactly flourishing. After due warning and perhaps an avuncular pat on the head, John advised his nephew to do some further reading. As an antidote to romance he recommended Euclid, Robertson's *Navigation*, and John Hamilton Moore's *Practical Navigator*.[2] He may have thought, or even hoped, such a regimen would discourage the boy. Not so. Matthew set to work by himself, and ploughed through the three treatises within a year. Perhaps he did get rid of some of the romance, but instead of giving up, he found himself stimulated by the mathematics, particularly as it applied to navigation.

Perhaps his daydreams, certainly his interest in navigation as a science, led him to hope that he might someday become an officer in His Majesty's navy. Clearly he had more stuff, as well as more ambition, than a rating needed. But according to the custom of the time, the only entrée to the navy open to an

[1] *Naval Chronicle*, vol. xxxii (1814), p. 178.

[2] Ernest Scott, *The Life of Captain Matthew Flinders, R.N.* (Sydney, 1914), p. 16. This is the first full-length biography of Matthew Flinders ever published. It emphasises the role of the French in Flinders's career, but must be used with caution. Professor Scott presents further details of Flinders's background and early life. Hereafter cited as Scott, *Life*.

ambitious boy lay in the sponsorship of a ranking commander, preferably a Captain. This system of recruitment, known as the 'interest', was a form of patronage the proper use of which could easily place even a child upon the quarterdeck, and on his way to a flag. Without a helping hand, however, little if anything could be expected beyond the onerous life of the forecastle.[3]

By good fortune, a cousin of the Flinders's was serving at the time as a governess in the household of Captain (later Vice-Admiral Sir Thomas) Pasley, then commanding H.M.S. *Scipio*. The cousin agreed to arrange an interview between Matthew and the Captain, with the happy result that on 23 October 1789 Flinders entered upon his naval career as a 'lieutenant's servant' in H.M.S. *Alert*. There he received his first indoctrination into navy life. Some six months later, when Pasley learned he was to take command of the *Bellerophon* (74) he called the boy from the *Alert* into the *Scipio* as an A.B. Three days later he took him along into the *Bellerophon*, and the following day Matthew was entered upon the books as a midshipman, a billet on the quarter-deck where Pasley could keep a watchful eye on him. There Flinders spent about eight months, largely cruising in the Narrow Seas. Then Pasley sent him on his way. On 14 April Flinders transferred into a vessel called the *Dictator*. It may be that the *Bellerophon* was going to sea, and his next ship was not yet ready to receive him. Then, on 8 May he carried his gear into the *Providence*, at that time fitting out for a South Sea voyage.

2

Following the miscarriage of the *Bounty's* mission, William Bligh had quickly acquitted himself of all responsibility for her loss, and received command of the *Providence*. Once again, at the behest of Sir Joseph Banks, President of the Royal Society, he had orders to transfer a quantity of breadfruit trees from Tahiti to Jamaica. In addition Bligh was instructed to examine the best way by which ships might in future pass through Torres Strait, separating New Holland from New Guinea.

[3] For a discussion of this system, see Michael Lewis, *A Social History of the Navy 1793–1815* (London, 1960), chap. 6.

A letter from Captain Pasley to Matthew, written not long after the boy had left the *Bellerophon*, reveals the intimate relationship that had grown up between patron and protégé :

*Bellerophon* Spithead June 3, 1791

'Dear Flinders

I am favoured with your letter on your return from visiting your friends in the Country and I am pleased to hear that you are so well satisfied with your situation on board the Providence. I have little doubt of your gaining the good opinion of Capt. Bligh if you are equally attentive to your duty there as you were in the Bellerophon. All that I have to request in return for the good offices I have done you, is, that you never fail writing me by all possible opportunitys during your Voyage, and that in your letters you will be very particular and circumstantial in regard to every thing, and place you may chance to see, or Visit, with your own observations thereon. Do this my young friend, and you rest assured that my good offices will not be wanting some future day for your advancement. All on board are well. Present my kind remembrances to Captain and Mrs Bligh and believe me

Yours very sincerely Thos. Pasley.'[4]

It would appear that, having satisfied himself as to the boy's competence as well as to his interest in voyaging, the benevolent Pasley had personally recommended Flinders to his acquaintance, William Bligh.

With the two botanists, Christopher Smith and James Wiles, on board, the *Providence* sailed from Deptford on 3 August 1791 in company with *Assistant*, Nathaniel Portlock. As the ships crossed the tropics on the way to the Cape of Good Hope, Flinders felt for the first time that 'inaccessible serenity of the sky' which in later years would be so familiar to him. But such were the dreams of the off-watch hours. Bligh had more serious matters for the young midshipman to attend to. After confidence had been established, Bligh gave over some of the chartwork and the care of the chronometers to the lad. (And God help anyone who permitted the timekeepers to run down!)

[4] N.M.M. 60/017. FLI/1.

Following a two months' stay at the Cape, the *Providence* sailed directly for Van Diemen's Land (modern Tasmania) where wood and water were taken on board, and where Bligh did some surveying. It was there that Flinders constructed his first chart of a new land.[5]

After rounding South Island, New Zealand, Bligh set a north-easterly course for Tahiti. Some six weeks later, after an uneventful passage, he arrived at Matavai Bay, and the botanists began the work of collecting and potting the breadfruit trees. At the end of three months, and after considerable experience in the ways of Tahitian natives, the voyagers departed on a westward course for Torres Strait that took them past the Tonga Islands, and on through the Fijis, which Bligh had visited three years before. The two main objects of the voyage lay ahead, and no time could be lost delivering the plants to Jamaica.

Years later, with Bligh's sanction, Flinders published his account of the investigations in Torres Strait.[6] The reefs were entered on 31 August 1792. Each day brought some forward progress with either the *Assistant* or a ship's boat leading the way. On several occasions Smith and Wiles went ashore to botanise, but the unfriendly attitude of natives discouraged their diversions. Indeed, it was here that Flinders first saw the wisdom of caution in dealing with the aborigines of New South Wales, for in one skirmish, when arrows and musket balls flew, a member of the *Assistant's* crew died of his wounds.

On 16 September Bligh took possession of the islands in the western approach to the strait, calling them the Clarence Archipelago, after William, third son of George III. As if to provide a climax to the passage, Flinders wrote that during the last night at anchor in the strait, the wind blowing a fresh gale, and with a tide of between four and five knots, the vessels were 'so closely surrounded with rocks and reefs as scarcely to have swinging room.' Small wonder the captain called this 'Bligh's Farewell'.

Curiously, Flinders made no allusion in his account to the

---

[5] Reproduced in George Mackaness, *The Life of Vice-Admiral William Bligh* (London, 1951).

[6] Matthew Flinders, *A Voyage to Terra Australis* . . . (2 vols., atlas, London, 1814), vol. 1, p. xix sqq. Hereafter cited as Flinders, *Voyage*.

shortage of drinking water; but between New Guinea and Jamaica he and his companions are known to have suffered acutely from thirst. Whether or not this contributed to his later kidney disease is past knowing, but it is recorded that he was occasionally reduced to licking the drops of water that fell from the cans used to freshen the breadfruit.[7]

Flinders ended his description of the strait with the following paragraph:

'Thus was accomplished in nineteen days, the passage from the Pacific, or Great Ocean, to the Indian Sea; without other misfortune than what arose from the attack of the natives, and some damage done to the cables and anchors. Perhaps no space of $3\frac{1}{2}°$ in length, presents more dangers than Torres Strait; but, with caution and perseverance, the captains Bligh and Portlock proved them to be surmountable; and within a reasonable time.'[8]

By the time he wrote this, he himself had negotiated these waters and knew what he was talking about.

A short stay at Kupang, Timor, another at St Helena, and the mission was accomplished. While the ships lay at Jamaica, however, France declared war on England, and it was four months before they could be permitted to leave, their presence being thought necessary to local defence.

For some unknown reason, although it was not unheard of, Flinders was dropped back on 2 April to A.B., and remained at that rating until he was discharged from Bligh's command.

At last, on 15 June, the *Providence* left the West Indies, and arrived back at Deptford on 7 August 1793.

Considering Bligh's career as a whole, both as naval officer and as Governor of New South Wales, during all of which he was involved in three mutinies, the question of the relationship between the captain of the *Providence* and midshipman Flinders naturally arises. If, as has been alleged, Bligh was 'notorious for a foul mouth,' and a 'nagger . . . with the immense power of a navy captain,'[9] one can scarcely believe that young Matthew

---

[7] S.L.V., 'Flinders Papers'.
[8] Flinders, *Voyage*, vol. I, p. xxix.
[9] David Hannay, *Ships and Men* (Edinburgh, 1910), p. 170.

would take kindly to him as a person. However that may be—
and the midshipman may indeed have had a difficult time of it—
he was then hardly in a position to make his feelings known.
Later, however, Flinders felt strongly that he and Bligh neither
would nor could ever get on together. In a letter to Banks,
dated 8 December 1806 from the Île de France, Flinders
remarked on Bligh's 'prepossession' against him, and expressed
the hope that he would in future 'not be placed under his
immediate orders since the credit, if any [which] should be due
to my labours, would be in danger of being monopolised.'[10]
Again, in another letter to Banks, 1 July 1807, Flinders alluded
to Bligh's 'considering me with an unfavourable eye.'[11] What
reason lay behind these reflections we do not know. They were
probably real enough. But later on Bligh went out of his way to
be obliging and attentive to Flinders. Thus, in 1812, when
Flinders had a reputation, Bligh introduced him to the Duke of
Clarence, and seemed, as Flinders thought, 'proud to have had
me for his disciple in surveying and nautical astronomy.' Bligh
was not always wrong.

What, then, did Flinders gain from these months in the
*Providence*? On the side of hard experience, he must have learned
that reading a treatise on navigation was not at all the same
thing as handling a heavy brass sextant on a rolling deck. He
discovered, too, that making a track through mazes of coral
reefs, as Bligh had done, required a kind of nerve that he would
have somehow to find within himself. Aesthetically, he came to
know all the delicious sensations one feels with seeing the Southern Cross by night, and the garish loveliness of the tropical seas
by day. Adding colour, these experiences became an indispensable part of the life he had begun to live for.


3


One of the very first things Flinders did when the *Providence*
anchored in the Downs the day before she entered Deptford was

---

[10] *Historical Records of New South Wales*, vol. VI, p. 207. Hereafter cited as
*H.R.N.S.W.*
[11] *Ibid.*, p. 274.

to write to Captain Pasley. The captain replied by return post from Plymouth :

'Dear Flinders,

I am favoured with your very acceptable letter from the Downs, and I believe all yours from the different places you wrote me . . . I do not know what are your plans now you are returned back to England. I expect to sail in a day or two to join my Lord Howe on board the Bellerophon. I shall receive you with pleasure after so long an absence. You will no doubt wish to see your friends [and] pay them a short visit, and return to join me, by that time I shall possibly be returned into Port. If not you will easily find a conveyance from Portsmouth or Plymouth by applying to the respective Admirals. They are both my friends. . . .'[12]

Presumably Flinders did go on leave, for it was not until 6 September that he was paid off. The following day he was entered once again on the books of the *Bellerophon*, still as an A.B. Some weeks later he was reinstated as midshipman, and served with Pasley for upwards of ten months.

It was during his second tour in the *Bellerophon* that Flinders took part in the only major naval action of his career, Earl Howe's 'Glorious First of June,' 1794, some 400 miles off Ushant. Pasley, now a Rear-Admiral, with his flag in the *Bellerophon*, led a light squadron intended to bring the French to battle. In the hot fighting that ensued, Flinders, then serving as Pasley's aide-de-camp, is said to have 'had a shot' at the French, quite against the Admiral's orders.[13] But whatever portion of wrath he incurred for his impetuosity was short-lived. A few moments later Pasley lost a leg.

After the battle the Admiral never went to sea again. Although he was advanced to Vice-Admiral of the Blue, and held

[12] Pasley to Flinders, 7 August 1793. N.M.M. 60/017. FLI/1. Pasley then adds a sentence : 'Your Capt. will meet a very hard reception—he has Dam'd himself.' In his biography of Bligh, Professor Mackaness says that the reception was indeed 'cool'. Pitt is known to have refused to see him. However competent professionally he may have been—and he was very competent—Bligh seems all his life to have been trouble-prone.

[13] Scott, *Life*, p. 45.

several shore commands after his recovery, his power in the navy had now passed its peak. Flinders had good reason for gratitude to Pasley; but how deeply he felt this loss we do not know.

He remained two more months in the *Bellerophon*, and then, suddenly, his life took a decisive turn.

Captain Cook's career, ended by his death in 1779, had brought the exploration of the southern hemisphere to a close. Man had at last learned the sum of the lands he could conquer, claim, or settle. The Dutch had discovered and charted the western parts of New Holland early in the seventeenth century. Thus, when in 1770 Cook had come upon, charted, and claimed its eastern coasts for the British Crown, only cartographic detail remained. But for eighteen years thereafter, no one had revisited it—no one, that is, but the Macassans who came yearly to fetch trepang for the bazaars of China. The French had no interest there; the Dutch lay powerless; and George III was too busy frittering away his American empire.

Anticipating the worst possible consequences of the American war, as early as 1779 Lord North's ministers had inquired into the transportation of convicts, the 'lower orders of society'. The problem was simply where to send these wretches in the event that the colony of Georgia might be lost. Sir Joseph Banks, who had sailed with Cook in the *Endeavour*, testified at these hearings in favour of Botany Bay as a suitable alternative. He had cited his reasons. First was its remoteness from home; 13,000 miles is a good long way for convicts. Second, he recommended the fertility of its soil, which would argue for self-sufficiency. And third, he bespoke its salubrious climate. Actually Banks, having been there for only a short time in the autumn, knew very little about the place; but even that little was more than anyone else either knew, or apparently cared to know. With the surrender of Cornwallis at Yorktown in 1781, a solution to the problem became stark necessity. The hulks in the Thames were nothing but cesspools, rotting ships and rotting men dying together.

Even so, it was not until 1786 that Lord Sydney, the Home Secretary, actually fixed upon Botany Bay.[14] In 1787 the First Fleet sailed for New South Wales, carrying Arthur Phillip, the

[14] Thomas Townshend, first Viscount Sydney. *H.R.N.S.W.*, vol. i, pt. 2, p. 14 sqq.

first Governor, to his post. With him went the first consignment of convicts, and the New South Wales Corps, sent along to enforce what order they might.

It is critical to all that follows here to understand that Sydney had acted apparently on no stronger evidence than 'the accounts given by the late Captain Cook,' and the 'representations of persons who had accompanied him. . . .' The cartographic detail that remained was not insignificant.

Moreover, in view of the risks to which Sydney was exposing the colony, albeit with good intentions, the only possible hope for the settlers lay in the maintenance of a lifeline from home, that is to say, in the employment of sea-power as an instrument of imperial policy.

As he left for his post, the position of Arthur Phillip was unenviable to say the least. The early history of the colony is a story of degradation almost beyond belief. Here was a mass of 750 outcasts, policed by a soldiery as rapacious as any then living, ruled over by a naval captain, and expected to scrape a livelihood from a soil whose productive qualities had scarcely been guessed at. Furthermore, a ruinous inflation at home nearly strangled the infant colony. Small wonder that after nearly six years Phillip, worn out by his exertions, should have wished to return home.

Exactly when Captain John Hunter, then serving in Howe's flagship, *Queen Charlotte*, heard of Phillip's resignation and return is not clear. It is also not clear whether Hunter actually volunteered his services for the post. Nor does it matter a great deal. What does matter is that the Home Secretary, in consultation with the Admiralty, and probably with Banks, settled not upon an experienced colonial administrator, but upon another naval captain, a 'pensioner', whose good intentions were exceeded only by his administrative ineptitude.

Hunter's commission was dated 6 February 1794. His ship was to be H.M.S. *Reliance*, which would be accompanied on the outward voyage by H.M. brig *Supply*, carrying, among other necessities, a town clock and 'the principal parts of a large wind-mill.'[15] Just how much advance notice Flinders had of these

---

[15] David Collins, *An Account of the English Colony in New South Wales* . . . (2 vols., London, 1798–1802), vol. I, p. 428.

impending events we do not know. It would seem, however, that his selection as Master's mate of the *Reliance* depended largely upon who knew whom. Hunter had served directly under Phillip as Second Captain of H.M.S. *Sirius* in the First Fleet. He now selected one Henry Waterhouse to be Captain of the *Reliance*. Waterhouse had served under Hunter as lieutenant in the *Sirius*, and was now the Fifth Lieutenant of the *Bellerophon*. In the absence of documents it requires but little speculation to suppose that Waterhouse, knowing of Flinders's hopes, and his competence as a navigator, invited him to join the company. Flinders, now twenty years of age, seized the opportunity. Commenting later, he wrote: '. . . the author of this account [*A Voyage to Terra Australis*], who was then a midshipman, and had not long before returned from a voyage to the South Seas, was led by his passion for exploring new countries, to embrace the opportunity of going out upon a station which, of all others, presented the most ample field for his favourite pursuit.'[16]

There were many delays in the sailing, not the least of them being caused by the presence of French war vessels which had first to be cleared from the Channel before the convoy could venture out. In one last letter to cousin Mary Franklin at Spilsby, Matthew spoke eloquently, yet bravely, of the breaking of family ties. He had written to his father, but had received no answer. He had dreamed 'continually' of the Chappells, and of Mary. Even in the midst of hurry and confusion he found himself longing for a Spilsby fireside. But he was committed. A few days later, on 15 February 1795, to be exact, he was gone, not to return home for nearly six years.

[16] Flinders, *Voyage*, vol. I, p. xcvi.

# CHAPTER TWO

# Van Diemen's Land

## 1795-1800

### 1

After more than a year of preparation and delays, the *Reliance* sailed in a huge convoy, guarded out into the open Atlantic by units of Admiral Lord Howe's fleet. On 6 March she stopped first at Santa Cruz Roads, Teneriffe, in the Canary Islands. There Flinders found a few moments to write to his bevy of sisters and cousins.[1]

If Matthew's family were concerned lest he felt any homesickness, this first letter would have done nothing to cheer them up. He was homesick. In spite of a brave chattiness, it contains all the homiletic advice, especially on the subject of letter-writing that young men in every age, gone out on foreign duty, have always given. He did inform them that the run to the Canaries had been a 'long and boisterous passage'; and that their next port of call would be Rio de Janeiro. He also reported that his brother, 'my little Samuel', on board the *Reliance*, had 'stood the Gales of Wind exceeding well, he is in high Spirits and has lost no Part of that enterprising Spirit which brought him on board with me.' So the surgeon of Donington had lost not one but two sons to the naval service.

As expected, the *Reliance* and *Supply* put in at Rio, where they took on food and water, enough of both to take them to Port Jackson without stopping at the Cape of Good Hope, then in Dutch hands. At Rio Flinders got another taste of war and its amenities when Hunter, as a matter of official courtesy, attempted to pay a visit to the Portuguese governor, and succeeded only after he had been rebuffed six times in as many days.

[1] Flinders to family, 10 March 1795. N.M.M. 60/017. FLI/4.

15

The two ships arrived at Sydney Heads on 7 September, following an uneventful passage of seven months. Some two months later, on 25 November, Waterhouse promoted his Master's Mate to Acting Lieutenant of the *Reliance*. Most probably it was this change in his status that affected Flinders's relationship with the Master, a Mr Moore. But that the two did not get on appears from a letter Flinders received some years later from Christopher Smith, late botanist in the *Providence*. It seems that Smith, at that time working for the Bengal government, had come across Mr Moore at Amboina, and hearing he had been Master of the *Reliance*, inquired after his friend Flinders. 'But I plainly saw,' he wrote, 'that you were not a favourite of his, therefore I did not trouble him more.'[2] That is all we, too, know of the matter. That Moore's jealousy of Flinders's competence, or perhaps his acquaintance with the Captain, played a part, would not be an unreasonable guess. Or it may have been a political difference, for Moore was, as Smith put it, 'a violent Republican', which was in his view, an 'unpardonable crime'. In any case, it is not an easy thing to get away from a personal rancour on board a ship; and it is no more possible for the Master's Mate to ignore the Master than for the Master to ignore his mate.

It is a curious fact that in all his published writings Flinders never once described the internal conditions at the convict colony. To be sure the mechanisms of colonial administration would scarcely concern an explorer. Moreover, beholden as he was to both Hunter and, later, Philip Gidley King, he would be understandably disinclined to write anything damaging to them. But without any doubt, what he saw and heard he decided to keep to himself. He had no remedies.

The social climate of Sydney in the 1790s did in no way resemble the New Jerusalem the pious local clergy—and a few long-winded politicians in London—hoped for at its founding. The best contemporary report, from the hand of David Collins, sometime Judge Advocate and Secretary of the colony, presents a dismal story of human affairs.[3] The place was rife with civil disorder, worse than mere discord. It was in fact a stew, where

[2] Smith to Flinders, 30 June 1799. N.M.M. 60/017. FLI/1.
[3] Collins, *op. cit.*, throughout.

capital crimes were a commonplace. The weather, ranging from
desiccating drought to disastrous flood, conspired with the
distance from home to produce a continual shortage of food.
The absolutely sinful behaviour of the convict population,
coupled with the cupidity and brutality of the soldiers who ruled
them, reduced whatever creative challenge a governor might
feel to a nullity. Friction with the retreating natives could be,
and was, taken as a constant in all frontier society. That much
the British had learned in their American experience. But why
it took them so long to bring the traffic in American rum and
Dutch arrack under control in this situation is a mystery.

Such, in generalised, abstract terms, was what Flinders saw
and probably made of the murder, thievery, arson, fraud, and
drunkenness he might have seen any day or night along the
untidy streets of Sydney in the year 1795. Such was the un-
promising context in which, only a month after his arrival there,
he began his life's work exploring the continent.

It would seem only rational that before the British government should have attempted to organise a colony in New South
Wales, they ought to have had a detailed survey made of the
chosen site. Yet that was precisely what they failed to do. It
seems to have occurred to no one, either at the Parliamentary
hearings in 1779, or in 1786 when Lord Sydney announced his
decision in favour of Botany Bay; and then the government
lacked the excuse of a war. In consequence of this lapse, the first
thing Arthur Phillip had done, even before the first boatload of
convicts went ashore in 1788, was to take to a boat himself and
look about. What he saw displeased him, and on his own authority he moved the site of the colony out of Botany Bay, northward to a place within Sydney Heads. Altogether an inauspicious
beginning. However incomprehensible such administrative pro-
cedures at the Home Department may seem, the fact is that,
seven years later, practically nothing further had been done.
Many years after, when he had learned something about the
subject, Flinders described the state of Australian cartography
as he first found it :

'The first advantage to maritime geography which arose from
the new settlement, was a survey of Botany and Broken Bays

and Port Jackson, with most of the rivers falling into them.
Botany Bay had, indeed, been examined by captain Cook; but
of the other two harbours, the entrances alone had been seen.
This survey, including the intermediate parts of the coast, was
made by captain [then lieutenant] John Hunter, and was
published soon after its transmission to England by governor
Phillip. . . .

'On arriving at Port Jackson in September of the same year
[1795], it appeared [to Flinders and Hunter] that the investigation of the coast had not been greatly extended beyond the
three harbours; and even in these, some of the rivers were not
altogether explored. Jervis Bay, indicated but not named by
captain Cook, had been entered by lieutenant Richard Bowen;
and to the north, Port Stephens had lately been examined by
Mr C. Grimes, land surveyor of the colony, and by captain
W. R. Broughton of H.M. ship Providence; but the intermediate
portions of coast, both to the north and south, were little further
known than from captain Cook's general chart; and none of the
more distant openings, marked but not explored by that celebrated navigator, had been seen.'[4]

Thus the extreme limits of the explored coast were, in 1795,
only one hundred miles apart, and even then the shore had been
exposed to only the most superficial study.

This remarkable state of affairs reflected a combination of
factors persisting in London for a time beyond reason, or so it
seemed in the colony. Assuming that the need for a survey had
at least been noted at the Home Department, the slow progress
of the war with France prevented what very likely seemed a
prodigal waste of ships and men. Moreover, New South Wales,
13,000 miles away from the comfortable office in Whitehall,
must have been little more than an abstraction to the bureau-
crats. Then too, was it not notorious then, as it is today,
that penal institutions are usually the objects of neglect, if not
worse?

Actually, the idea for systematically charting the coasts of
New South Wales had been suggested to Sir Joseph Banks by

---

[4] Flinders, *Voyage*, vol. I, p. xcvi sq.

William Bligh as far back as 1791[5]—not that there was anything particularly brilliant about the idea, even then. Whether Hunter had discussed the matter with Banks before the *Reliance* sailed we do not know. But certainly the subject came up more than once during the seven-month voyage out to Port Jackson—with or without the approbation of Mr Moore. Furthermore, it is entirely possible that the issue was raised not by Hunter or Flinders, but by the surgeon of the *Reliance*.

George Bass was one of this world's projectors. He was born at Aswarby, Lincolnshire in 1771, three years before Matthew Flinders. Not a mere adventurer, he had a lively, inquiring mind, a mind driven by an unusually prolific imagination. Apart from his profession as surgeon, he was also a self-taught naturalist, which at that time implied an interest in both botany and zoology. It was he, in fact, who first worked out the taxonomic description of the wombat, and of the white albatross as well. Bass once told Sir Joseph Banks that he had gone out to New South Wales 'with the professed intention of exploring more of the country than any of my predecessors'.[6] From the record he made it is not hard to believe. In addition to his exploits along the coasts, he led an attempt to cross the Blue Mountains, far to the west of Sydney, turning back only to avoid death from thirst. Bass disappeared from sight in 1802, and is believed to have died either in Peru, where he had gone to trade, or somewhere in the south Pacific.

These were Bass's vintage years, and Flinders's life in New South Wales at this time can be considered only in terms of the association that had grown up between them. About a month after the arrival of the *Reliance* at Port Jackson there began that series of preliminary examinations of nearby shores and rivers later described by Flinders as 'intimately connected with the Investigator's voyage, of which they were, in fact, the leading cause'.[7] Whatever the statement reveals of Flinders, it suggests also Bass's influence with him, if not over him. Although Flinders was both restless and determined, of the two Bass

[5] Bligh to Banks, 17 December 1791. Writing from Capetown, he suggested that government send out two vessels for the purpose. M.L.

[6] Bass to Banks, 27 May 1799. M.L. For a study of Bass's life, see K. M. Bowden, *George Bass, 1771–1803* (Melbourne, 1952).

[7] Flinders, *Voyage*, vol. I, p. xcvi.

3

probably had the more vivid personality. We can fairly hear him promoting their joint excursions, first persuading Captain Waterhouse to release Flinders from duties on board the *Reliance*, and then, having done so, going to the Governor for his consent, arguing that they could use the rowing-boat he had brought out from England, the 'Tom Thumb'.

The first 'voyage' of the 'Tom Thumb', lasting from 26 October to 3 November 1795, was a mere reconnaissance, and had been intended as nothing more. The boat was manned by Bass, Flinders, and Bass's servant, a boy named Martin. These three sailed out of Sydney Heads, turned south, and then ran into Botany Bay. After travelling some distance up the George River at the head of the bay, they reversed their course and returned home promptly. The real importance of the voyage lies not in the tangible gains, which were negligible, but in the confidence Governor Hunter gained in his two young explorers. As Flinders later remarked, 'projects of this nature, when originating in the minds of young men, are usually termed romantic; and so far from any good being anticipated, even prudence and friendship join in discouraging, if not in opposing them.'[8] Hunter and Waterhouse had been careful in this first instance, and had been repaid. As a gauge of the future, here was a successful experiment.

Some time during 1795, when Flinders was in his twenty-first year, he suffered his first kidney attack. Perhaps it was nothing but a temporary infection, with no permanent damage. Bass's remedies seem to have succeeded. Nevertheless, occurring at so early an age, it must have warned him of trouble ahead; and indeed, we must look upon it with deep foreboding, for it has the ring of the Fate motif in a Wagnerian opera. But Bass could then predict nothing.

From 21 January to 5 March the *Reliance* went out on colonial duty to Norfolk Island, Britain's 'Devil's Island', some 900 miles east of Sydney. Further exploration, if not the planning for it, had therefore to be suspended. But just three weeks after their return, on 25 March, Bass, Flinders, and Martin went back to work. Their purpose was 'to explore a large river, said to fall into the sea some miles south of Botany Bay, of which there was

[8] *Ibid.*, p. xcvii.

no indication in captain Cook's chart.' This time they took a different boat, also called 'Tom Thumb,' of the same size as Bass's, also equipped with a sail, but built in the colony.[9] The 'large river' turned out to be an inlet of the sea, which they named Port Hacking, after Henry Hacking, late quartermaster of the *Sirius*, who had first discovered it. In the course of their journey they made a number of interesting observations of the surrounding country. Their reports on the fertility of the soil, and upon some 'black lumps, apparently of slaty stone,' later identified as coal, had significance. But they had not gone out equipped for detailed study, and as a result their examination was 'confined, by circumstances,' as Flinders put it, 'to a general view'.

Actually this voyage achieved more notoriety for its perils and hardships than fame for its accomplishments. On the second day out, the boat was thrown up on the shore by heavy surf, 'arms, ammunition, clothes, and provisions thoroughly drenched, and partly spoiled'. Natives whose attention had been attracted began congregating in increasing numbers, adding menace to physical discomfort. A playful interlude of trimming the beards of a few natives did nothing to diminish the threat which, however, eventually came to nothing. Then on the fourth night, while running along the shore, the boat was nearly overwhelmed by so furious a thunderstorm that for an hour, 'a single wrong movement, or a moment's inattention, would have sent us to the bottom'.[10]

Thus was laid the groundwork for larger, more ambitious schemes. Flinders had had his first experience of boat-handling in heavy surf; and he had met with natives outside the pale of the colony. Such dangers had produced thrills that might be turned to use, whenever time allowed.

But time would not allow. For over a year and a half, duty on board the *Reliance* precluded all thought of exploration. After six months on the ground, the Governor now began to carry his long-term plans for the colony into effect. Perhaps John Macarthur, the enterprising captain in the New South Wales

[9] For a discussion of the two 'Tom Thumbs', see Bowden, *op. cit.*, Appendix I.
[10] Flinders, *Voyage*, vol. I, p. ci.

Corps, had been urging him to more decisive action.[11] In any case, Hunter had by now recognised the precarious folly of trying to feed and clothe his wards at long range and irregular intervals. He therefore determined to send both the *Reliance* and the *Supply* to Capetown for a breeding stock of cattle and sheep, that he might improve the self-sufficiency of the economy.

The two ships left Port Jackson late in September 1796. Taking advantage of the westerlies, they sailed by way of Cape Horn, stopping first, once again, at Norfolk Island. On this outward leg Flinders qualified himself for promotion to lieutenancy. A few days after they arrived at Table Bay on 16 January, Captain Waterhouse recommended him to Rear-Admiral Pringle, then commanding at the Cape; whereupon Flinders, on the morning of the 24th 'attended at the Admirals, and after being ask [*sic*] a few questions' duly received his certificate.[12]

Three months of heavy work followed in refitting, replenishing stores, and taking aboard the livestock and feed. Soon after departing for Port Jackson on 10 April the *Reliance* was overtaken by storms so murderous that Waterhouse feared she would go down. It was probably the worst weather Flinders ever met with. They managed somehow to survive, though much of the livestock did not, and arrived back at Port Jackson on 26 June. The passage of seventy-eight days was nearly double the normal time for what has always been a rough, but not a dangerous, run.

The storms had battered the old *Reliance* so badly that for some months she lay in port quite unfit for sea. Since the services of the Second-Lieutenant were essential during the repairs, further exploration was again postponed. Most likely the dull routine in port chafed Flinders's nerves. Yet we can only imagine what his disappointment might have been if he had learned what Hunter wrote to Banks on 1 August of that year. The 'black lumps of slaty stone' had indeed turned out to be coal. Hunter naturally looked forward to exploiting the find, and beyond that, to further prospecting :

[11] For an excellent study of this ebullient character, see M. H. Ellis, *John Macarthur* (Sydney, 1955).

[12] Flinders's seniority as Lieutenant dated as from 31 January 1798. N.M.M. 60/017. FLI/5.

'I earnestly wish Government would send a Maritime Surveyor
here with fit Vessels & have this coast Examined; I am much
inclined to think many useful discoverys would be made. We
have much Ore in this land, beside Iron: at least, I think so.
This would be good amusement for a Mineralogist; but we are
such an abandoned set, that my time is wholly taken up in
looking after the Public Concerns, & in endeavouring to establish some decency & order. I have not a Moment to bestow on
many things which I delight in, & which might well deserve my
attention.'[13]

The harassed Governor evidently did not feel that Flinders
was ready for the command he suggested to Banks. He was
probably right. Yet the need for a thorough examination had
now become a matter of public urgency.

In describing his colony as 'abandoned' Hunter probably
meant to convey to Banks the notion of licentiousness. But
Banks could also read neglect into his meaning, for neglected
they surely were, and would remain. Under Jervis the British
had won at Cape St Vincent. But then the Mutiny at the Nore
had sent the Admiralty Commissioners reeling. Napoleon,
having given up his plans for invading England, now gathered
his forces for Egypt, and even flattered himself that he might
take India. The Battle of the Nile was only a year away. Under
the circumstances the Admiralty Board must be excused for failing
to take seriously a proposal for surveying New South Wales. It
was the old story, and Hunter would simply have to carry on
as best he could.

2

When Edmond Halley set about constructing his magnificent
sea-chart of the world (c. 1700) he had only the scantiest
information on New Holland.[14] William Dampier had touched
the north-west coast; but Dampier was no surveyor. And the

---

[13] Hunter to Banks, 1 August 1797. B.M. (N.H.) D.T.C. 10(2). 108.
[14] *Nova & Accuratissima totius terrarum Orbis Tabula Nautica Variationum
Magneticarum Index.*

Dutch charts, reliable up to a point, left much to the imagination. Thus the north, the west, and part of the south coasts are there. The Gulf of Carpentaria is there. But Halley connected Cape York to New Guinea; and he knew nothing at all about the east coast. Therefore, when James Cook went out on his first voyage, three problems confronted the map-makers with regard to this land: first, the longitudinal limits to the eastward; second, the relationship of New Holland to New Guinea, if any; and third, the configuration of the south coast, including Van Diemen's Land. Cook solved the first by sailing north along the east coast, inside the Barrier Reef. Then, turning westward at Cape York, he solved the second by finding the navigable water in Torres Strait. After Cook, only the southern portion remained a mystery. With nothing but a suggestion of a strait separating Van Diemen's Land from New South Wales, and no positive evidence, he declined to speculate. He solved his cartographic problem by simply interpolating an arc from St Peter's Island (133° 30' E.), the farthest reach of the Dutchmen, to the southern capes of Van Diemen's Land.[15]

Subsequent navigators also treated the Van Diemen's Land question conservatively. In 1789, while in the *Sirius*, Hunter himself had experienced a strong easterly current and 'an uncommon large sea' there. He had suggested the existence of 'either a very deep gulf, or a straight [sic] which may separate Van Diemen's Land from New Holland'.[16] Bligh never published his journal from the *Providence* voyage, so his views were not known. Then in 1793, the Frenchman, Labillardière, also became convinced of the strait; but again, on insufficient evidence.

Hunter knew as well as anyone, perhaps better, what a boon to navigation a strait in that region might be. Vessels coming out from India or the Cape might save days when every day counted. He therefore decided to settle the question then and there, with or without help from home.

Flinders still could not be diverted from the damaged *Reliance*.

[15] James Cook, 'A General Chart: Exhibiting the Discoveries made by Captn. James Cook in this and his two succeeding voyages'.

[16] John Hunter, *Historical Journal of the Transactions at Port Jackson and Norfolk Island* . . . (London, 1793), p. 125 sq.

But Surgeon Bass was both free and eager. On 3 December 1797, therefore, Bass set out in a fine whaleboat, manned by six seamen chosen for the purpose from the *Reliance* and the *Supply*. Hunter provisioned the party for six weeks, but by fishing and shooting they were able to remain away for something over eleven. Doubtless this possibility had been foreseen, for no rescue attempt seems to have been made. On the outward leg the party happened upon a band of seven escaped convicts stranded on a small offshore island. Two who were in a debilitated condition Bass picked up on his return. The other five he set over on the mainland, provisioned and lightly armed for a trek back to Sydney. They were never heard from again.

But for one dangerous night, no emergency occurred to detract from Bass's solid accomplishment. Running close inshore to southward, he found convincing, if not conclusive, evidence in favour of a strait. For one thing, at Cape Howe he followed the mainland first west, then north as it trended away from Van Diemen's Land. During all this time he encountered a heavy easterly swell, moving as from an oceanic fetch thousands of miles long. Moreover, as he worked along he became aware of a strong 'Venturi effect', characteristic of a tidal current constricted between two bodies of land. He had set the stage for a circumnavigation of Van Diemen's Land. The discovery of Western Port at the farthest end of his voyage seems almost incidental, a bonus added to the value of his more important achievement.

This feat was the apogee of George Bass's career in exploration. Long after he had disappeared, Flinders wrote of it in most extravagant terms:

'Our previous knowledge of the coast scarcely extended beyond the Ram Head; and there began the harvest in which Mr Bass was ambitious to place the first reaping hook. . . . A voyage expressly undertaken for discovery in an open boat, and in which six hundred miles of coast, mostly in a boisterous climate, was explored, has not, perhaps, its equal in the annals of maritime history. The public will award to its high spirited and able conductor, alas! no more, an honourable place in the list of those whose ardour stands most conspicuous for the promotion of useful knowledge.'[17]

In a more material way, the Governor saw fit to reward Bass by making him a grant of one hundred acres of government land in Banks Town, on the George River he and Flinders had explored.

Three weeks before Bass returned, Hunter dispatched the colonial schooner *Francis* south to Preservation Island, off the north-east coast of Van Diemen's Land. Her mission was to bring in what remained of the cargo of the *Sydney Cove*. This little vessel carrying goods from Bengal to Port Jackson, had been wrecked at the island upwards of a year before. Having already sent out once for crew and cargo, Hunter was going back to finish the work. This time he allowed Flinders to go along as a passenger, hoping he might examine the islands, mainly the Furneaux Group, lying just south of Cape Howe. Here was another approach to the question of the strait.

As a passenger Flinders could add little to what was already known. He not only lacked authority to move the vessel where and when he wished, but his instruments had none of the accuracy demanded of hydrographic work. Nevertheless, the results were not disappointing. For one thing, Flinders began work on his first chart of the region. He obtained confirmatory evidence, if it were needed, of a strong east-west tidal current flowing off Cape Howe. Finally, he realised for the first time how deceptively the magnetic compass could behave. He found that with the ordinary steering compass he used, not only were his bearings off by two or three degrees, but more, 'they showed that a change in the course steered produced an alteration in the compass'. He was actually observing magnetic deviation. What he did about it years later changed the design of the magnetic compass.[18]

Bass returned in the whaleboat on 24 February, while the *Francis* was still out. Flinders followed him in on 9 March. Three days later Hunter began a letter to Banks in which he discussed the results of these excursions. After reporting Bass's

[17] Flinders, *Voyage*, vol. i, p. cxix sq.
[18] *Ibid.*, p. cxxvi.

part, he told Banks, 'I have since had occasion to send the
Colonial Schooner to the Southward, to take from an Island the
remaining crew & effects of a ship wrecked there. I sent in the
Schooner the Second Lt. of the *Reliance* (Mr Flinders) with
directions to make such observations among the islands as he
could.'[19] So began, at a distance of 13,000 miles, the relationship
between Sir Joseph Banks and Matthew Flinders. No formalities,
only a name in a letter. At this stage, neither Flinders nor Banks
could possibly have foreseen, in even the haziest way, what this
might all lead to. But Hunter's confidence in the young man was
growing. Doubtless, too, the Governor discovered a friendship
here. Not only was Flinders able to carry out a few of the
positive projects Hunter himself had wanted to do; but here was
an honest, forthright young man, who seemed a ray of light in
the lonely, darkening world enveloping Government House.

Some time after the return of the *Francis* the *Reliance* went
once again to Norfolk Island. The delay in the Van Diemen's
Land project did no harm, however, because the winter months
in the 'roaring forties' hardly favour the risks of coastal exploration. In September 1798 it was arranged that a final attack
should be made, beginning the following month, by Flinders
and Bass together. Their ship, the twenty-five-ton sloop, *Norfolk*,
built at Norfolk Island, was placed under Lieutenant Flinders's
command. The sloop carried a crew of eight men chosen from
the *Reliance* and the *Supply*. Hunter's instructions to Flinders
were 'to penetrate behind [i.e. to the west of] Furneaux's
Islands; and should a strait be found, to pass through it and
return by the south end of Van Diemen's Land; making such
examinations and surveys on the way as circumstances might
permit.'[20]

These orders to circumnavigate Van Diemen's Land were
precisely what Flinders and Bass needed. For Flinders, the only
thing lacking was a chronometer, a serious, but not fatal handi-
cap. Relatively free of responsibility, Bass was in an excellent
position to assist in making observations or, if he chose, to roam
the shores and hills, botanising and searching out new animal
life.

[19] Hunter to Banks, 12 March 1798. B.M. (N.H.) D.T.C. 10(2). 246.
[20] Flinders, *Voyage*, vol. I, p. cxxxviii.

On 7 October the *Norfolk* sailed out of Port Jackson in company with a private sealing vessel, *Nautilus*. She carried provisions for a twelve-week cruise, but with luck in shooting ducks and kangaroo, she might be able to remain away longer if necessary. After setting his trigonometric base for the survey along the coast of the mainland, Flinders crossed over to the Furneaux Group, where the *Nautilus* would remain for her work, and the *Norfolk* would begin hers. There, on Cape Barren Island, Bass caught the wombat he described, and pronounced to be 'very economically made'. By 1 November Flinders was running close inshore off Cape Portland, having at times as little as four fathoms of water beneath him. After a rapid advance westward to Low Head, he halted further movement for an examination of the Tamar River. There, for the first, but not the last time in his life, he felt his ship touch the ground. Fortunately, no damage was done. Then, caught by a gale, he retreated to the Furneaux Group once again to avoid being driven ashore. Weather had put him behind schedule, and as soon as the winds abated he went back, obliged to quicken the pace of his work.

By 8 December the sloop had nearly reached the northwest extremity of Van Diemen's Land. For several days both Flinders and Bass had been disturbed by the northwest trending of this coast, fearing they might end their cruise in Western Port, so recently discovered by Bass in the whaleboat. Then a look at the tides lifted their spirits. For the first time, they noticed that low water occurred, not when the tide ran from the west, but when it ran from the east. They quickly realised that the flood tide must therefore come from the west. 'This', Flinders wrote, 'we considered to be a strong proof, not only of the real existence of a passage betwixt this land and New South Wales, but also that the entrance into the Southern Indian Ocean could not be far distant.' The very next day, 9 December, the coast turned sharply south. As they turned with it and saw the long swell Bass had noted in the whaleboat, 'Mr Bass and myself hailed it with joy and mutual congratulation, as announcing the long-wished-for discovery of a passage into the Indian Ocean.' Of the same moment Bass wrote that he then 'began to taste the enjoyment resulting from the completion of this discovery'. They now knew that Van Diemen's Land was indeed an island.

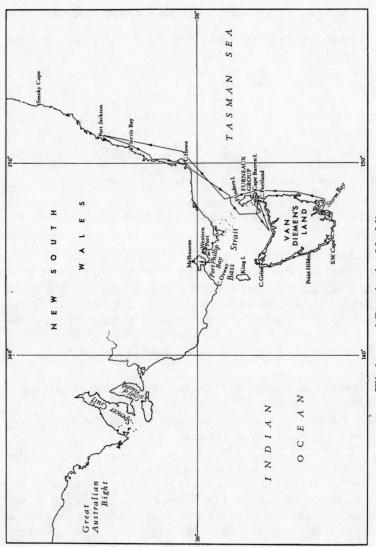

Flinders and Bass in the *Norfolk*, 1798–9

The day was a memorable one for yet another reason:

'A large flock of gannets was observed at daylight, to issue out
of the great bight to southward [i.e. off the land to the south of
Cape Grim;] and they were followed by such a number of sooty
petrels [*Nectris brevicaudis*] as we had never seen equalled.
There was a stream of from fifty to eighty yards in depth, and
of three hundred yards, or more, in breadth; the birds were not
scattered, but flying as compactly as a free movement of their
wings seemed to allow; and during a full *hour and a half*, this
stream of petrels continued to pass without interruption, at a
rate little inferior to the swiftness of a pigeon.'

In his methodical way, Flinders added the following computa-
tion:

'Taking the stream to have been fifty yards deep by three
hundred in width, and that it moved at the rate of thirty miles
an hour, and allowing nine cubic yards of space to each bird, the
number would amount to 151,500,000. The burrows required
to lodge this quantity of birds would be 75,750,000; and allowing a square yard to each burrow, they would cover something
more than 18½ geographic square miles of ground.'[21]

From this set of facts Flinders and Bass deduced that somewhere to the southward they must be on the look-out for uninha-
bited islands where these birds might nest undisturbed, and from
which they would fly at daybreak for food.

The *Norfolk* had now been out of port for nine of the allotted
twelve weeks. Flinders made haste accordingly, and arrived at
South-west Cape in four days. He attempted, without much success, to fix the position of the Cape. In fact, he failed by several
miles—a critical difference for ships approaching a lee shore at
night. It appeared later that either his sextant had been damaged,
or he had made an error in reading it.[22]

[21] *Ibid.*, p. clxx.
[22] The modern figure for the latitude of South West Cape is 43° 35′ S. H.M.S.O.,
*Australia Pilot*, vol. II (1956), p. 222. Flinders gave 43° 29′ S.; Furneaux, 43° 39′
S.; Cook, 43° 37′ S.; P. P. King, 43° 39′ S.; and Stokes, 43° 34′ S. Flinders himself
believed he had misread his sextant in a hurry to get the noon bearings for the day.

For the last two weeks of the year the *Norfolk* lay in Storm Bay on the south-east coast of the island. On Christmas Day the party were out in boats exploring in the Derwent River area. At last, on 4 January 1799, Flinders left the shore and headed for Port Jackson, where he arrived on the 11th.

In the main, two real advantages had been gained from the voyage. First, the existence of the strait was firmly established, and the principal dangers and shelters in it had been charted. From this it followed that the voyage to Sydney from India or the Cape could be shortened by about a week. Second, the work in the Tamar valley along the north shore, and in the Derwent to the south, supplied the government with information useful for future colonisation. Thus the cities of Launceston and Hobart.

As soon as he could begin work on his charts at Sydney, Flinders needed names for prominent features of the coasts. It was a common enough practice to use terms descriptive either of the place, as North-west Cape, or Circular Head, or, of some remarkable event in the voyage, as Albatross Island. But Flinders decided also to pay his compliments to people. In some cases the persons were government officials, as the Duke of Portland, then Secretary of State for Home Affairs, Alexander Dalrymple, Hydrographer to the Admiralty, and Governor Hunter. Some were friends. Thus Point Hibbs was named after the colonial master of the *Norfolk*, and Isle Waterhouse after his own captain. The Chappell Islands, a small cluster in the Furneaux Group, still keeps the name of the girl Flinders would marry in a year or so. With characteristic generosity he requested of the Governor that the strait, 'which had been the great object of research,' be called Bass Strait. 'This was no more,' he said, 'than a just tribute to my worthy friend and companion, for the extreme dangers and fatigues he had undergone in first entering it in the whaleboat, and to the correct judgment he had formed from various indications, of the existence of a wide opening between Van Diemen's Land and New South Wales.'[23] This favour Hunter was happy to confer.

[23] Flinders, *Voyage*, vol. i, p. cxciii.

3

That Hunter had gone ahead with this survey on his own was
just as well. His letter to Banks, suggesting a maritime survey,
and reciting the ageless difficulties of proconsuls, had arrived.
On 1 February Banks replied : '. . . the situation of Europe is at
present so critical & His Majesty's Ministers so fully employed
in business of the deepest importance, that it is scarce possible
to gain a moment's audience on any subject, but those which
stand foremost in their minds; & colonies of all kinds, you may
be assured, are now put into the back ground.'[24]

Eager as he was to see New South Wales thrive and grow,
Banks enjoyed writing this letter no more than Hunter did reading it. If only the two could find a handle for the Ministers to
grasp, perhaps something might befall. Time would tell.

For the next six months Flinders remained with the *Reliance*
in Port Jackson. Little is known of his activities during the
period, and still less of his plans for the future, if he had any.
That something was in the wind, however, appears from a letter
Flinders wrote to 'my dearest Friend', Ann Chappell, on
16 March.[25] The letter began, 'Short as may be the time before
we sail . . .,' and went off from there into a lovesick rhapsody.
No further reference to the matter of sailing home was made.
But most probably Waterhouse had been led to expect orders.

A week or so later, Flinders was given work to do of the most
disagreeable kind. A reformed convict, one Isaac Nicholls, who
had made a favourable impression upon Hunter, stood accused of
receiving stolen property, tobacco, from a thief. The trial court
consisted of the Judge Advocate, Richard Atkins, a bibulous
reprobate and remittance man, who loathed Hunter; three
officers of the New South Wales Corps; and three naval officers,
Captain Waterhouse, Captain Kent, of the *Supply*, and Lieutenant Flinders. In arriving at its verdict the court split, four to
three, with the navy on the short end standing for acquittal.
Nicholls was sentenced to fourteen years on Norfolk Island, a

[24] Banks to Hunter, 1 February 1799. B.M. (N.H.) D.T.C. 11. 187.
[25] Flinders to Ann, 16 March 1799. N.M.M. 60/017. FLI/25.

punishment that so outraged Hunter that he forthwith set up a
Court of Inquiry to look into the matter. He appointed to it,
among others, George Bass. Nicholls had evidently been framed.
In any case, he never served his sentence, and was eventually
pardoned by the Colonial Office in 1802. This trial had no
further repercussions for Flinders; but while it lasted he had
thought of little else.

By May of 1799, at the conclusion of the Nicholls affair, the
tour of duty in the *Reliance* had begun to pall. Four years of
complete isolation from the greatest events of the age was as
much as young, active, ambitious men could take. So far as
Flinders and Bass were concerned, after the discovery of the
strait, anything further they could do would only be anticlimax.
Inevitably, restlessness set in.

The earliest perceptible manifestation of this change in mood
had been Matthew's nostalgic letter to Ann, back in February.
Now another appeared. George Bass had for some time been
declining in health, from what specific cause we do not know.
For one of his temperament, idleness can be a serious problem.
Moreover, it is not improbable that he had already begun to plan
his future commercial speculations. One of his principal partners
in the first venture was one Charles Bishop, who had gone south
in the sealer *Nautilus* with the *Norfolk* a few months back. Bass
was granted a leave for sickness and left for England, by way
of China, on 29 May 1799. Flinders remained behind.

Now that winter was setting in, nothing could be done to the
south of Sydney, although the coast beyond Western Port had
never even been seen. On the other hand, an examination to the
north, short of the Barrier Reef, might be profitable, and it was
certainly feasible. Once again Hunter assigned the *Norfolk* to
Flinders, and provisioned her this time for six weeks. Evidently
the *Reliance* was not expected to sail for home very soon.
Flinders took with him substantially the same crew as before,
with the additions of midshipman Samuel Flinders, and a Port
Jackson native named Bongaree, who was to act as intercessor
with whatever natives might appear. The object of the expedition was to examine Moreton Bay, at the head of which the city
of Brisbane now stands, and, farther north, Hervey Bay, both of
which openings Cook had passed and noted without entering.

Hunter had hopes that a navigable river might be found falling into one of these bays from the interior.

The *Norfolk* sailed out of Port Jackson on 8 July and reached the entrance to Moreton Bay on the 14th. Almost immediately the party met up with natives who, they found, were quite unrelated to those of Port Jackson. Bongaree could do nothing to communicate with them. Since Flinders wished to spend some time ashore he tried at once to establish a friendly intercourse with these strangers, just as he had in Port Hacking three years before. This time the plan failed, for one of the natives, without warning or provocation, suddenly threw his spear. Flinders had no choice but to assert his authority then and there if he were to carry on with his work. Having his musket loaded with buckshot, he fired, wounding the offender. It was not a pleasant affair, but it effected its object. His survey party was menaced no further.[26]

Of the hydrographic results Flinders wrote that he had been disappointed in not being able to penetrate into the interior of New South Wales by either of the openings. He concluded his report by saying that, 'however mortifying the conviction might be, it was then an ascertained fact, that no river of importance intersected the East Coast between the 24th and 39th degrees of south latitude.'[27] Mortifying indeed; but he would have been appalled if, during his lifetime, he had learned of the Clarence River, '240 miles in length,' and 'of considerable importance and the outlet for the produce of large and rich agricultural and pastoral districts.' He had in fact anchored off its mouth only three days after leaving Port Jackson. But what was even worse, he also missed the Brisbane River after running the entire length of Moreton Bay into which it empties.

It is no use trying to explain away these mistakes. He should not have made them. As for the unfortunate incident with the natives, it seems clear that the experience had value, if not for the natives, at least for the whites at Sydney, and possibly for sailors who might land along these lonely coasts.

The party arrived back safely in the evening of 20 August, just six weeks and a day after they had left. For Flinders the preliminaries were over. He had performed his last service for

[26] Cf. Collins, *op. cit.*, vol. ii, chaps. 19–21.
[27] Flinders, *Voyage*, vol. i, p. ccii.

Hunter, soon to retire, and his last survey until the voyage of H.M. Sloop *Investigator*.

Of his last half year at Port Jackson we know next to nothing. We do know that on 1 January 1800 Hunter made over a grant of 300 acres in Banks Town to Matthew Flinders, 'Lt. of the Reliance'.[28]

The time for quitting the colony was now at hand.

[28] *H.R.N.S.W.*, vol. IV, p. 48. Flinders presently sold it to a Mr Bowles for £280. See records of Flinders's London agent, W. A. Standert, in N.M.M. 60/017. FLI/6.

# PART II

# H.M. Sloop *Investigator*

## 1800-1803

# CHAPTER THREE

# Flinders Proposes, Banks Disposes

## 1800

### 1

It is not to be supposed that Matthew Flinders, navigator, rose from obscurity to eminence, from strength to strength, with never a doubt in his soul about where he was going. The *Voyage to Terra Australis*, being a public account of his career, naturally enough presented only a narrative of events. His private correspondence told another tale.

The year was 1800. At twenty-six, Flinders had already served in the navy for ten years. He had now fallen quite hopelessly in love with Ann Chappell, and clearly foresaw the difficulty, perhaps even hardship, of supporting a wife on a lieutenant's pay. He saw officers in the fighting fleet growing fat on prize-money that was not available to explorers. Misgivings filled his mind. In the letter he wrote to Ann in March 1799, he had confessed to her that, after they had parted four years ago, he had 'never since been satisfied with my profession; and, strange as it may appear when mature deliberation was called to decide upon the question, it aided the sentiment, and condemned the sea.'[1]

Late in June 1799, Christopher (Paddy) Smith, the *Providence* botanist, in the same letter in which he referred to Mr Moore, late Master of the *Reliance*, also told Flinders that he had directed his agents at Calcutta to send Flinders a gift of: 'Six dozen of Madeira wine, one doz. shirts, marked M.F., one doz. Towels, two black stocks, one case of Spirits, and Twenty pounds Sterling.'[2] These handsome luxuries arrived at Port Jackson on

[1] Flinders to Ann, 16 March 1799. N.M.M. 60/017. FLI/25.
[2] Smith to Flinders, 30 June 1799. N.M.M. 60/017. FLI/1.

12 February 1800, ahead of Smith's letter. The gift and the sentiment that prompted it took Flinders by surprise, and in an access of feeling he disclosed the current state of his mind. In a letter to Smith, after saying he had more than £100 in hand and would therefore return the money, and then, after relating how he and his friends had saluted Paddy Smith with a bottle of his Madeira, he came to the point: 'The main purpose of my letter [is] to ask you how far I might benefit myself by entering into the Country Service.' He had in mind borrowing some capital, and running his own ship in the cotton trade between Calcutta and China. He went on:

'The thing is, my dear friend, I am tired of serving for a pittance, and as it were living from hand to mouth, whilst others, with no better claim are making hundreds and thousands. The examples which have occurred in this place have opened my eyes a little to my own interest; and besides, I want to be my own master, and not to be subject to the caprices of whomsoever the Lords above may please to set over me. . . . Between ourselves, I have some hopes that my relations in England will advance me two or three thousand pounds to forward my mercantile plans, which if they do, and moderate success should attend me, a few years will probably see me independent of the world. . . . The honour of being an honest man and ranked as a gentleman is sufficient for me. . . . As I sincerely believe you wish me well, I make no scruple to ask for any information you can get, and to point out any opening that may be suited to my capacity.'[3]

Nothing could be plainer or more ingenuous. Just how much George Bass's recent defection from the navy had had to do with

[3] Flinders to Smith, 14 February 1800. N.M.M. 60/017. FLI/4. Only a month before, he had written to Captain P. Malcolm, of H.M.S. *Suffolk*, saying that 'we are now given to understand that it is in the contemplation of Government to send out one or two vessels, to carry on the examination of this still immense island, *the command* of which report has given to me' [italics mine]. S.L.V., 17 January 1799. When Hunter had received news of the approach of the *Lady Nelson*, later Flinders's tender, is not known. It is doubtful whether the decision to place Flinders in command had yet been taken, for on 3 May 1800 Philip Gidley King had written to Banks: 'I am concerned Flinders is going, but I hope arrangements will be made so as he will be ready to come out to take the Lady Nelson. . . .' *H.R.N.S.W.*, vol. IV, p. 82 sq.

turning Matthew's mind is impossible to say. Nor is it clear who the successful, if undeserving, models Flinders had observed might be. What is clear is that, from a combination of causes, Flinders had grown disenchanted with the naval service, just as had his Uncle John before him. The ancient lures of independence, money, and status now occupied his mind.

The letter may have been addressed to Smith; but actually Flinders was talking to himself. As nothing further was ever said of the matter, much less done about it, we may put it down to passing fancy, a fit of envy, neither frivolous nor deadly serious. In his advancing maturity, he had found himself confronted by conflicting values. He is entitled to be measured by his choice.

The enterprise of H.M. Sloop *Investigator* dates from 3 March 1800, the day on which the *Reliance*, with Flinders aboard, cleared Sydney Heads bound for England. Naturally his mind on that day was dominated by thoughts of home. Deeper down, however, he sensed the enormous prospect of discovery. To throw away the fruits of four years' work seemed an absurdity. But now he faced a different problem. How should one proceed in inducing politicians, harassed by Ireland and drawn taut by the demands of war, to support an ambitious scheme of exploration 13,000 miles away? What, at the worst, were the risks of being simply dismissed with a smile? The issue was essentially political in character, having little to do with the seamanship he had learned under Bligh, and even less with the romance of *Robinson Crusoe*. All this was new to Flinders, and it was by no means simple. Although his commission in the Royal Navy clothed him with a certain respectability, the Flinders family hardly belonged to the Establishment. Quite the reverse. Yet, if he were to achieve his ambition, he had now to gain a hearing at the very pinnacle of power in London, a London to whose people and ways he was a complete stranger. What he needed was the entrée that only a patron of the first rank could provide.

Most likely Hunter had guided him, for Flinders chose his patron with real sagacity. When occasion required, The Right Hon. Sir Joseph Banks, Bart., P.R.S., could exert as much sheer influence upon affairs which happened to interest him as anyone in contemporary London. Universally respected, often feared, he quite literally ruled the world of science over which he reigned.

Although thirty years had passed since he had sailed with Cook to the discovery of New South Wales, he had always retained a lively interest in the place. Since its establishment in 1788, he had kept a watchful, informed eye upon the little colony. He was, in fact, regarded as the authority on the subject. Not least, the study of its natural history intrigued him.

Flinders's decision to dedicate his *Observations on the Coast of Van Diemen's Land* . . . to Sir Joseph was therefore as logical as it was shrewd. It seems likely that by the time the *Reliance* sailed for home, Flinders had decided to enter his opening bid for command of an expedition directly to Banks. There were in fact, however, three other centres of power to which, given his plan, he might have addressed himself. As a naval officer in active service, he might reasonably have proceeded through Admiralty channels, perhaps with the help of his friend, Pasley. But the Admiralty at that time had no administrative machinery for dealing with questions of scientific research. The Hydrographic Office was still an infant, a one-man operation. Sooner or later, confronted by a reasonable proposal, the Admiralty Commissioners themselves would have had to turn to Banks. Alternatively, a project for surveying New Holland might have been placed before the Home Department, where responsibility for the colony rested.[4] Such a course might have had a certain logic, but as the record showed only too clearly, only a scant hope of success.

One other possible source of support was the Honourable East India Company, semi-autonomous, quasi-official, with huge resources of both money and power invested east of the Cape of Good Hope. In fact, the Company enjoyed exclusive trading rights in all the waters surrounding New Holland and beyond. French privateers working in the Indies were threatening the Company's China trade.[5] Indeed, the *Walpole* had actually gone round Australia. It therefore seemed plausible to assume that in order to minimise losses the British merchants would wish to learn as much as possible about the seas on the eastern flank of

---

[4] The office of Secretary of State for War and the Colonies was not created until 1801.

[5] C. N. Parkinson, in *War in the Eastern Seas, 1793–1815* (London, 1954), discusses this phase of the Napoleonic threat.

their China run. In point of fact, this, chronologically, is where Flinders began the discourse. On her way home, the *Reliance* put in at St Helena, then under the Company's control. There he talked with the Governor, Lieut.-Colonel Robert Brooke. No record of the interview remains, but subsequent transactions indicate that Flinders showed Brooke a copy of his manuscript on Van Diemen's Land, and asked him for advice. Evidently Brooke encouraged Flinders, and gave him a letter of endorsement for use in London.

After a brief stay at St Helena, the *Reliance* departed in convoy, arriving at Portsmouth on 26 August 1800. She had been out of England for just over five and a half years.

2

Eleven days after his arrival, on 6 September, Flinders sent off a letter to Banks. He opened with a short account of his work along the east and south-east coasts of New South Wales, and then moved on to a more general—and hopeful—statement of the problem:[6]

'This more minute examination of the coast, and of the above bays in particular, seems to point out, that New Holland is probably not of that extent as has usually been supposed, for had it been so, some considerable rivers would most likely have been found to fall into the sea in the extent of 18° of latitude, that is, from 21° to 39°. Probably it will be found, that an extensive strait seperates [*sic*] New South Wales from New Holland by the way of the Gulph of Carpentaria; or perhaps a southern gulph may only peninsulate New South Wales. The commander of an American ship, by name Williamson, reported his having sailed from the latitude 45° to 10° 15' south, in nearly a north direction, without seeing any land: his longitude being somewhat to the west of the south-west cape of Van Diemen's Land.[7] This is related to us by the commander of the Bombay ship Hercules,

---

[6] M.L., Banks Papers, vol. xx: 'Australia and the South Sea Islands', p. 59 sqq.
[7] Williamson's navigation was not flawless: he would have had to sail through dry land.

Mr. Mc Farlane, and was noticed in a London paper about two years since. Should such a strait exist, the advantages that would result from it to any settlements in Van Diemen's Land, New South Wales, or the eastern parts of New Holland, by the very expeditious communication with India, seem almost incalculable.

'It cannot be doubted, but that a very great part of that still extensive country remains either totally unknown, or has been partially examined at a time when navigation was much less advanced than at present. The interests of geography and natural history in general, and of the British nation in particular, seem to require, that this only remaining considerable part of the globe should be thoroughly explored. The brig Lady Nelson has lately been sent out partly with this view, as reported; but if Sir Joseph Banks will excuse me, I presume she must be very inadequate to the task, as perhaps would any single vessel. A further knowledge of the strait between New Holland and New Guinea, and of the south coast of the latter, are perhaps desiderata of importance, and might possibly be explored during the circumnavigation of New Holland without much lost time; and during those intervals when the examination of the coasts might be thought too dangerous, that extensive group the Feegee or Bligh's Islands would afford ample employment, as well as refreshment, to the crews.

'If any similar plan to the above should ever be entered upon, Sir Joseph Banks will immediately see that two vessels ought to be employed upon it, one of which, at least, ought to be considerably larger than the Lady Nelson. Then a person or persons could be accomodated [sic] who should examine into the natural production of this wonderful country, for surely what has already been found is materially different from all others; and the mineralogical branch would probably not be the least interesting.

'If His Majesty should be so far desirous to have the discovery of New Holland completed, as to send out a vessel after the Lady Nelson proper for the execution of it, and the late discoveries in that country should so far meet approbation as to induce the execution of it to be committed to me, I should enter upon it with that zeal which I hope has hitherto characterized my services.

'The detention of the Reliance at Spithead, prevents me from paying my respects in person to Sir Joseph Banks, and delivering the letters intrusted to me by His Excellency governor Hunter and lieutenant-colonel Paterson, for which reason they are now inclosed, together with a small parcel of the seeds of flowers, shrubs and trees of New South Wales. By the first opportunity I shall do myself the honour of calling in Soho Square to give every further information within my knowledge; as also of laying the charts before the Admiralty; but previously thought it proper to make this private communication to Sir Joseph Banks, pleading on behalf of any informality there may be in thus addressing him, that almost constant employment abroad, and an education amongst the unpolished inhabitants of the Lincolnshire fens, have prevented me from learning better; but not from imbibing the respect and consideration with which the Right Honourable president of the most learned society in the world will always be held by his most devoted and obedient servant.

Mattw. Flinders'

So much for the Country Service. Flinders had now opted for rewards other than money and status, either in or out of the navy.

Here began a voluminous proliferation of letters, orders, memoranda and diplomatic exchanges which, after ten months, sent the *Investigator* on her way. Gathering their forces week by week, and on the whole quite rapidly, Flinders and Banks together mounted what was at once, and for its time, a scientific research project of extraordinary proportions, as well as a naval mission for tightening Britain's strategic control in the Far East.

Flinders sent his letter to Banks's residence in Soho Square. But Banks at the moment was not in town. He was in fact at Overton in Derbyshire, and would not come up to London before November, when he had to prepare for the Royal Society's annual meeting. Until then he would spend most of the time at his country house, Revesby Abbey, in Lincolnshire. Thus, Flinders was obliged to possess his soul in patience.

It was a difficult moment, not made easier by news of his sister's death. A letter written to Ann from the *Reliance* at the Nore, on 25 September, reveals how deep had been his family attachment. Yet at the same time, he was looking to the future:

'My dear friend

'Have you received my letter of March 16 and Sept. 1, 1799, and another of Sept. 2, 1798? You answer yes. Then my dear friend the last letter which I have received from you is dated September 1797! If you think that I esteem you and value your friendship, it will be in your power to form a judgement of the uneasiness I have suffered on your account. From Thomas [Franklin?] I learn that you are in the land of the living, and at present on a visit at Barton. My imagination has flown after you often and many a time, but the lords of the admiralty still keep me in confinement at the Nore. You must know, and your tender feelings have often anticipated for me, the rapturous pleasure I promised myself on returning from this antipodean voyage, and an absence of six years; and if I mistake not your feeling heart will well picture my disappointment and distress on finding my best beloved sister [Elizabeth] and the friend of my bosom [Mary Franklin] both torn from my arms by that scythe bearing villain. It is a shock to my spirits . . . that will not hastily be done away. I shed no tear—the world is full enough of sorrow without my plaints being added to the sum; but a stupid langour seems to have taken possession of me, and all the flattering marks of attention which the friends I have already met have honoured me with, seem to have nothing more than a momentary effect. . . .

'As you are one of those friends whom I consider it indispensibly [sic] necessary to see, I should be glad to have some little account of your movements, where you reside and with whom; that my motions may be regulated accordingly . . . as soon as we shall be ordered up to Woolwich or to Deptford, which we expect daily, to be paid off, I shall go up to London occasionally to put the business I have got to do into a fair training; and after the ship is paid off I shall reside there altogether till the principal part is executed; and this will probably take two months and more. But if the absence of people from London at this time should oblige me to defer some part till they return, then I shall take that opportunity of coming into Lincolnshire, if so long a time as three weeks can be spared.

'You see that I make everything subservient to business. Indeed my dearest friend, this time seems to be a very critical period of my life I have been long absent, have done services abroad that were not expected, but which seem to be thought a good deal of. I have more and greater friends than before, and this seems to be the moment that their exertions may be most serviceable to me. I may now perhaps make a bold dash forward, or may remain a poor lieutenant all my life.

'P.S. . . . I ought to have begun my letter by saying that six different times before this, I have been going to write you, but the melancholy subject of my dearest Betsey and my dear friend Mary . . . was too ready to aid the ink's blackness and tinge the whole sheet with its hue; I therefore desisted till a more favourable moment should occur for writing a miscellaneous letter.'[8]

It is a curious document. For a man of only twenty-six, who had more than once faced mortal danger, and was so full of ambition, his profound introspection, and an almost total lack of *élan*, are really astonishing. He saw more clearly than most men that he stood at a turning point, and privately he was troubled and unsure.

3

Presumably his 'business' in London had to do with either the publication of his manuscript, or with conversations about his new proposal. Probably both. Precisely who his new-found friends were, and what the nature of their exertions, is not known. In any case, his next important step appears not to have been taken until 16 October, when he wrote a letter to the Court of Directors of the East India Company. Doubtless he enclosed Brooke's endorsement, and perhaps also an abstract of his *Observations*.[9] Without question, he petitioned the Court for financial help in some way commensurate with their interests as he read them. It took nerve to go ahead without Banks. In their Minutes the Court recorded receipt of Flinders's letter and his 'Petition';

[8] Flinders to Ann, 25 September 1800. N.M.M. 60/017. FLI/25.
[9] A search of the India Office Library has failed to bring to light either the Flinders or the Brooke letter. It may be presumed that they were destroyed with other records of the Committee of Shipping in 1860. Professor Scott overlooked this East India Company business, and was thus led into difficulties over the chronology of events at this crucial juncture of Flinders's life. See Scott, *Life*, chap. 12.

and further, they referred the documents to the Committee of
Shipping for study and recommendation.[10] This too would take
time. But now the thing was done, Flinders felt free to apply for
leave to visit his family and his 'Annette.'

Doubtless his reunion with friends and relatives was as happy
as might be following so soon after Elizabeth's death. Doubtless,
too, Matthew grasped this opportunity to win the hand of Ann.
Thereafter his letters to her shed all pretence at formality.
Whether it was this new fact, whether Matthew's father resented
his sons' intentions of remaining in the navy, or whether from a
concatenation of other circumstances, late in November, after
Flinders had returned to London, his father wrote him a long
and bitter letter, denouncing his elder children for their continued dependence upon him for their support. That he should
take out his resentment upon either Matthew or Samuel, neither
of whom he had supported for five years or more, was not a
reasonable thing to do, and Matthew knew it. 'All concealments
now done away,' he repeated the charges back to Ann, and
apologised in staccato, grief-stricken sentences for dragging her
into his family predicament. Professing his love, he closed his
letter hoping she would understand.[11]

Nothing further ever came of the incident. Matthew's father
died in May 1802, having made his eldest son co-executor of his
estate, and leaving him a more than nominal sum. The net effect
of the father's outburst seems, however, to have been to draw
Matthew and Ann all the closer together.

Just as these dire domestic problems were coming to a boil,
Flinders received another letter, perhaps the most important of
his life :

Soho Square Novr. 16 1800
'Sir

Jos : Banks presents his Compts to Mr Flinders he is sorry
indeed to have been prevented by bad health from answering a
Letter he Received some time ago from Mr Flinders will be
happy to see him in Soho Square at any time when he will be so
good as to Call upon him.'[12]

[10] I.O., East India Company, Minutes, vol. cix, pt. A, p. 643 (22 October 1800)
[11] Flinders to Ann, 29 November 1800. N.M.M. 60/017. FLI/25.
[12] Banks to Flinders, 16 November 1800. N.M.M. 60/017. FLI/1.

At last! Whether in trepidation or not, Flinders lost little time in going round to the top of the Square. Obviously the first interview was an astonishing success, even if Banks could scarcely give his visitor a promise.

Precisely what happened during the ensuing week is not at all clear. Flinders later wrote that 'a plan [for completing the investigation of Terra Australis] was approved by that distinguished patron of science and useful enterprise; it was laid before Earl Spencer, then first Lord Commissioner of the Admiralty; and finally received the sanction of His Majesty, who was graciously pleased to direct that the voyage should be undertaken.'[13] No documents describing these events in detail have come to light. Probably Banks, once convinced, had only to speak to Spencer over a glass of port, and the thing was done. Again, whether Privy Council ever debated the proposal is not known. No reference to the matter appears in Council Minutes. What can be said is that, while Banks was always careful to observe protocol if it meant avoiding a collision, he certainly knew when to use—and when to disregard—official channels. At any rate, the project now became a special case of Admiralty administration; and one cannot help being struck by the celerity with which arrangements began to be made on all sides. No time could be wasted. Six months had passed since the Pitt government had issued a passport—at Banks's urging—for a French expedition under Captain Nicolas Baudin intended for similar work in the same area.[14] Banks knew that Baudin's two ships, *Naturaliste* and *Géographe*, had already left the Canaries for Mauritius a month before. A strong element of competition now interjected itself.[15]

On 21 November, only five days after Banks had written to

[13] Flinders, *Voyage*, vol. i, p. cciv.

[14] Cf. Sir Gavin de Beer, *The Sciences were never at War* (London, 1960), pp. 65, 90 sq., and 112.

[15] That the French believed this to be the case appears in a passage in the first edition of *Voyage de Découvertes aux Terres Australes.* . . . (2 vols. and atlas, Paris, 1807–16) ed. by François Péron, Tome I, p. 8 : 'L'histoire de notre navigation et de nos propres dangers fera mieux ressortir encore toute l'étendue de ces difficultés, et la perte des deux vaisseaux du capitaine Flinders, *envoyé par le gouvèrnement anglis pour rivaliser avec nous* [italics mine], n'en fournira que trop une nouvelle et déplorable preuve.' In publishing the second edition (1824) M. Freycinet, editor, saw no reason to alter this text. Tome i, p. 71.

Flinders, the Admiralty directed the Navy Board to take a three-masted vessel named the *Xenophon* up on the ways at Sheerness, and to make her defects good.[16] Less than three weeks passed before the Navy Board was instructed to complete the *Xenophon's* provisions to six months for foreign service, 'with all possible dispatch'.[17] And on 19 January 1801, another direction from the Admiralty desired the Navy Board to 'cause His May. sloop *Xenophon* to be registered upon the List of the Royal Navy, from this time, by the Name of the *Investigator*'.[18]

That Flinders had been immediately caught up in a storm of effort by his commitment to Banks appears in a letter he wrote to Ann a week before Christmas.[19] His intended ship was indeed the *Xenophon*, soon to be renamed *Investigator*—at whose choice is not known. He spoke of a hoped-for promotion in rank, of the possibility of going down to Lincolnshire the day after Christmas with Sir Joseph. Then the tone of the letter turned sombre.

Apparently Ann, the realist, had put the issue of their future to him squarely : did he wish to marry her and settle down; or did he intend to remain explorer, leaving her forever behind to fend for herself? He answered with reckless bravery, but appalling fatuity. Next week, he wrote, 'let us meet as lovers, and part as friends—Ah me!' He would—he must—return to New South Wales. For his part, he would bury himself in work, and never look back. He admonished her to 'learn music and the French language,' to study 'geography and astronomy, and even metaphysics'. 'Write a great deal, work with thy kneedle [*sic*] and read every book that comes thy way save trifling novels.'

His answer showed her just how well he understood women. 'Meet as lovers, and part as friends!' Needlework and reading indeed! Somehow, perhaps by the very frenzy of activity to which events compelled them, their love survived this *crise de coeur*.

Banks too entered the new project with vigour and enthusiasm.

[16] Admiralty to Navy Board, 21 November 1800. P.R.O., Adm. 2/293: 484. Virtually nothing can be gleaned from either Flinders's writings or extant archives to describe the *Investigator*. Files at the National Maritime Museum do contain a working drawing of the orlop deck, but nothing else on the subject.
[17] Admiralty to Navy Board, 10 December 1800. P.R.O., Adm. 2/294: 51.
[18] Admiralty to Navy Board, 19 January 1801. P.R.O., *Ibid*. 247.
[19] Flinders to Ann, 18 December 1800. N.M.M. 60/017. FLI/25.

Lacking staff, the Admiralty happily relied upon his scientific experience to draw up a programme for the voyage. Certain changes were required in the *Xenophon*, both above and below decks, to accommodate the plants Banks hoped to retrieve. Designs must be sent to the yard as soon as possible. General instructions for the commander's guidance must be drawn. Lists of instruments, equipment, books, and charts were needed. But these problems, while certainly important, even vital, were by no means as serious as the recruitment of a competent group of 'scientific gentlemen'. Here Banks's prestige and his wide acquaintance in the world of savants, gave him a strong field from which to draw. Even so, since he wanted only the best, he was quite prepared to spend whatever time and effort were required to get them.

True to his own interest, Banks began by looking for a naturalist, a young man who could take responsibility for both botany and zoology. No comprehensive field studies, let alone taxonomy, had ever been made in New Holland. He turned first to a young man named Robert Brown, whom he had met in London the previous year, and to whom he had opened his collections and his library. Brown, then twenty-seven, not quite four months older than Flinders, had finished his course of studies in medicine at the University of Edinburgh. In 1795 he had entered the regiment of Fifeshire Fencibles in which he was, in 1800, still serving in Ireland as both Ensign and Assistant Surgeon. What attracted Banks's attention was Brown's evident enthusiasm for natural history, displayed only a year before, supported by the fact that, when he was only eighteen, Brown had published an original paper on the flora of Scotland.

On 12 December Banks wrote his invitation:

'Sir

'A ship is this day ordered to be Fitted out for the purpose of exploring the natural history (among other things) of New Holland, & it is Resolved that a naturalist & a Botanic Painter shall be sent in her.

'The salary of the naturalist will be £400 a year & I conclude that the expenses of the mess &c canot [*sic*] cost him so much as £100, if you choose to accept the appointment I will certainly

5

recommend you, but if you do it will be necessary for you to
Come here as speedily as you can for the admiralty are inclined
to use great expedition in the outfit, & say that they will be
ready for the next Convoy, which will sail at the Latter end of
this month, at all Events however you may depend upon it that
I will not recommend any other person till I have heard from
you, & I hope you will be the messenger of your own answer
the voyage will I conclude Last 3 years at least. . . .'[20]

Brown's later career, as first observer of 'Brownian Movement,' and as 'Princeps Botanicorum' throughout Europe,
proved Banks's shrewd perception in choosing men. Whatever
the need for haste, the hope of the Admiralty that the ship might
sail 'the latter end of this month', betrayed more enthusiasm than
good sense. In fact, if she had, Brown among others would have
been left behind because, although he accepted instantly, nego-
tiations for his release from the regiment grew both heated and
protracted.

Nothing so well reveals Banks's industry and his powers of
persuasion as these efforts to put together a team of scientists.
Having sent his letter to Brown, he set to work immediately to
find a botanic draughtsman, a landscape artist, a miner, and a
gardener. Thus, in the only known letter from Banks to Earl
Spencer on the subject of this voyage, dated 14 December 1800,
he wrote :

'I hope tomorrow to have it in my power to offer for your
Lordships approbation a Botanic Painter for the voyage who in
my opinion is as good as can be found in all Europe his name is
Ferdinand Bauer a german who travelled with Dr. Sibthorpe in
Greece. I am sorry to say that Mr. Alexander declines the
appointment of Landscape painter on account of the ill health of
his wife but he expresses his infinite regret at not being able to
become a candidate for an appointment which would in all other
respects have been particularly suitable to him. I mean to wait
upon Lady Spencer tomorrow to ask her if her Ladyship can
assist me by thinking of any other person.'[21]

[20] Banks to Brown, 12 December 1800. B.M., Add. MSS. 32439. 24 sq.
[21] Banks to Spencer, 14 December 1800. Spencer Collections, Althorp. Bauer
was in fact an Austrian, born 20 January 1760, died 17 March 1826. For accounts

It was fortunate that Banks secured Bauer, for in him he had both a mature artist and a congenial colleague for Brown. The loss of William Alexander as landscape artist was a pity. Alexander had a wide reputation as both traveller and artist, having gone with McCartney's embassy to China in 1792, and having later prepared the final landscapes for Vancouver's narrative. Failing Alexander, Banks turned next to William Daniell, nephew of the celebrated artist, Thomas Daniell. He also declined. Finally, he fixed upon William Westall, another brilliant choice. Whether Lady Spencer had any part in this appointment is not clear; but Banks's astuteness in consulting her is.

As the year 1800 drew to a close, Flinders was living in rooms at 16 King Street, Soho, an address now long buried in the history of Shaftesbury Avenue. Living so close to Banks—no more than a ten-minute walk—he was no doubt too busy with his own future to dwell overmuch on the departure of his old friend Bass for Port Jackson. Whether Flinders watched the *Venus* sail down the Thames does not appear. They never met again, and perhaps that was just as well—for both.

of his life, see: John Lhotsky's biographical sketch in *Linn. Soc. Proc.*, vol. I, p. 39 sq. (1839); W. T. Stearn, 'Franz and Ferdinand Bauer . . .', *Endeavour*, vol. XIX, p. 27 sqq. (Jan. 1960); and Bernard Smith, *European Vision and the South Pacific, 1768–1850* (Oxford, 1960), p. 141 sq. The author is indebted to Mr Warren R. Dawson for the transcription of Banks's letter to Spencer. The quotation given is the last paragraph of a letter which otherwise deals with quite unrelated matters.

# CHAPTER FOUR

# The *Investigator*

## January–July 1801

1

As the new year opened, Great Britain found herself trapped in deepening crisis. The inflation of prices brought about by the wars appeared to be out of hand. A four-pound loaf of bread which in 1780 had cost 7d. now cost 17½d., and no end was in sight. Irish nationalists chose the moment to bring the problem of political settlement to a boil. Pitt's solution, involving Catholic emancipation, drove George III into frenzied opposition. Determined to stand by his Coronation Oath, he resisted his Prime Minister so fiercely that Pitt, broken in health, was forced to resign. Charles Jenkinson, 1st Baron Hawkesbury, took over the Foreign Office on 20 February. The next day Spencer turned over the Admiralty to John Jervis, Earl of St Vincent; and a month later Henry Addington replaced Pitt at the Treasury.

On the international scene matters were equally bad. Late in December, under the bullying of Russia, the Scandinavian powers had joined together in opposing the British in the Baltic. Since the Royal Navy was then procuring all its masts and spars in those countries, so dangerous a confrontation was intolerable. The issue was decided on the afternoon of 2 April 1801, the day on which Nelson outfought the Danish fleet at Copenhagen.

For all their peril and drama, however, these events had little apparent effect upon Flinders's preparations. Food and clothing were dear, and wages low; but apart from that, the *Investigator* seems to have been strangely isolated from outside perturbances. Even the change from Spencer to St Vincent, a fighting Admiral, caused not a ripple in Flinders's life. The commitment to the voyage remained alive.

After the Christmas holidays, Banks went about his work methodically. From his general correspondence it would appear that Sir Joseph was not burdened with his usual miscellany of projects. At least not for the moment. Aside from working on the importation of hemp seeds for the East India Company, and a minor quarrel over enclosure of his property in Lincolnshire, he was relatively free to put his energies on the *Investigator*. There was work to be done on the plant cabin designs. Lists of various kinds of equipment had to be made up. The burden of drafting the instructions for the voyage fell on him. But for the moment, his most important problem was the recruitment of scientists.

Quite unexpectedly, the release of Robert Brown from his Fifeshire regiment became a troublesome, acrimonious affair. As he was bound to do, Brown had consulted his immediate superior, one Lieut.-Colonel Thomas Durham, and had requested to go on leave for one month. The Lieut.-Colonel had immediately assented, and had so advised not only his brother, colonel James Durham, commanding, but also Lord Cornwallis, Lord Lieutenant of Ireland.[1] The Colonel exploded. The issue was not whether Brown might go, but whether in going, he might retain his Ensigncy in the regiment. Naturally, the Colonel regarded his stated complement of officers inviolate; but by agreeing to let Brown go on leave, he would in effect be admitting that the billet was not needed, and no replacement would be allowed. In righteous anger Colonel Durham accused Brown of attempting to deceive him, suggesting that Brown really intended to extend the leave for the duration of the voyage.[2] Brown's reaction was sharp and angry. Finding himself caught in a misunderstanding between the two brothers, he took refuge in his own honour.[3] This instantly ended his friendship with the Lieut.-Colonel.[4] Recriminations flew. Finally, Banks was forced to intervene.

[1] T. Durham to Cornwallis, 17 December 1800. B.M. (N.H.) 'Brown Correspondence', vol. III, p. 100.
[2] J. Durham to Brown, 13 January 1801. *Ibid.*, p. 103.
[3] Brown to J. Durham, 20 January 1801. *Ibid.*, p. 104.
[4] T. Durham to Brown, 27 January 1801. *Ibid.*, p. 107.

Having written to Colonel Durham, and received no answer, he wrote directly to Cornwallis. After explaining the case, he ventured to hope that Cornwallis would allow Brown to retain his Ensigncy, and added:

'. . . I am sorry to say that Col. Durham appears by Letters written to Ensign Brown disinclined to give his Consent to the measure. I have however written to the Colonel & used every argument I could draw from the importance of the Service in which Government wishes to Employ the Ensign, to induce the Colonel to approve it,[5] & as I have not in three days Received any answer from him, I have taken the Liberty of applying to your Excellency, hoping that the indecision which is apparent by the Colonels postponing an answer to my Letter, may by your Excellency's good offices be Converted into a Consent, in which Event I have no doubt of a Favourable answer from your Lordship's well known attention & patronage of usefull Science & beneficial discovery.'[6]

It was a masterly combination of pressure with tact: 'the Service in which *Government* wishes to employ the Ensign,' 'your Excellency's *good offices*,' 'your Lordship's *well known* attention & patronage of useful Science and beneficial discovery.' Whether he touched Cornwallis's common sense, his vanity, or his overburden of work made no difference to Banks. What he wanted was results, and he got them. On 3 March his Lordship directed Brown's release, as he put it to Banks, 'agreeably to your Desire'.[7]

So much for the Durhams. Once again, as in the cases of Bligh and Vancouver, Banks had effected a liaison between scientific enterprise and the Admiralty where, only a few years before, he had felt 'natural history must be considered as mere rubbish.'[8]

Meanwhile Flinders, after returning from his holiday in Lincolnshire, remained in London, finishing his monograph and awaiting orders to proceed to Sheerness. That he was able to

[5] *Ibid.*, p. 113.
[6] Banks to Cornwallis, 23 February 1801. *Ibid.*, p. 114.
[7] E. Cooke to Banks, 3 March 1801. *Ibid.*, p. 115.
[8] Banks to Major W. Price, 31 March 1796. B.M. (N.H.) D.T.C. 10(1). 29.

keep busy was just as well, for after his visit to Ann he found himself in an agony of unrequited love. For perfectly good reasons she had not taken kindly to his last letter, and he was now quite certain he had lost her. 'On love I *must* not think,' he wrote, ' . . . it has constituted the greatest happiness and the greatest misery of my life . . . I dare not think on thee, Annette. . . .' 'Thou hast promised to inform me when thou art married. . . .'[9] So on and on, in page after page of brokenhearted letters which inevitably drained his energy.

On 19 January, Evan Nepean, Secretary to the Admiralty, signed Flinders's commission as 'Lieutenant of His Majesty's Sloop the Investigator, Willing and Requiring you forthwith to go on board and take upon you the Charge and Command of Lieutenant in her accordingly.'[10] Losing little time, Matthew arrived at Sheerness on 24 January. After looking her over, he wrote to Banks describing the *Investigator* as a 'comfortable ship,' having, in fact, rather 'too much room for the commander'.[11] The following day, Sunday, 25 January 1801, with resolution Flinders took pen to fresh-ruled paper and began the Journal of H.M. Sloop *Investigator*:

'His Majesty's ship Xenophon of 334 tons and 75 men, having undergone a thorough examination and been newly coppered in dock at Sheerness was pitched upon to proceed upon a voyage of discovery to the South Seas; and on 19 January a commission was signed by the Lords of the Admiralty for Matthew Flinders, late second lieutenant of His Majesty's ship Reliance to be lieutenant of the Investigator to which name the Xenophon was changed by this commission, and being the senior officer, I took command and John Henry Martin, Esqr considered himself to be superseded.

'Mustered the ship's company and read my commission as lieutenant. Received fresh beef. Snow at times.'[12]

[9] Flinders to Ann, 16 and 27 January 1801. N.M.M. 60/017. FLI/25.
[10] N.M.M. 60/017. FLI/5. Sir Evan Nepean (1751–1822) became Governor of Bombay, 1812–19.
[11] Flinders to Banks, 24 January 1801. M.L.
[12] Matthew Flinders, 'Journal', P.R.O., Adm. 55/75, p. 1. Hereafter cited as Flinders, 'Journal', vol. I.

Had the *Xenophon*, then, only been 'pitched upon'? However
—Flinders and his crew got down to business, much of which
revolved around the daily routine of the port:

'Employed clearing the holds to receive coal.'
'Answered the signal for weekly accounts.'
'Read the articles of war and punished John Fuller marine with
12 lashes for contempt to his serjeant. Washed and aired
below.'
'Received beer and bread from the lighter.'

So it went, day after day. Each laconic entry, however insignificant by itself, added nevertheless to a record of feverish activity
generated by forces of which the crew, enlisted for their muscle,
were wholly innocent.

Flinders faced a formidable assignment. He knew that in order
to put in a full southern summer he ought to arrive at New
Holland no later than December next. Thus, from the day he
took command he had at the most eleven months, of which a half
at least would be spent on the outward journey. In less than six
months he had to supervise the fitting-out and provisioning of
his ship. He had to rebuild his crew, taking such of the *Xenophon's*
men as wished to go, and finding other volunteers as he could in
the fleet. But more, there were a thousand details about the
project itself that only he and Banks could settle, sitting down
together. All of this he now undertook to do.

The day after assuming command, Flinders wrote again to
Banks, urging the need for a new establishment of men. The
special service of the *Investigator* required a rebalancing of the
crew. Officers would be requested for abilities not needed in the
fighting navy. This new establishment could be authorised only
by the Admiralty, and 'I am not,' he wrote, 'without hopes of
seeing a commander included in it.' Cook had been only a
lieutenant when he took *Endeavour* to the South Seas. So had
Bligh in the *Bounty*. Times had changed.

He was concerned, too, about overloading. Even though the
ship was commodious, she seemed roomy in the wrong places.
So much so, in fact, that Flinders feared for her safety: 'Should
we be obliged to clear for action, it would be necessary to throw

a great deal overboard.' The condition argued, he thought, for lighter guns, providing he could be furnished with a French passport.[13]

Then there was the problem of accommodating the plants Brown would collect. The greenhouse was being properly fitted on the quarterdeck; but the joiners at the yard said they had no plans for a plant cabin, only word that there was to be one.[14]

To all such matters as Flinders reported to him, Sir Joseph gave the minutest attention, conferring personally at the Admiralty when necessary, and writing notes when not. Thus on 2 February, the Admiralty directed the Navy Board to change the ship's guns.[15] On 3 February, they set the complement at eighty-three men.[16] Still Flinders expressed impatience. Orders to the yard came more slowly than he thought necessary. Boats were not right. Casks for salt and dry provision, and for water, had not been requisitioned. To top it all, no Master for the ship had been found.[17] Flinders kept up the pressure.

In fact, however, progress was being made. The time had come to send in lists of the many small items of equipment that had to be purchased. More paperwork. The Navy Board could easily handle provisions and sea stores; but books of a very unusual kind were needed for this mission :

H.M.S. Investigator Sheerness Feb. 8, 1801

'Sir Joseph

The above are the lists of what appear to me requisite to be taken on our voyage. You will probably see some things super-abundant, and many useful things left out. I thought to have kept it till my arrival in town, that I might have had the advantage of your advice upon various things; but as that time will probably be yet prolonged, and orders from the admiralty are come down to hasten the outfit and to the Nore, the time requisite to propose them, makes it necessary to forward it immediately.

'I understand from Mr Whidbey, that the admiralty, on

[13] Flinders to Banks, 26 January 1801. M.L.
[14] Flinders to Banks, 29 January 1801. M.L.
[15] Admiralty to Navy Board, 2 February 1801. P.R.O., Adm. 2/294: 320 sq.
[16] Admiralty to Navy Board, 3 February 1801. Ibid., 322; and Admiralty to Flinders, 5 February 1801. P.R.O., Adm. 2/141: 97 sq.
[17] Flinders to Banks, 4 February 1801. M.L.

application being made, will order the Navy Board, their book-seller, their stationer, and Arrowsmith to furnish the lists on the first page; and that the treasury purveyor will provide the last on the application of the admiralty; but if you, Sir Joseph, will take the trouble, I wish to leave this matter entirely to you, and I only send the lists as containing my ideas upon what is necessary. No fishing gear are inserted, because we shall get supplied from this yard; but I have inserted shooting materials in the lists of articles for presents, but which are certainly meant to provide ourselves with food, and for defense. I think it right that these should be found to us.

'On receiving the new establishment for the Investigator, I wrote to the Admiralty for the boatswain, gunner and carpenter; and represented, that there were several people now on board who were unfit to go the voyage, and submitted it to their consideration, whether the whole company should not consist of volunteers. This morning I find, that V. Adm. Graeme has received orders to take out such men as I object to, and to complete the complement with volunteers; but these changes are not to take place until we get to the Nore. I did not mention the Reliance people now in the Jamaica, lest it might interfere with what you had done.

'In answer to another application to the Navy Board about the master, they desire me this morning to pitch upon some body; and refer me to a letter of Feb. 26 which I never received. But since I find that they depend entirely on me, I shall fix upon somebody immediately, from the necessity of having one before much is done in the holds.

'The victualling office have yet sent us nothing; but informed me, that the provisions I requested, are ordered to be got ready. The shipwrights are now getting on with us, and if we had but the master, the water and provisions, we should have little to wait for, but the articles contained in the present lists.

'No application has yet been made to the Sick & Hurt Board for the concrete acid of lemon, or other antiscorbutics; but I trust that Dr. Blane will have every thing necessary prepared for us.

'I hoped to have received a line from you, Sir Joseph, this morning, and trust that I shall be gratified by next post. I am anxious for your opinion about my coming to town, and to know if any progress is made with the charts and memoir.'[18]

There was the matter of scientific and nautical instruments to be supplied by Edward Troughton, instrument maker, up in London. Apart from the chronometers, Flinders would need, or at least he would get, these items as follows:[19]

'A List of Instruments to be supplied for the use of Captain Flinders of His Majesty's Sloop Investigator.

> '1—Eight Inch Sextant
> 1—Stand for Ditto
> 2—Small Hadleys for Surveying
> 1—Military Telescope
> 2—Strait bars & 1 Horse Shoe Magnet
> 2—Circumferenters with Telescopes
> 1—Protractor of 3 or 4 Inches radius
> 3—Common Pocket Compasses
> 3—Pedometers
> 1—Copying Glass
> 1—Parallel Ruler
> 1—Surveying Chain
> 2—Ebony ruling Scales of 3 & 5 Feet
> 2—Thermometers
> 1—Pocket Ditto
> 2—Quick Silver Horizons, complete in a box
> 1—box of Instruments [drawing?]
> 1—Beam compass
> 1—Set of graduating Scales
> 1—Walkers new invented Compass
> 1—Common Azimuth Compass, Walkers Construction.'

Finally, for purposes of barter with—or pacifying—natives, the ship would have to carry prodigious quantities of trinkets and tools:[20]

---

[18] Flinders to Banks, 8 February 1801. M.L.
[19] Admiralty to Navy Board, 7 March 1801. P.R.O., Adm. 2/294: 477 sq.
[20] Admiralty to Navy Board, 15 April 1801. P.R.O., Adm. 2/295: 172–5.

'List of Articles requisite for His Majesty's Sloop Investigator, to take on her Voyage of Discovery, for use, Presents to Natives &c.

'A Marquee compleat

| | |
|---|---:|
| Bell tents | 3 |
| Canteens containing every necessary for excursions | 3 |
| Dust shot to kill specimens | 6 Bags |
| No. 6 | 6 |
| No. 4 | 10 |
| No. 2 for Do. and food | 12 |
| No. 1 | 12 |
| Swan shot | 20 |
| Small Buckshot | 20 |
| Large Do. | 20 |
| Buck and Swan shot casters | 2 prs. |
| Lead for Casting | 1000 Cwt. |
| Axes for Presents &c. | 50 |
| Hatchets | 300 |
| Small Adzes | 50 |
| Tohees of sizes | 200 |

These are pieces of thin bar Iron about Six inches long, sharpened at one end, and turned a little at the other, they are meant to be a substitute for an adze.

| | |
|---|---:|
| Hammers of sizes | 100 |
| Casks of nails of sizes | 4 |
| Cross-cut Saws | 5 |
| Pit Saws | 5 |
| Hand Saws | 100 |
| Pocket knives | 500 |
| Shoemakers Do. | 100 |
| Scissors of Sizes | 300 Pairs |
| Files of sorts | 200 |
| Looking glasses of sorts | 500 |
| Coarse combs | 100 |
| Blue beads | 50 strings |

| | |
|---|---|
| Red beads | 50 strings |
| White Do. | 50 |
| Yellow Do. | 50 |
| Ear Rings | 100 Pairs |
| Rings for Fingers of sizes | 200 |
| Red gartering | 500 yds. |
| Blue Do. | 500 |
| Red Caps | 100 |
| Small Blankets | 100 |
| Red Baize thin | 100 yds. |
| Coloured linen | 100 |
| Red thread | 5 lbs. |
| Needles | 1000 |
| Medals of His Majesty ⎫<br>or some new common coins ⎭ | some |

> Bar iron for the purpose
> of making Tools, suitable
> to the taste of the Indians,
> that may be met with, with a
> proportion of Steel for
> edging them.'

These lists had to be compiled, copied, priced, and the goods purchased, checked, and delivered; and being out of the ordinary, the whole business probably produced among the clerks at the Navy Board nothing but vexation of spirit. For some of these objects they would have to chase all over London.

Victualling was a difficult problem from start to finish. Of course, while the ship was in a home port, the crew received the same food as the rest of the fleet. But provisioning for a long voyage required hours of consultation. As Flinders was not only commander, but also the designated Purser, the responsibility for stores was his. He was personally accountable, indeed liable, for all the food delivered. Shortages occurred which would not be discovered for months. With space in the *Investigator* at a premium, and food in short supply at Port Jackson, plans had to be laid for shipping extra provisions to the colony for Flinders's account.[21]

Finding two commissioned officers had been easy. The First

[21] Flinders to Admiralty, 17 July 1801. P.R.O., Adm. 1/1800: F73.

Lieutenant was one Lieutenant (later Captain) Robert Fowler who, having been in the *Xenophon*, had requested leave of the Admiralty 'to remain in her during her intended voyage'.[22] Matthew's brother, Samuel, wanted to go, and, having passed his examination for lieutenancy[23] was welcome to serve as second lieutenant. But the Master came only too slowly:

'I fear that we shall scarcely be able to find a good master to go the voyage, the pay being so small. If the Navy Board would hold out some encouragement, such as the pay of a superior rate, or something else considerable which it might be convenient to them to give, I could get one immediately. Mr John Engledus the present master of the Iris frigate, would engage under such circumstances, and he is a man who might answer very well, but he objects to leaving a superior for an inferior pay. . . .'[24]

There were also to be found and signed on, three Warrant officers: a Boatswain, a Gunner, a Carpenter, as well as four Midshipmen, a Clerk, a Sailmaker, an Armourer, and a Surgeon. The difficulty lay in the fact that the *Investigator's* mission would remove her from the realm of enemy action, and hence by definition preclude the possibility of prize money. So Flinders had to take what volunteers he could persuade. On the whole, and for no obvious reason, he did very well indeed.

2

'Read my commission as Commander. Employed as necessary.'[25]

The promotion had come as no surprise to either Flinders or Banks. Yet mutual congratulations seemed in order:

'I have the satisfaction to inform you, that my commission as commander of His Majestys sloop Investigator, came down here

[22] Fowler to Admiralty, 31 December 1800. P.R.O., Adm. 1/2875: F155.
[23] Flinders to Admiralty, 5 March 1801. P.R.O., Adm. 1/1800: F58.
[24] Flinders to Banks, 9 March 1801. M.L. In May the Navy Board adjusted the pay of the Master to a level which equated the *Investigator* with a first rate. *See* Flinders to Banks, 10 May 1801. M.L.
[25] Flinders, 'Journal', vol. I, p. 2.

this morning, and for which, Sir Joseph, I felt myself entirely indebted to your influence and kindness. Panegyric, or a long train of sentences of gratitude, would be unpleasant to a mind like that of Sir Joseph Banks. I will therefore only add, that it shall be my endeavour to shew by my conduct and exertions that your good opinion has not been misplaced.'[26]

Banks answered immediately:

'I give you sincere joy at the attainment of your wish in your appointment of Commander. I have long known that it was certain, but I am glad it is now placed beyond the reach of accident, or the change of administration.'[27]

Other important news in the same letter told Flinders that his memoir on Van Diemen's Land had gone to the printers.

By early February Banks had finished selection of his scientists. He had arranged personally with the First Lord, Earl Spencer, that their salaries were to be paid by the Admiralty.[28] But the use of public funds, subject to audit, required that the undertaking be placed upon a more formal footing. Moreover, approval of the arrangements in writing, by the full Board of Admiralty Commissioners, would guarantee their survival, too, against political upheaval. Thus on 9 February, Evan Nepean, the able, industrious Admiralty Secretary, wrote to Banks, 'I wish you would have the goodness to let me know the salaries to be given to the different persons who are to go out in the Investigator.'[29] It must have seemed strange to Banks that Nepean did not have this information from Spencer. Anyway, Banks replied immediately:

| 'To the naturalist | £400 |
| To two draftsmen | 600 |
| To a gardener | 100 |
| To a miner | 100' |

These were salaries per annum.

[26] Flinders to Banks, 18 February 1801. M.L.
[27] Banks to Flinders, 19 February 1801. N.M.M. 60/017. FLI/1.
[28] It is important to note that the Royal Society as such had absolutely no connection with the enterprise.
[29] Nepean to Banks, 9 February 1801. H.R.N.S.W., vol. IV, p. 298.

Banks added, 'The astronomer, you know, is appointed by the Board of Longitude, and receives £400 a year, the same as was given in Cook's voyage, a salary at present thought rather too low by the astronomer.'[30]

On 1 March the Admiralty authorised Flinders to receive the six scientists, together with four of their servants, on board, to give them proper cabins, and to victual them 'in the same manner as your Sloop's Company'.[31] Two weeks later, Mr Crosley, the Astronomer, proposed to join the ship. But by 2 April none of the scientists had left London. Sir Joseph had advised his people not to go on board the ship until the terms under which they were employed had been settled.[32] Doubtless the severe attack of gout Banks had suffered at the beginning of March had delayed these arrangements. But on 15 April final agreement on questions of compensation was reached. Salaries were to be computed in guineas instead of pounds, were to run as from 10 February, the agreed date on which Banks had engaged the men; and, in order that they might purchase their outfits, a half-year's salary was to be advanced immediately.[33]

It was the best offer to the men. But what of the other side of the bargain? Drafting terms of employment under which the scientists would serve had not yet been done. In reply to a detailed query on the matter from Banks, Nepean astutely wrote, 'Any proposal you make will be approved. The whole is left entirely to your decision'.[34]

The document Banks drafted, not without significance today, was signed by Brown, Westall, Bauer, Peter Good, the gardener and John Allen, the miner, .[35] It read as follows:

[30] *Ibid.*, p. 299. This memorandum was printed by the editor of *H.R.N.S.W.* 'from a draft in the handwriting of Sir Joseph Banks, which is neither signed nor addressed'. After thirty years of inflation it is scarcely surprising that the Astronomer demurred.

[31] Admiralty to Flinders, 1 March 1801. P.R.O., Adm. 2/141: 491 sqq.

[32] Navy Board to Admiralty, 2 April 1801. P.R.O., Adm. 106/2227: 174.

[33] Admiralty to Navy Board, 15 April 1801. P.R.O., Adm. 2/295:169–72.

[34] Nepean to Banks, 28 April 1801. *H.R.N.S.W.*, vol. IV, p. 348. As an illustration of the workings of government sponsorship of research in Britain at the time, the importance of this document cannot be overestimated. It says as much for the pragmatic intelligence of the Admiralty Commissioners as it does for Banks's competence.

[35] It will be recalled that Crosley was employed not by the Admiralty, but by the Board of Longitude. The document is printed here *in extenso* to show in what

'In order to prevent all misunderstandings between the Lords Commissioners for executing the office of Lord High Admiral of the United Kingdom, and the persons employed by their Lordships as scientific assistants on board His Majestys ship the Investigator, for the purpose of exploring the country of New Holland, their Lordships have been pleased to issue the following instructions and commands, to be obeyed by the persons so employed; and it is expected that every person so employed do sign his name to the same in testimony of his acquiescence in the terms on which their Lordships are pleased to employ him.

'1st Their Lordships require every person employed as a scientific assistant on board the Investigator, to render voluntary obedience to the Commander of the ship, in all orders he shall from time to time issue for the direction of the conduct of his crew, or any part thereof.

'2d Their Lordships require that all persons so employed do on all occasions conduct themselves peaceably, quietly, and civilly to each other; each readily assisting the other in his respective department to the utmost of his ability, in such manner as will best promote the success of the public service in which they are jointly engaged, and unite their individual endeavours into one general result.

'3dly Their Lordships require the Draughtsman employed for natural history to pay due attention to the directions he shall receive from the Naturalist, and the Draughtsman employed for landscape and figures to pay regard to the opinion of the Commander, in the choice of objects most fitting to be delineated, and their Lordships moreover require the gardener and the miner to pay obedience to the Naturalist, in all such orders as he shall think fit to give them.

'4thly Their Lordships consider the salary allotted to each person* employed, as a full compensation for the whole of his time; they therefore expect, that all journals, remarks, memorandums, drawings, sketches, collections of natural history, and

---

* Naturalist 400g. per an°. Draughtsmen 300g. Gardener and Miner 100g. per annum.

---

particulars the aims of science on the one hand, and of government on the other, had—and still have—to be made explicit. It is a masterpiece of its kind.

6

of habits, arms, utensils, ornaments &c of every kind, be delivered up on the return of the ship, to such persons as their Lordships shall direct to receive them.

'5thly In order, however, to encourage the persons engaged in this undertaking to exert themselves to the utmost in accomplishing the object of their mission, their Lordships hereby declare, that if the information collected during the voyage is deemed of sufficient importance, it is their Lordships intention to cause it to be published in the form of a narrative, drawn up by the Commander, on a plan similar to that pursued in the publication of captain Cooks voyages and to give such picuniary [*sic*] assistance as their Lordships shall see fitting, for the engraving of charts, plans, views, figures, &c and that in such case, the most interesting observations of natural history, and the most remarkable views of land and delineations of people &c will be inserting [*sic*] therein.

'6thly Their Lordships moreover declare, that in case the persons employed in the undertaking as scientific assistants are industrious in their several departments, civil and obliging to each other, and co-operate together on all occasions, in making the general work in which they are engaged complete, by assisting each other and uniting their efforts for the advantage of the public, it is intended that the profit derived from the sale of the said publication shall be divided between the Commander and the Assistants, in proportion to the good conduct each shall have held during the voyage, and the comparative advantage the publication shall, in the opinion of their Lordships, derive from the labours of each individual.

'7th Their Lordships moreover declare, that after such descriptions and sketches as shall be found necessary for the illustration and embellishment of the intended publication, shall have been selected by such persons as their Lordships shall be pleased to appoint; and such specimens of natural history, arms, implements, habits, ornaments &c as their Lordships think fitting shall have been applied to such purposes as their Lordships shall approve, the remainder of the descriptions of plants and of animals &c and the sketches of all kinds shall be at the disposal of the persons who have made them for the purpose of being published by them whenever it is thought proper at their own risk, and for their own advantage; provided however, that all such drawings as shall be finished during the voyage, and such sketches as their Lordships shall order to be finished after the return of the ship shall be considered as the property of the public and lodged in the depôt of the Admiralty when required so to be; and that the remainder of the collections of natural history, arms, habits, implements, ornaments &c shall be at the disposal of the persons who have collected them; all this, however, on condition that each person shall during the voyage have behaved himself with propriety to the rest; their Lordships reserving to themselves the power of punishing all deviations from good humour and perfect harmony among the parties, by withholding from the persons offending, such parts of the benefits above described as they shall think proper.

'We the undersigned Robert Brown, naturalist, &c in testimony of our concurrence in the above terms, and as a pledge of our obedience to all such instructions and commands as their Lordships shall be pleased to issue to us during the time we shall be in their Lordships employ, have signed our names to this engagement on the 29th day of April in the year of our Lord 1801

> Robert Brown, naturalist
> Ferdinand Bauer, botanic draughtsman
> William Westall, landscape & figure painter
> Peter Good, gardener
> John Allen, miner

'Note—This was not one of the papers inclosed to me from the Admiralty, but I think it necessary to insert it, from its importance to the intended voyage.
                    M. F.'[36]

For the scientists all was now settled except the division of the mess money. Back in January the East India Company's Committee of Shipping had invited Flinders to attend them at India House to testify on his petition for support.[37] On 4 March

[36] Flinders, 'Journal', vol. I, p. 21. See also *H.R.N.S.W.*, vol. IV, p. 349 sqq.
[37] So Flinders reported to Banks on 26 January. M.L.

the Committee had acted favourably, and reported its findings
to the Court of Directors.[38] The Court accepted the recommendation. They authorised their secretary, William Ramsay, to
notify Flinders that he would be 'paid the sums as are usually
allowed by the Company to Masters and Commanders in His
Majesty's Service in India, and that a similar Allowance be made
to the Lieutenants for their Mess as is paid to the Officers of
Vessels of the same rate as the Investigator. . . .'[39] They thought,
however, that as the protection of commerce in Indian waters
was a more dangerous form of activity than surveying the coasts
of New Holland, Flinders and his officers should be paid only for
such time as they were actually employed on the survey.

Doutless the Court intended by this Resolution that Flinders
and his officers should be paid 'batta,' an extra allowance for
subsistence given their officers in India and to naval officers
employed in their service east of the Cape of Good Hope. It does
seem curious, however, that, knowing as they did of Banks's
patronage of the project, they omitted all reference to support
of the civilian scientists. Most probably they expected Banks to
come back with more precise suggestions.[40]

What means Sir Joseph chose to clarify these questions is not
known; nor does it matter. What does matter is that, on 12 May,
Flinders was in a position to inquire what steps he should take
to withdraw the sum allowed.[41] Under pressure of negotiation
the terms of the agreement had emerged as follows:

*First*, Flinders was allowed 40 guineas for the support of
Good, the gardener, and Allen the miner.

*Second*, in lieu of a regular allowance of 'batta,' that is, subsistence paid as additional compensation, Flinders, as Purser,
was given outright the sum of £1,200, to be used as 'Table

[38] I.O., East India Company, Court Minutes, vol. CIX, pt. A, p. 1165 sq.,
11 March 1801.
[39] *Ibid*. Sir Francis Baring, founder of the House of Baring, was among those
who voted favourably on the motion.
[40] It is not irrelevant to point out that Banks had dealt with the Court on many
matters during the previous fifteen years. Most recently, in January 1801, the
Directors had thanked him for his help in procuring the hemp seeds for their use
in India.
[41] I.O., East India Company, Court of Directors, 'Letters Received by the Court,
Miscellaneous Letters Received', vol. CIV, f. 208.

Money,' for himself, his officers, and the 'scientific gentlemen'.

*Third*, this £1,200 was in addition to the 40 guineas allowed for Good and Allen, neither of whom was classed as 'gentleman'. (No mention was ever made of the four servants.)

*Fourth*, payment of the £1,200 was to be made in two parts : £600 immediately, and £600 at the conclusion of the voyage.[42]

Flinders's past services aside, essentially what the Company were paying for was information. Information not, as Flinders had earlier suggested, about a shortened passage from India to Port Jackson, but about what the west and north-west coasts of New Holland offered by way of safety for their outward-bound ships. They needed a hedge against the closure by the enemy of Sunda and Macassar Straits.[43]

This matter was by no means ended with the allocation of the grant-in-aid by the Court of Directors. There remained an annoying and protracted, if not acrimonious, debate between Banks and Flinders over distribution of the £1,200. The Company's directors declined to interfere in the matter, saying only that the fund was to be used as Table Money for the Cabin Mess—the Commander and the four scientists—and the Gunroom Mess—Lieutenants Fowler and S. W. Flinders, the Master, and the Surgeon. Banks suggested that the scientists receive double the allowance to the officers, but refused to dictate because Flinders had to live with the situation. Flinders, on the other hand, wanted to set his officers on an equal footing with the scientists; but as this would substantially increase his own share, looked about for some third person to decide. Impasse quickly developed, and lasted for well over a month. In principle, Flinders prevailed, the formula being approximately as follows :

| | |
|---|---|
| Commander | £300 |
| Four scientists | 150 |
| Four officers | 150 |
| | £600 |

[42] I.O., East India Company, Committee of Correspondence, Minutes, No. 1A, 13 May 1801; Committee of Correspondence, 'Memoranda', No. 39, 13 May 1801; and Court of Directors, 'Miscellanies', No. 41, p. 535, 14 May 1801.

[43] Flinders, *Voyage*, vol. I, p. 10.

Actually, as the Astronomer, Crosley, left the ship at the Cape of Good Hope, and was not replaced, the distribution changed :[44]

| Commander | £300 |
|---|---|
| Three scientists | 150 |
| Four officers | 150 |
| | £600 |

3

While these problems were being ironed out at India House and elsewhere, Flinders himself had been far from idle. During wartime Sheerness was a busy yard. Docking and mooring space was at a premium, so that ships whose hulls and masts were in good condition were ordered out as soon as possible. Some went directly to sea; those needing only deckwork were moved a few miles out to the Nore anchorage. Thus, with her hull newly coppered, the *Investigator* was ordered to complete stores and provisions, and 'having so done repair to the Nore and remain there until you receive further Order'.[45] This order was signed on 5 February. On 15 March Flinders wrote to the Admiralty saying that the ship was nearly ready for sea, and that he hoped to sail for New Holland 'in a month from this time'.[46] Delays in provisioning held up the move for some ten days.

'Thurs. March 26. Hoisted in the launch and furled sails. Received beer and water, and returned empty casks. Employed cleaning ship and securing for sea.'

'Frid. March 27. A.M. Thick weather and almost calm. At 7 made the signal for a pilot with a gun. At 10 slipped the moorings, and made sail out of the harbour. At 11 brought to at the little Nore, and furled sails in 11 fathoms water, with small bower.'[47]

[44] Flinders to Brown, 9 December 1810. B.M., Add. MSS. 32439. 346.
[45] Admiralty to Flinders, 5 February 1801. P.R.O., Adm. 2/141 : 99.
[46] Flinders to Admiralty, 15 March 1801. P.R.O., Adm. 1/1800 : F61.
[47] Flinders, 'Journal', vol. I, p. 3 sq.

Thus the first few miles under way. It had not been a momentous event, certainly not such as would distract him from a more serious difficulty. Only ten days after moving to the Nore he wrote once again to Ann, his first to her since late in January. Evidently she had warmed toward him once again, and had in fact reopened the subject of marriage. On 6 April he replied:

'My dearest friend,
'Thou hast asked me if there is a *possibility* of our living together. I think I see a *probability* of living with a moderate share of comfort. Till now I was not certain of being able to fit myself out clear of the world. I have now done it; and have accommodation on board the Investigator, in which as my wife, a woman may, with love to assist her, make herself happy. This prospect has recalled all the tenderness which I have so sedulously endeavoured to banish. I am sent for to London, where I shall be from the 9th to the 19th or perhaps longer. If thou wilt meet me there, this hand shall be thine forever. If thou hast sufficient love and courage, say to Mr. and Mrs. Tyler [her mother and stepfather] that I require nothing more than a sufficient stock of clothes, and a small sum to answer the increased expenses that will necessarily and immediately come upon me; as well for living on board, as for providing for it at Port Jackson; for whilst I am employed in the most dangerous part of my duty thou shalt be placed under some friendly roof there. I will specify this sum to be £200, or if great inconvenience will result from advancing it, I will say £150; and I leave everything future to the justice and generosity of thy parents and friends.

'It is but a bad specimen of my stability to change in this manner, as appearances will bespeak I do; but it is no change. It is only just now that I see attendant comfort; the want of which only, kept me back.

'I need not, or at this time have I time to enter into a detail of my income and prospects; it will, I trust, be sufficient for me to say, that I see a fortune growing under me, to meet increasing expenses. I only want to have a fair start, and my life for it we will do well, and be happy. I will write further tomorrow; but shall most anxiously expect thy answer at 86 Fleet St. London on my arrival on Friday; and I trust thy presence immediately afterwards. Mr. or perhaps Mrs. Tyler will most probably accompany thee . . . .

'It will be much better to keep this matter entirely secret. There are many reasons for it yet, and I have also a powerful one. I do not exactly know how my great friends might like it.'[48]

Something can be said of Matthew's *volte-face*. Although the reason he gave for it was the improvement of his financial prospects, a better guess would be that theretofore he had been simply muddle-headed about the matter—as all lovers are entitled to be. But when he expected to secure a 'fortune,' as he called it, remains far from clear.

The secrecy he enjoined was a mistake, not because his plans to take Ann with him did not work out, as indeed they did not, but because he should have taken counsel with Sir Joseph. He and Banks had established a mutual confidence which Flinders now chose to ignore.

Whatever his business in London, it did not detain Flinders until the 19th. Indeed, he obtained an extension of his leave from the *Investigator*. Writing from London, he told the Admiralty he thought his presence 'may be more useful *here* [italics mine] than at Sheerness'.[49] Then, after giving Banks his mailing address in Boston, he went off to take his bride. Evidently plans had changed, because the marriage took place at Partney, Lincs, on Friday, 17 April.[50] This was not camouflage, it was deception, and in the event several people were badly hurt. The couple arrived back in London the following Monday, neither Sir Joseph nor the Admiralty any the wiser.

---

[48] N.M.M. 60/017. FLI/25. This copy differs significantly from that given by Scott in his *Life*, p. 166 sq., which he quoted from the Flinders Papers in the State Library of Victoria. The Melbourne copy lacks any mention of an amount of dowry money Flinders requested Ann to bring. Moreover, Scott omitted the short paragraph beginning, 'It is but a bad specimen of my stability . . .', although the paragraph appears in the copy he used.

[49] Flinders to Admiralty, 15 April 1801. P.R.O., Adm. 1/1800: F63.

[50] A note in the Flinders Papers, S.L.V., reports that the wedding took place in London. This is erroneous, *vide* Flinders to Ann, 13 April 1801. N.M.M. 60/017. FLI/25.

4

From the days of the American Revolution, when Benjamin Franklin was serving as Minister from the Congress of the United States to the French government, the practice had grown among the Great Powers of exempting ships, of whatever nation, engaged in the pursuit of science, from the hazards of war. In this way, at Franklin's request, James Cook was able to carry on his explorations unmolested. In June 1800, at the request of French scientists, Banks had persuaded His Majesty's government to issue a passport for a similar enterprise under Nicolas Baudin, going to New Holland.[51]

Now in 1801, Flinders and Banks both felt that the *Investigator* should carry French papers. The guarantee of immunity would enable Flinders both to conserve space and weight otherwise given to heavy guns, and to spare gun-crews for the fighting fleet. What he needed was not only a safe-conduct, but also an assurance that, for reasons of humanity, he might feel free to ask assistance in case of need. Thus, on 20 March, at Flinders's urging,[52] St Vincent wrote to Addington, 'Would not this be a favourable moment to apply to the Government of France for a Passport for H.M. Ship Investigator going out upon discovery?'[53] At the same time, he wrote to Hawkesbury at the Foreign Office, formally requesting him to take appropriate steps in the matter.[54]

Whether Hawkesbury was unaware that communication between the two hostile governments could be ponderous and chancy, or whether he failed to sense any urgency in the matter, the fact is that the Foreign Secretary did nothing about it until 8 May. On that date, Hawkesbury blandly acknowledged receipt of St Vincent's letter of 20 March, and reported that he had '*lost no time* [italics mine] in making an immediate application to the

[51] For a discussion of the history of this subject, *see* Sir Gavin de Beer, *The Sciences were never at War* (London, 1960), chaps. 3, 7, and 9.
[52] Flinders to Admiralty, 15 March 1801. P.R.O., Adm. 1/1800: F61.
[53] St Vincent to Addington, 20 March 1801. B.M., Add. MSS. 31169, f. 104.
[54] Admiralty to Hawkesbury, 20 March 1801. P.R.O., F.O. 27/58.

French Government. . . .'[55] He had indeed—on that very day![56] But Hawkesbury's application to the French chargé d'affaires recited none of the particulars about the ship, so that, by the time Otto received Hawkesbury's letter, forwarded it to Paris, and received back their perfectly natural inquiries as to tonnage, size of crew, and armament,[57] nearly a month had passed. Not until 23 June—three months after the first Admiralty request —did the passport arrive.[58]

'Le Premier Consul de la République Française, sur le compte qui lui a été rendu de la demande faite par le Lord Hawkesbury au Citoyen Otto, Commissaire du Gouvernement Français à Londres, d'un Passeport pour la Corvette Investigator, dont le Signalement est ci-après, expédiée par le Gouvernement Anglais, sous le commandement du Capitaine Matthew Flinders, pour un voyage de découvertes dans la mer Pacifique, ayant décidé que ce Passeport seroit accordé, et que cette expédition, dont l'objet est d'étendre les connoissances humaines, et d'assurer d'avantage les progrès de la Science nautique et de la Géographie, trouveroit de la part du Gouvernement Français la sureté et la protection nécessaires.

'Le Ministre de la Marine et des Colonies ordonne en conséquence à tous les Commandants des Bâtiments de guerre de la République, à ses agens dans toutes les Colonies Francaises, aux Commandants des Bâtiments porteurs de Lettres de Marque, et à tous autres qu'il appartiendra, de laisser passer librement et sans empêchement, la dite Corvette Investigator, ses Officiers, équipage, et effets, pendant la durée de leur voyage; de leur permettre d'aborder dans les différents ports de la République, tant en Europe que dans les autres parties du Monde, soit qu'ils soient forcés par le mauvais tems d'y chercher un réfuge, soit qu'ils viennent y reclamer les secours et les moyens de réparation nécessaires pour continuer leur voyage. Il est bien entendu, cependant, qu'ils ne trouveront ainsi protection et assistance, que dans le cas où ils ne se seront pas volontairement

[55] Hawkesbury to Admiralty, 8 May 1801. P.R.O., Adm. 1/4187.
[56] Hawkesbury to Otto, 8 May 1801. P.R.O., F.O. 27/58.
[57] Hawkesbury to Admiralty, 5 June 1801. P.R.O., Adm. 1/4187.
[58] Otto to Hawkesbury, 23 June 1801. P.R.O., F.O. 27/58.

détournés de la route qu'ils doivent suivre, qu'ils n'auront commis, ou qu'ils n'annonceront l'intention de commettre aucune hostilité contre la République Française et ses alliés, qu'ils n'auront procuré, ou cherché à procurer aucun secours à ses ennemis, et qu'ils ne s'occuperont d'aucune espéce de commerce, ni de contrebande.

'Fait à Paris le quatre Prairial an neuf de la République Française.

Le Ministre de la Marine et des Colonies

[Signed] Forfait.

Par le Ministre de la Marine et des Colonies

[Signed] C^hrs M. Jurien.

Signalement de la corvette.

La corvette l'Investigator est du port de 334 tonneaux. Son équipage est composé de 83 hommes, outre cinq hommes de lettres.

Son artillerie est de 6 carronades de 12.
            2    ditto      de 18.
            2    canons   de 6
            2    pierriers.

'Le soussigné, Commissaire du Gouvernement Français à Londres, certifie le signalement ci-dessus conforme à la note qui lui a été communiquée par le ministre de Sa Majesté Britannique.

Londres le 4 Messidor an 9.

[Signed] Otto'. [59]

Of all the anxieties attendant upon his preparations for the voyage, perhaps none caused Flinders so much uneasiness as the delay in receiving this document. Yet, during the month of May, troubles of even greater moment developed. On top of Banks's annoyance over the distribution of the scientists' Table

---

[59] N.M.M. 60/017. FLI/3. This document failed Flinders on the first occasion when he was obliged to use it. It is reprinted here in order that the reader may see from its wording why. It should be noted that the only reason for arming the *Investigator* at all was to repel attack from natives.

Money, and still with no Master appointed to the ship, Flinders ran into four mishaps which, taken together, nearly finished his naval career. Although there was no causal connection between them, all four reached the notice of the Admiralty Commissioners in such rapid succession as to undermine their confidence in his ability. Only Banks saved him from destruction.

Immediately after his mariage, Flinders had taken Ann to London, and on to Sheerness. Whether or not she actually set up housekeeping on board the *Investigator* is not certain. But at precisely the wrong moment she did convey that appearance. At some time near mid-May, 'being seen by the Lords of the Admiralty when inspecting the ship, seated in the captain's cabin without her bonnet, they considered that too open a declaration of that being her home'.[60]

Thus was the secret out. Banks heard of the marriage in a Lincoln newspaper, but got wind of it also at the Admiralty. He warned Flinders not to violate the King's Regulations by taking his wife with him: '. . . I am convinced,' he wrote, 'by the language I have heard, that their Lordships will, if they hear of her being in New South Wales, immediately order you to be superseded, whatever may be the consequences, and in all likelihood order Mr. Grant to finish the survey.'[61]

To this warning Flinders responded passionately:

'It is true that I had an intention of taking Mrs Flinders to Port Jackson to remain there until I should have completed the purpose of the voyage, and to have then brought her home again in the ship. . . . The Admiralty have most probably conceived that I intended to keep her on board during the voyage, but this was far from my intention.' He hoped for an indulgence that would permit him to take Ann out to Sydney, but failing that, he had made his decision. 'If their Lordships sentiments continue the same [was it a question of sentiment?] whatever may be my disappointment, I shall give up the wife for the voyage of discovery; and I would beg of you, Sir Joseph, to be assured that even this circumstance will not damp the ardour

[60] S.L.V., 'Flinders Papers'.
[61] From a rough draft, unsigned, dated 21 May 1801, quoted in *H.R.N.S.W.*, vol. IV, p. 372.

I feel to accomplish the important purpose of the present voyage.'[62]

One can scarcely imagine the effect these transactions produced upon Ann. Had not Matthew promised her before the wedding that he would take her along? Even if it were common practice, why had he not warned her of the consequences of discovery by the Admiralty, instead of requiring secrecy without explanation? Could nothing be done?

Banks offered to intercede. But Flinders declined, anticipating the rebuttal that 'her presence would tend to increase the number of, and to lengthen my visits; I am, therefore, afraid to risk their Lordships ill opinion, and Mrs. Flinders will return to her friends immediately that our sailing orders arrive.'[63]

The same letter went on to report progress aboard ship, including the fact that he had at last found a Master who volunteered, and that he had applied for him to the authorities. It said nothing, however, about three other recent, unfortunate incidents which had also come to their Lordships' attention.

Just as the difficulty over Ann had reached its climax, Flinders received a communication from the Admiralty: 'You are hereby required and directed to proceed without loss of time in the Sloop you command to Spithead and remain there for further order.'[64]

This order, suggesting as it surely did, her husband's imminent departure, could not have given Ann much comfort. Flinders closed out all the shipboard work he could, and prepared to leave the Nore. On 25 May, he recalled a party of fifteen men he had been ordered to lend for work aboard the *Advice* brig. Unfortunately, only twelve came back, the other three having changed their minds about voyaging, deserted, and vanished.[65] It was not a good beginning.

Late the next day, 26 May, with a harbour pilot on board, the *Investigator* unmoored, and moved out of the Nore to an

[62] Flinders to Banks, 24 May 1801. M.L.
[63] Flinders to Banks, 3 June 1801. M.L. This turn of events produced upon Ann so strong a shock that her health gave way. She remained in a sickly condition until after the *Investigator* had sailed.
[64] Admiralty to Flinders, 22 May 1801. P.R.O., Adm. 2/141 : 399.
[65] Flinders, 'Journal', vol. I, p. 8.

English Channel, 1801

anchorage in the Downs. There she lay through the 27th, awaiting an easterly wind inside the Goodwin Sands before proceeding down Channel. The following afternoon, having discharged the pilot in the Downs, Flinders weighed anchor with winds in the south-east and began the run to Spithead. After only a few miles—'At 6 the ship touched the ground. Hove all aback. The leadsman having found no bottom with fifteen fathoms at ¼ before six had left the chains without being relieved, and the supposed distance of the land by the officer of the watch being six miles, the lead had not been attended to minutely at the time.'[66]

He had come upon the Roar, a bank in Dungeness Roads.

Flinders lowered the boats, sounded round the ship, and in less than two hours was able to float her off. Since the ship made no more water after the grounding than before, she could have had little if any damage. Nevertheless, it being evening, he returned to the Downs for the night. Diligently, he filed a report of the incident to the Admiralty.[67]

At 1 p.m. of the 29th, together with other ships in the roadstead, the *Investigator* 'fired a royal salute on the anniversary of the Restoration. At 2 moored a cable each way. Wrote to Admiral Lutwidge informing him of the desertion of the Carpenter of the Trent who had been sent on board at the Nore for a passage.'[68]

Next morning Flinders weighed again, left the Downs, and passed down the Channel without further incident. He arrived at Spithead on 2 June, reported his arrival to the Admiralty, and mentioned, quite in passing, the loss of his three deserters.[69]

Following only a week after the trouble over Ann, all this was too much for their Lordships. On 4 June, just when official displeasure had erupted, Banks walked into the Admiralty to inquire about the *Investigator*. He was appalled—'mortified' was the word he used: 'I heard with pain,' he told Flinders, 'many severe remarks on these matters, and in defence I could only say that, as Capt Flinders is a sensible man and a good

[66] *Ibid.*, p. 10.
[67] Flinders to Admiralty, 29 May 1801. P.R.O., Adm. 1/1800: F66.
[68] Flinders, 'Journal', vol. I, p. 11.
[69] Flinders to Admiralty, 2 June 1801. P.R.O., Adm. 1/1800: F67.

seaman, such matters could only be attributed to the laxity of
discipline which always takes place when the captain's wife is
on board, and that such lax discipline could never again take
place because you had wisely resolved to leave Mrs. Flinders
with her relations . . . I think that your character would have
been better supported yesterday had I known from you what had
happened.[70]

It was a clever response, and probably smoothed the official
feathers. By next day, Nepean's mood had improved:

'The questions that remain not quite cleared up are why was
not the lead going when the ship went ashore and why was there
not an officer in charge of the quarterdeck at the time the
prisoner [the Carpenter of the *Trent*] escaped. You tell me
that the man was not delivered into your charge as a prisoner.
If this is so I advise you to state the fact to the Board [of
Admiralty Commissioners] who will call upon the Port Admiral
for an explanation.'[71]

There was no need for Flinders to go up to London to answer
formal charges. But he did reply in writing. As for his three
deserters, they were not under his control when they absconded.
Moreover, he had warned the commander of the *Advice* against
allowing his men to go ashore. Again, he took no special
precautions to guard the Carpenter of the *Trent* because he had
not been advised to. Furthermore, stationing only a midshipman on the quarterdeck was normal procedure in an English
roadstead.[72]

He could dispose of these queries easily. But the matter of
grounding at The Roar wanted a more elaborate explanation.
Not only had the ship been endangered, but her commander's
professional competence was at stake. His report to Banks throws
light upon both Flinders's character and, incidentally, upon the
current state of British hydrography:

'The chart of the Channel supplied me by Arrowsmith, published by J[ohn] H[amilton] Moore was the principal cause of

---

[70] Banks to Flinders, 5 June 1801. *H.R.N.S.W.*, vol. IV, p. 383 sq.

[71] Banks to Flinders, 6 [?] June 1801. *Ibid.*, p. 387 sqq.

[72] Flinders to Admiralty, 5 June 1801. P.R.O., Adm. 1/1800: F68; and
Flinders to Banks, 6 June 1801. M.L.

the ship having touched the ground, from not having a sand laid down in it called the Roar . . . .[73] Finding so material a thing as a sand 3 or 4 miles from the shore, unlaid down in the chart, I thought it a duty incumbent upon me to endeavour to prevent the light accident from happening to others by stating the circumstance . . . . The Admiralty do not seem to take it into consideration that I had no master appointed who ought to be the pilot; or that having been constantly employed myself in foreign voyages, I cannot, consequently, have much personal knowledge of the channel. . . .'

That the leadsman had left his station was Flinders's fault, and he offered no excuse. But bad charts were not his fault. Dover Straits had been silting up for centuries. That the charting of the Channel should have been neglected when so many English ships used it overbalanced any case against a misled commander. Flinders's report was forwarded to the Hydrographer for examination and comment, and the incident was closed. Late in 1802 the Admiralty did indeed order a survey of Dungeness harbour, where the *Investigator* had gone aground. The surveyor was Captain William Bligh.[74]

Perhaps the affair might have ended differently if the examination of the *Investigator* at Portsmouth had disclosed some injury. But Flinders had been lucky.

5

By the middle of June these troubles had evaporated, and all the complex preparations of six months began to fall into place. Only farewells remained. Closing his letter of 6 June, Banks wrote:

'My paper is exhausted, and I have little more to say. I there-

---

[73] *Ibid. See also* Flinders, *Voyage*, vol. I, p. 6 sq. Nathaniel Bowditch (1773–1838), American mathematician, gained his reputation by publishing the *American Practical Navigator* in 1802 as a corrective to Moore's treatise.

[74] George Mackaness, *Life of Vice-Admiral William Bligh* (London, 1951). p. 329.

fore put an end to our correspondence for some months, con-
cluding you will sail immediately, and with sincere good wishes
for your future prosperity, and with a firm belief that you will
in your future conduct do credit to yourself as an able navigator
and to me as having recommended you, and conclude with
sincere esteem and real regard.'[75]

On 12 June, John Allen, miner, signed his Last Will and
Testament.[76]

On 14 June, Robert Brown set out from London, joining the
ship at Spithead the following day. Having got himself unpacked
and organised, he began to enjoy life. He started his Journal,[77]
and set about a daily regimen of reading, everything from
Brisson's *Physique* and Buffon's *Théorie de la Terre* to
Shakespeare's plays and Johnson's *Rambler*. Tiring of that, he
often went on shore with Flinders, or botanised with Bauer on
the Isle of Wight. Or else he enjoyed the finer things:

'. . . Drank about a pint of Wine.'
'. . . A glass of grog.'
'. . . Drank upwards of a pint of Port.'
'. . . Drank my usual quantity of Wine, Port and Sherry.'
'. . . Drank nothing.'

Only receipt of the formal Instructions for the voyage held
the ship; and apparently only the illness of Mr Nepean postponed their delivery. Early in July Annette had returned to
Lincolnshire to live with her parents. Without her the waiting
became nearly unbearable for Matthew. 'Can I live without
thee and be happy? Indeed I think at this moment it cannot
be. . . .'[78] He wrote a last letter to his father, whom he would
never see again, and several more to Banks and Ann. But this
was just marking time.

On 15 July the long-sought Master, Mr Thistle, late of the
*Buffalo*, came aboard.[79]

---

[75] Banks to Flinders, 6 June 1801. *H.R.N.S.W.*, vol. IV, p. 389.
[76] Sutro Library, San Francisco, Cal. Banks Collection.
[77] Robert Brown, 'Journal and Diary for the Period 1801–1804'. B.M. (N.H.)
W.O. 778. Hereafter cited as Brown, 'Journal'.
[78] Flinders to Ann, 30 June 1801. N.M.M. 60/017. FLI/25.
[79] Thistle had returned from New South Wales only three weeks before this day.

At last, on 17 July there came a substantial packet of papers from the Admiralty:[80] Instructions for the voyage—'By the Commissioners for executing the Office of Lord High Admiral of the United Kingdom of Great Britain & Ireland &c.'[81] With the Instructions were a letter from His Grace of Portland instructing King to place the *Lady Nelson* under Flinders's command;[82] a memoir from the Hydrographer on the weather along the south coast of New Holland; the French passport; a minute on the proper conduct of the *Investigator* toward enemy ships;[83] and copies of lists of various articles and nautical instruments already on board.

The long wait was over. While Brown wrote to his mother, and prepared his cabin, Flinders acknowledged receipt of his orders,[84] notified Sir Joseph, 'received provisions, lashed and secured for sea'. He would be gone the next fair wind.

[80] Flinders, 'Journal', vol. I, p. 14.
[81] P.R.O., Adm. 1/1800 (undated draft); or N.M.M. 60/017. FLI/3, 22 June 1801.
[82] Portland to King, 26 June 1801. P.R.O., Adm. 1/4187.
[83] *See* Flinders to Admiralty, 2 July 1801. P.R.O., Adm. 1/1800: F72, and the Admiralty answer to the effect that he was to behave toward them as if the war did not exist.
[84] Flinders to Admiralty, 17 July 1801. P.R.O., Adm. 1/1800: F73.

CHAPTER FIVE

# Shakedown Cruise

## July–December 1801

1

'Whereas the Sloop under your Command has been fitted &
stored for a Voyage to remote Parts; and whereas it is our
intention that you shall proceed in her to the Coast of New
Holland for the purpose of making a complete Examination and
Survey of the said Coast, on the Eastern side of which His
Majesty's Colony of New South Wales is situated; You are
hereby required & directed to put to sea the first favourable
opportunity of Wind & Weather, and proceed with as little
delay as possible in execution of the Service above-mentioned,
repairing·in the first place to the Cape of Good Hope in order to
take on board such Supplies of Water & Live Stock as you may
be in want of.'[1]

Flinders had calculated that with only fifty-eight tons of
potable water on board he would be unable to reach the Cape
unless he either put the ship on rations, or else made an intermediate stop.[2] Madeira was therefore inserted in the final
version. But why Madeira? Only weeks before, on 6 June to be
exact, Napoleon had blackmailed Portugal into signing the
Treaty of Badajoz. Under its terms Portugal undertook to
close her ports to British ships. By this means Napoleon hoped
both to choke Portugal's lucrative trade with England and to
deprive the British of their bases on the Atlantic. Yet here was

---

[1] Instructions for executing the voyage of H.M. Sloop *Investigator*. P.R.O.,
Adm. 1/1800. For complete, final version of these instructions, see Appendix A
of the present work, from Flinders, *Voyage*, vol. I, p. 8 sqq.
[2] Flinders to Banks, 24 May 1801. M.L.

the Admiralty having the audacity to order a naval vessel, as a matter of course, to stock up on food and water in Funchal, the principal harbour of Portuguese-owned Madeira. There was, of course, nothing either the Portuguese or Napoleon could do about it, for by the time Flinders arrived there the 85th British regiment had landed and taken over control of the islands. As Flinders himself got the story, the Portuguese position there was not a strong one: '. . . magazines, forts, gun carriages &c. are in a state almost incapable of defense, and were the Portuguese left to themselves would most probably remain so.'[3]

## 2

Over the centuries the sailor's practical habit of mind has made of the ship's log one of the least dramatic, most laconic modes of record known to man. Generally speaking, neither the typhoon's fury nor the awful moment of combat can change this habit. That being the case, certainly the mere departure of a ship on a four-year cruise would betray nothing of a disciplined captain's private thoughts. Thus Flinders on 18 July 1801: 'At 10 made the signal and weighed. Moderate breezes with fine weather.'[4]

Doubtless the crew had fallen in at morning muster wearing their glazed hats, 'decorated,' as *The Times* had reported, 'with a globe and the name of the ship in letters of gold'.[5] In any case, with Fowler taking the first watch, H.M. Sloop *Investigator* stood out of Spithead anchorage and turned to starboard. For about a hundred miles she hugged the shore through the dangerous waters lying off Dorset and Devon to Start Point. There she took her departure and sailed out the channel to the sea.

Off and on for the first several days merchant vessels of various descriptions came in sight. On the fourth day out Flinders fell in with the Channel Fleet, on station guarding the

[3] Flinders, 'Journal', vol. I, p. 38.
[4] *Ibid.*, p. 25.
[5] Cf. *The Times*, 27 June 1801, p. 3.

Western Approaches off Brest. 'Spoke the *Windsor Castle*, Vice-Admiral [Sir Andrew] Mitchell, and went on board by desire. At 5½ [o'clock] returned. Cheered the admiral's ship and made all sail again.'[6]

At about eight o'clock in the morning of the following day there appeared on the horizon two luggers. One, hoisting English colours, fired a shot to bring the *Investigator* to. Flinders hoisted his ensign and cleared for action, upon which the luggers, thought to be Guernsey privateers,[7] broke off and disappeared.

Otherwise, traffic in this usually busy quarter was relatively light. Three days passed without another sail in sight. 25 July. Flinders made the private signal to a ship, and the signal not being answered, once again cleared for action. This time it was the *Investigator* that fired first. But the enemy turned out to be a brig from Lisbon to Stockholm, and nothing further ensued.

Running along at a mere five knots, Flinders must have counted each day a day lost from the survey work ahead. Yet at this stage there was work enough to fill any day, simply training the crew. This crew, while not exactly green, had yet to develop that teamwork aloft that might some day save the ship in a tropical squall. Again, hours of exercise at the great guns might pay off in an emergency. Or again, for the sake of health, cleaning and airing the ship below became almost a fetish of the young captain.

On 29 July, only twelve days out, he got his first disquieting hint of trouble ahead. 'We have the mortification to find the ship makes more than two inches of water per hour. This leak commenced yesterday, and keeps increasing something.'[8] With some investigation by the Carpenter, the probable source was found to lie above the waterline. Even so, it was a danger he could never quite get off his mind.

By way of diversion for the scientists, just off Madeira, Flinders stopped to capture a Hawksbill turtle[9] asleep on the surface. Brown examined it and took its temperature (84°), Bauer sketched it, and the Surgeon, to Brown's infinite disgust, cut it up 'in a very rude and slovenly manner'.

[6] Flinders, 'Journal', vol. i, p. 30.    [7] Brown, 'Journal', vol. iA, p. 18.
[8] Flinders, 'Journal', vol. i, p. 35.    [9] *Eretmochelys imbricata imbricata*.

Porto Santo, northernmost of the Madeiras, came in sight on 31 July, and Flinders headed straight for it. Next day after breakfast the captain with a party went ashore at Bujio, the southern Dezerta. There Flinders made his first original discovery of the voyage, a dangerous ledge of rocks projecting from under the cliffs at the south-west part of the island.[10]

3 August. 'Entered Funchal Road, being towed in by the boats, in company with a Portuguese sloop of war and an American brig.' On arrival, Flinders waited first upon Captain James Bowen, of H.M.S. *Argo*,[11] and soon after upon the governor, with whom he arranged for the scientists to go exploring. While for the next two days the Carpenter patched and caulked the leaky seams, and working parties turned to, bringing provisions and water aboard, Flinders discoursed on local politics with the British Consul.

What Flinders saw at Madeira he later recorded in his journal, as Pasley and Bligh had taught him to do:

'The appearance of the town of Funchal from the bay is pretty and picturesque; it acquires this from being placed at the feet of those majestic hills that occupy all the central parts of the island. Behind the town, and considerably raised above it, are the country houses of many of the richer inhabitants, situated amongst groups of trees and surrounded by vineyards; these with a convent dedicated to Nostra Seignora del Monte, which is white but partly hid by the green foliage of the vines and trees, as indeed are the houses, add very much to its appearance. The town is rather large, and there was more trade and activity in it than I expected to see. The students of the college and the different ecclesiastics appear to form no inconsiderable part of the superior class of its inhabitants. Several British merchants reside here, who besides their houses of business in the town have country houses behind it. I visited the hospitable seat of Mr Murdock, and thought it the prettiest place I had ever seen. The house of Joseph Pringle, Esq. the British consul was

[10] *Oriental Navigator*, 3rd edn (London, 1816), p. 10.
[11] Captain Bowen (1751–1835) was at this time on convoy duty in the Atlantic. He retired a Rear Admiral, having once distinguished himself as master of Howe's flagship, *Queen Charlotte*, on 1 June 1794.

my home when on shore, and indeed the hospitality of our
countrymen prevented me from experiencing the accommodation
which is afforded to strangers by a house in the town dignified
with the name of hotel. Some of our gentlemen complained of
its being miserable enough, even without the addition of such
swarms of fleas and other vermin with which they were
annoyed.'[12]

Of only one thing did he find reason to complain: 'Wine for
the ship's company was charged at the enormous price of 5s. 8d.
per gallon . . . For good Madeira we paid as much as £42 the
pipe'.[13]

On 7 August, having reported by dispatch to the Admiralty,[14]
and completed his provisioning, Flinders got under way for
the Cape. Now began the more interesting, more challenging
effort, southward through the slot separating Brazil from
Africa. 8 August. 'Saw the island of Palma, westernmost of the
Canaries, ten or twelve leagues distant. Flying fish about,
steady breezes and fine weather. 14 August. Sighted the island
of St. Antonio, Cape Verdes, approached it for inspection without going ashore, and pushed on. 17 August. Stopped to pick
up a man that had fallen overboard. 28 August. Passed a strange
sail, the first since Madeira.'

For some time Flinders had intended to look out for St
Paul Rocks consistently reported to lie somewhere in the western
Atlantic near the equator. But by the end of August he found
himself carried far to the eastward as he approached the line.
On 2 September, therefore, he altered course to westward.
By regulating the sails so as to slow down at dusk, he contrived
to retain nearly the same visible horizon overnight; and by
placing his three warrant officers on watch in the forecastle at
night, he reduced the probability of missing the Rocks to a
minimum.[15]

[12] Flinders, 'Journal', vol. I, p. 38.
[13] Flinders, *Voyage*, vol. I, p. 24. But see C. N. Parkinson, *Trade in the Eastern
Seas 1793–1813* (Cambridge, 1937), p. 74, where the author reckons Madeira
at £44 the pipe (about 40 dozen bottles) in 1805 'not a very expensive wine'.
[14] Flinders to Admiralty, 5 August 1801. P.R.O., Adm. 1/1800: F74.
[15] Flinders later felt called upon to excuse himself for thus trespassing on the
warrant officers' time: 'The leisure usually enjoyed by this class of officers,

On 17 September H.M. Sloop *Investigator* crossed the equator for the first time. At the appropriate moment the cutter was lowered upon the line. Then: 'In order to give the ship's company a day's amusement, I permitted the ceremony of shaving and ducking as usual . . . to be performed in its full latitude. At the conclusion, they had as much grog given them as they could drink, the ship having been previously put under snug sail. After the ceremony, hoisted the cutter upon the quarter again.'[16]

St Paul Rocks lie north of the equator, and about 850 miles west of the point at which Flinders crossed the equator. He had therefore failed in his search, and on 10 September broke it off, having already devoted as much time to it as he felt authorised to do. He shaped a course for the island of Trinidad and Martin Vas Rocks. After fixing their position as well as he could without going ashore, and taking a departure therefrom, he hurried on to yet another problem of the south Atlantic: the supposed island of Saxemberg.

In the third edition of the *Oriental Navigator*, John Stevens reported, for what it was worth: 'This island [Saxemberg] is said to have been first seen by J. L. Lindeman, of Monnikendam, 23d August 1670 . . . and, from his account, it was laid down in the charts at about 30° 45' S. and 19½° W.'[17]

Over the years a few other seamen had filed similar reports, but the evidence for its position lacked conviction. Flinders therefore proceeded to a point some 400 miles due west of the position given, and by parallel sailing ran due eastward, taking, as he said, the 'opportunity which presented itself of now adding 6° of longitude to the examined space . . . adopting the same

---

particularly by the gunner and carpenter, I conceived to admit of this abridgment, without injury to their ordinary sea duties.' *Voyage*, vol. 1, p. 30. Warrants in the navy remain today a leisure class, whose value lies in their ability to apply a venerated practical wisdom—if politely invited to do so.

[16] Flinders, 'Journal', vol. 1, p. 57. In his published narrative he resorted to a more guarded version: '. . . the ship being previously put under snug sail, the seamen were furnished with the means, and the permission, to conclude the day with merriment.' *Voyage*, vol. 1, p. 29.

Of the same occasion one of the sailors wrote: '. . . the greatest part of Officers & men was shaved, not having cross'd the line before At night Grog was serv'd out to each Watch, which caus'd the Evening to be spent in Merriment.' M.L. Samuel Smith, 'Journal', p. 6 sq.

[17] p. 16.

regulations for the look-out at night, as when searching for St Paul's.'[18]

He found nothing, and therefore reported only negative information. In the upshot, despite positive identification from the logs of other ships, the fact was the island did not, and does not, exist; and Flinders was the first respectable explorer who, after careful search, said so.[19]

The remainder of this leg of the outward voyage, from 1 October—the date, incidentally, on which the Preliminary Peace of Amiens was signed—to 16 October, passed uneventfully. At 6 o'clock in the evening of the 17th the *Investigator* lay at anchor in False Bay, off Capetown.

To all the ship's company, but most especially to Flinders, arrival at the Cape came as a welcome relief. Though they had plenty of work on board, all of it heavy, the sailors off watch could go ashore to taste the pleasures, eternally sought—but rarely catalogued—by their kind. They would not find them soon again.

The scientific gentlemen, too, could put the time to use according to their lights. The ship remained at the Cape for eighteen days, but, Flinders noted, '. . . in taking so early a departure, though it was to proceed to the untrodden and not less fertile region of botany, New Holland, I had to engage with the counter wishes of my scientific companions; so much delighted were they to find the richest treasures of the English hot-house profusely scattered upon the sides and summits of these barren hills.'[20]

To Flinders the Cape was only a springboard to the grand purpose. Each day there brought him measurably closer to the

---

[18] Flinders, *Voyage*, vol. I, p. 34.

[19] Flinders, 'Journal', vol. I, p. 71. A modern view comes from Professor Maurice Ewing, noted oceanographer: 'None of our charts show any evidence of such an island, and the position is far enough west of the axis of the mid-Atlantic Ridge that I would be somewhat surprized if one was ever there. . . . The best chance for such an island would be 100–200 miles east of the reported position. . . . As far as I know, it is not the habit of islands of the mid-Atlantic Ridge to appear and disappear as readily as they do in other parts of the world. So, if there ever was an island there, which has disappeared since, I would expect that it must have been a small, obvious, and possibly smoking, cone at the time it was reported, and that its disappearance would consist only of reduction to sea-level or slightly below by waves.' Private correspondence with the author.

[20] Flinders, 'Journal', vol. I, p. 82.

real beginning. Moreover, his arrival there ended the anxiety he had felt for weeks over the condition of the ship. With proper facilities and adequate help, her defects could be promptly and thoroughly corrected.

John Crosley, Astronomer, had been in declining health since the ship left Spithead. Perhaps it was chronic seasickness, perhaps not. At any rate, by the time he reached the Cape, he seriously doubted he could go on. After thorough discussion with Flinders, he decided to quit the voyage, and arranged forthwith to return to England. This was a blow to Flinders who had now to assume responsibility for making all the astronomical observations on the survey that were going to be made.

These matters were duly reported to both the Admiralty[21] and Banks.[22] Finally, on 4 November, when all work on the *Investigator* had ended, and the stores were loaded, Flinders sailed for New Holland.

3

The three-months' run from England to the Cape had been a shakedown cruise, a testing time for both ship and men. The critical element in the trial was Flinders's own capacity for command. How he had come through it is difficult to determine, for the only information we have is inferential. One may argue that any captain with both the wisdom and the courage to set his warrants to standing night watches has what it takes. Or again, the fact that in these three months he had to inflict punishment only once speaks well for his leadership.[23] However this may be, in his dispatches to the Admiralty reporting the visit and departure of the *Investigator*, Admiral Sir Roger Curtis, then commanding at the Cape, noted nothing at all unusual about the ship. On the contrary, he eagerly did all he could to further Flinders's interests.

[21] Flinders to Admiralty, [?] October 1801. P.R.O., Adm. 1/1801.
[22] Flinders to Banks, 21 October 1801. B.M., Add. MSS. 32439. 45–6.
[23] On 9 October: 'Punished Thos. Flint, seaman, and Andrew Robson, marine; the first with 12, and the last with six lashes, for fighting.' Flinders, 'Journal', vol. I, p. 75. Fowler adds, 'for fighting in the top-gallant sails' [!]. 'Journal', vol. I, p. 25.

Flinders, however, would not have been the one to analyse himself. During these first months at sea he had had just two concerns, the effectiveness of his crew, and the condition of his ship.

Once the routine of the day at sea had been firmly established, which might take a week or so, the captain could rely upon a regularised, if somewhat limited, range of tasks to keep the men off watch from idleness. These would include polishing bright-work, scrubbing down the deck, or working up junk. But apart from such normal practices at the captain's disposal, two other elements remained indispensable to the crew's welfare. One of these was a scheme of organised recreation on a reliable sched-ule; the other a rigid adherence to good dietary standards. Flinders paid strict attention to both.

26 August 1801. 'Drum and fife playing as usual to the people, who generally have a dance or some kind of play every evening.'[24]

Again, 'it was a part of my plan for preserving the health of the people, to promote active amusements amongst them, so long as it did not interfere with the duties of the ship.'[25] Where-fore he permitted the ceremonies usual when crossing the equator. All this was perhaps no more than common sense, but the point is Flinders planned for it.

As for diet, while Flinders was not an innovator, he did indeed give a good deal of thought to the matter. On 3 September 1801, within the tropics, and in order to conserve what time he might otherwise have to spend recruiting the health of the crew at the Cape, he consulted with Surgeon Bell as to the victualling, with the following results:

'Oatmeal boiled for breakfast, four days instead of three; and rice being served now in lieu of cheese, it was boiled for breakfast on the other three days.

'Pease boiled for dinner four days in the week as usual; and on the other three days we proposed to give one pint of portable soup to each man, consisting of two ounces of the soup, two ounces of scotch barley, and such onions, pepper &c. as the messes might have to add to it, with a sufficiency of water. Thus the people would have a hot breakfast every day, and also hot soup every day for dinner, besides the usual meat allowed them [salt pork and beef].

'On examining into the surgeon's stores, almost the whole of the barley was found to be spoiled; and when the portable broth was boiled by itself, no person chused to take it; I therefore directed that each man should be served with two ounces of it, in the cake, three times per week, threatening those who took it and waisted [sic] it, with punishment.

'I did not think it necessary to issue sour krout [as an anti-scorbutic] so long as the lime juice and sugar continued to be issued to them, but purposed to change these so soon as the weather should become somewhat cooler.'[26]

And what was the result of these measures? The *Investigator* arrived at the Cape with not a single man on the sick list.

There can be no doubt that the condition of the *Investigator*, ex-*Xenophon*, distracted Flinders constantly. At one point she took in water at the rate of five inches an hour. Occasional recaulking might reduce the flooding somewhat. But 'the blows of the sea,' he wrote, 'make her tremble in every part.' Inexorably the faults in construction would worsen. In after years, when he no longer had any hope of renewing his work, he recalled the warnings given him by the dockyard officers at Sheerness, and added:

'Should it be asked, why representations were not made, and a stronger vessel procured? I answer, that the exigencies of the navy were such at that time, that I was given to understand no better ship could be spared from the service; and my anxiety to complete the investigation of the coasts of Terra Australis did not admit of refusing the one offered.'[27]

A hard choice; a sad commentary.

[26] Flinders, 'Journal', vol. i, p. 54.
[27] Flinders, *Voyage*, vol. i, p. 28.

# CHAPTER SIX

# The Southern Portion

## December 1801–May 1802

### 1

'What a ship on discovery may do is not to be given as an example to others, whose sole objects are expedition and safety.'[1]

From Flinders himself, this is the perfect text on the theme of hydrographic surveying.

On 4 November, then, the *Investigator* set out from the Cape, heading due east for New Holland some 5,000 miles away. Relying upon Vancouver's plot of Amsterdam Island in the Indian Ocean, Flinders made for it to check out his chronometers. From whatever cause, however, he missed it and, wasting no time, proceeded on his way.[2] Averaging more than six knots, he arrived at Cape Leeuwin, after a passage of thirty-two days, on 6 December.

Until that moment in history only three navigators had ever laid eyes on this shore. Early in the seventeenth century the Dutchman, Pieter Nuyts, had picked it up at Cape Leeuwin and followed it eastward for 18°, about 900 miles. Then, only ten years before, Captain George Vancouver had struck the coast at the point he named Cape Chatham. He proceeded eastward to King George III Sound. After surveying the Sound he moved on to Termination Island, at 122° 8′ E., and from there departed for the Pacific. Finally, in 1792 the French Admiral,

---

[1] Flinders, *Voyage*, vol. I, p. 248.

[2] Flinders's own dead reckoning may or may not have been correct, but the position given by Vancouver, 38° 43′ S., 77° 40′ E., was clearly inaccurate. The correct position is 37° 50′ S., 77° 32′ E. Flinders probably passed some 50 miles north of the island.

Bruni d'Entrecasteaux, had run the coast from Cape Leeuwin
to a point just beyond the head of the Great Australian Bight.
There he too had broken off to southward.

The chartwork of these three needed no apology in their own
time, so far as it went. But eastward, beyond their farthest
reach, lay a long segment of coast, most of it claimed for Britain
by Cook, but in fact quite virgin. On the charts it appeared as
merely an interpolated arc, and within the hypothesis there lay
a puzzle. In Flinders's lucid prose :

'What rendered a knowledge of this part more particularly
interesting, was the circumstance of no considerable river having been found on any of the coasts of Terra Australis previously
explored : but it was scarcely credible that, if this vast country
were one connected mass of land, it should not contain some
large rivers; and if any, this unknown part was one of two
remaining places, where they were expected to discharge themselves into the sea.

'The apparent want of rivers had induced some persons to
think, that Terra Australis might be composed of two or more
islands, as had formerly been suspected by the Dutch, and by
Dampier; whilst others, believing in the continuity of the
shores, thought this want might arise from the interior being
principally occupied by a mediterranean sea; but it was generally
agreed, that one end of the separating channels, or otherwise
the entrance, if such existed, into the supposed sea, would most
likely be found in this unexplored part of the South Coast.'[3]

Thus the express admonition in the orders to examine any
creek or opening likely to lead to an inland sea or strait. It
was the single most significant problem Flinders undertook to
solve.

Anxious as he was to get on with it, however, he knew his
rigging and sails needed attention, and so from Cape Leeuwin
he hurried immediately on to King George Sound, the sheltered
roadstead entered by Vancouver. Four weeks he allowed for the
purpose, and in that time there was work enough and more for

[3] Flinders, *Voyage*, vol. i, p. lxxiii sq.

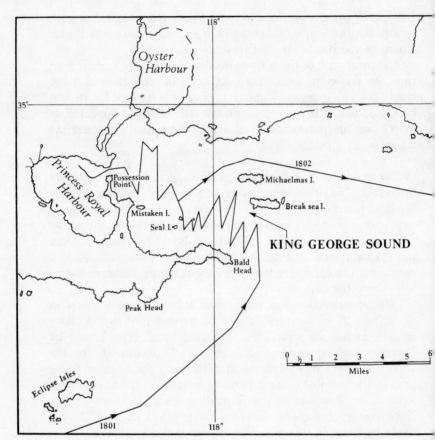

King George Sound, 1802

all. He anchored inside Princess Royal Harbour where, on
13 December, work began in earnest. Top-gallant masts came
down to the deck; water casks began their daily trips ashore;
working parties fanned out in search of firewood. And every
day thereafter, Sundays only excepted, the chores went steadily
on.

Leaving the ship to his warrant officers, Flinders and his
brother, who now assisted with the astronomical work, moved
ashore to a camp they used jointly with the scientists. While
he undertook a resurvey of the Sound, Bauer, Brown, and
Westall began acquainting themselves with the new land. A
two-day walking tour, ending on Christmas Eve, taught them
much. But at midsummer this barren country was unbearably
hot, and at the end the party were too fatigued to learn anything
more. After a Christmas Day given over to rest and amusement,
work began again. 30 December was moving day. Flinders had
finished his survey, and as soon as the top-gallant masts went
up, he broke camp and prepared to return aboard.

For the four weeks they lay in port, the entire ship's company
had one new duty : learning how to establish friendly relations
with the natives. Presumably there had been some lectures to
the crew on the subject; and if absence of hostility be taken as a
measure, the tuition had been a success. Just as the tents on
shore came down, the marines who had stood guard there
formed up for embarkation. Flinders recorded the scene :

'The red coats with white crossed belts were so much in their
[the natives'] way of ornamenting themselves, that they absolutely screamed with delight on seeing the men drawn up;
their vociferation and wild gestures could only be silenced by
commencing the exercise, to which they paid the utmost
attention. The fife, the drum, the motion of the exercise, all
excited curiosity and astonishment; and the old man who had
seen us on our way to the lagoons [on the walking tour] was so
absorbed with the latter, that with a stick in his hand he was,
almost unknown to himself, imitating the marines in their
exercise.'[4]

Flinders, 'Journal', vol. i, p. 107.

On this of all busy days, one last unhappy event thrust itself upon Flinders's notice: 'Punished William Donovan with 36 lashes for repeated drunkenness and fighting.'[5]

At last, on 5 January, the *Investigator* quit the Sound. The survey proper began. It is well known, of course, that Flinders's survey data have been largely superseded. Constantly changing coastal conditions, increasing ship traffic, and improved instrumentation have all made this more or less inevitable.[6] Nevertheless in its time his accuracy was of a very high order,[7] a fact that may with justice be attributed to his thoroughness of method. Thus, throughout the survey, he tried to keep as close inshore as he could without danger to the ship, so as to reduce the error of judging distances from ship to shore. When off-lying hazards, haze, the set of the current, or the winds forced him away, he himself went to the masthead to get his observations. To permit immediate verification he laid all bearings down while landmarks were still in sight; and every position taken during the day was plotted on a rough chart before he retired for the night. It goes without saying that he began each day's work where he had left off the day before. Commenting later on technique he wrote, 'this plan, to see and lay down every thing myself, required constant attention and much labour, but was absolutely necessary to obtaining that accuracy of which I was desirous. . . .'[8]

We picture him, then, standing at the binnacle or perched in the tops, taking sights and calling off time signals to his brother stationed nearby with a watch. We wonder how a man can go on hour after hour, day after day, repeating so laborious a process for a distance of 6,000 miles. Then we cease asking why, at the age of twenty-seven, Flinders was the doyen of English naval surveyors.

Moving quickly away from the Sound, Flinders reached the Archipelago of the Recherche within three days. Close inshore

---

[5] *Ibid.*

[6] Presentation of Flinders's data here would be both tiresome and useless.

[7] His latitudes were usually correct to within one mile, frequently less. His longitudes, if inaccurate, nearly always erred to the west; that is, because his watches were slow he had usually travelled farther eastward of Greenwich than the watches indicated.

[8] Flinders, *Voyage*, vol. i, p. 73 sq.

he found himself in a navigator's nightmare. Haze, submerged rocks, and onshore winds put to him the test at the very outset; but relying heavily upon d'Entrecasteaux he came out at the end of three weeks without accident, and indeed with some success. Then, no sooner was he free of these perils than he had to face the same problems over again, though for a shorter time, in Nuyts Archipelago. Here, unfortunately, his troubles were compounded. First he discovered that the ship was once again leaking badly. So it was chronic after all. Three inches per hour taken aboard on 1 February, and six the following day.[9] The only favourable thing to be said was that the leak seemed to be in the upper works, so that by trimming fore and aft the intake could be minimised.

Then it was just here that brother Samuel chose to complicate life. For some reason the youngster, who ought to have known better, decided he was working too hard. One can imagine Matthew's reaction. It had been a mistake to bring Samuel along in the first place. On so small a ship it must be embarrassing to say the least to punish any officer; but in any case, the captain's brother was the last person from whom any laxity could be tolerated.[10] Flinders acted firmly: 'The 2nd lieutenant not having given me all the assistance in the astronomical and surveying departments that I expected, he was ordered to keep his own watch during the night.' As a result, 'from the stimulus of pride, he chose to keep it in the day also, and to continue giving me the same proportion of assistance as he had done before.'[11]

It will be recalled that out in the Atlantic Flinders had detected an abnormal variation in the magnetic compass,[12] and

[9] Fowler, 'Journal', vol. 1, p. 44; Flinders, 'Journal', vol. 1, p. 134.

[10] Back at Amsterdam Island Samuel had fallen on deck and broken one of the two surveying sextants. Flinders, 'Journal', vol. 1, p. 134.

[11] Ibid., p. 127.

[12] For the benefit of those who may be unfamiliar with the problem of magnetic variation the following brief statement may help. The navigator requires a *geographical* reference direction, normally geographic north. The nearest indicator he has is magnetic north, which is *not* the same as geographic north. The magnetic needle points to magnetic north, not true north, and the difference between the two, expressed numerically, is known as 'variation'. This must be corrected to find true north. But further, every ship has its own magnetic field, created by the iron within the ship itself. This, too, deflects the magnetic needle, usually by a significant amount, which is called 'deviation'. Deviation must be corrected to

had vaguely suspected that local iron in the ship might be the cause. Now once again, on an unknown coast—for he had gone beyond any land seen by his predecessors—he noted an intolerable irregularity. So, despite potential danger from native attack, he struck two of his deck guns below. Still the error persisted, and he laboured under the constant worry that, knowing neither its cause nor its extent, all his observations with the compass might be worthless—or worse, disastrous.

2

Disaster!

Sunday, 21 February. 'Sent the master, Mr Thistle, over to the mainland to search for water. At 7 [in the evening] the boat was seen returning, but suddenly missed, upon which lieut. Fowler was sent in another boat to look after her. At $9\frac{1}{2}$ fired a gun, and soon after the last boat returned without any intelligence of the other boat, but had near been swamped herself among the strong ripplings of tide.'[13]

Faced with his first emergency, one of the most shocking kind, Flinders had reacted rapidly. He also behaved correctly: it would have been quite improper for him to have left the ship himself. His immediate reconstruction was melancholy:

'The sudden disappearance of the boat, and the dangerous ripplings of the tide that lieut. Fowler found about the place where she was last seen make us fear that she has been upset, or as she was under three lug sails, perhaps capsized over the people, only two of whom, unfortunately, were at all expert in swimming. The tide ran to the southward for an hour and a half after we missed the boat, it is therefore probable that she has drifted to seaward. Had it been daylight, there is no doubt that we should have picked up some or all of the people, but the hallooing and firing of musquets was ineffectual to procure any intelligence of their situation, and it was too dark to see any

yield a figure for the variation, which in turn must be corrected to find true north. Flinders's principal contribution to scientific knowledge was his analysis of deviation. (See Chapter 14 below.)

[13] Flinders, 'Journal', vol. I, p. 154.

thing. After the last boat had been gone two hours I became anxious for *her* safety, and fired a gun for her to return; it appeared that my fears had not been groundless, for she had narrowly escaped being swamped in a strong tide rippling.'[14]

So was lost the Master Flinders had sought so long.

It might have been easy to dismiss an incident of this sort as simply one of the perils of the sea. Sailors know that the sea claims whom it wishes. But Flinders took it hardly. That he had lost ten per cent of his working crew was not the point. He was kindly, not callous. The search began at daybreak, and lasted for three days, long after real hope had passed. But all he found were footprints on the beach, a sail and yard floating near the shore, and a bit of Thistle's gear. On Wednesday Flinders gave up the search, named the point of land off which the boat had foundered, Cape Catastrophe, and on the shore at a place called Memory Cove, he nailed a copper plaque to a tree:[15]

## Memory Cove

His Majestys ship Investigator—Mattw. Flinders— Commander, anchored here February 22, 1802.

Mr. John Thistle the master,— Mr. William Taylor—midshipman and six of the crew were most unfortunately drowned near this place from being upset in a boat. The wreck of the boat was found, but their bodies were not recovered.

Nautici cavete!—

One thing remained, a debt to simple justice. Flinders wrote in his Journal:

'I must take occasion to observe in this place, that Mr. Thistle was truly a valuable man, as a seaman, an officer, and a good

---

[14] *Ibid*, p. 155. The area remains notorious for its tide rips. *Australia Pilot* (London, 1949), vol. I, p. 142.
[15] Flinders, 'Journal', vol. I, p. 158.

member of society. I have know him since the year 1794, and
we have mostly been together since that time. He was constantly
one of those employed in the different excursions that were
made from Port Jackson for the further discovery of the neighbouring coasts of New Holland; and for his superior merit and
prudent conduct was advanced from before the mast to be a
midshipman, and afterwards a master in His Majesty's service.
His zeal in the cause of discovery induced him to join the
Investigator when at Spithead and ready to sail, although he
had returned to England only three weeks before from a distant
voyage of six years continuance.

'In a voyage like the present, his loss cannot be otherwise
than severely felt; and he is lamented by all on board, but more
especially by his messmates who better knew the goodness and
stability of his disposition.'[16]

The relationship between Flinders and his Master had been
an easy one. Trust and confidence well beyond the limits of
naval discipline; and beyond that a natural friendship. A competent pilot was not all Flinders lost at Cape Catastrophe.

7 March, the final entry in the journal: 'Sold the clothes of
the lost boats crew at the mast.'[17]

The delay in work imposed by the loss of the boat had been
no more wanted than the loss of the boat itself. For the autumnal
equinox was at hand, and Flinders knew next to nothing about
the approaching weather. What little he did know was based
largely upon Alexander Dalrymple's 'analogy of nature'.[18] That
is, the south coast of New Holland, being in the same latitude
as the Cape of Good Hope should, *ergo*, have approximately
the same climate. And without much question, that was the
best information available anywhere on the subject. But in any
event, Dalrymple warned, 'it is at all times dangerous to be on
a lee shore [as Flinders now was], but a lee shore on an
unknown coast is hazardous in the last extreme.'[19]

[16] *Ibid.*, p. 158. Thistle had gone with Bass in the second 'Tom Thumb', and
with Flinders both times in the *Norfolk*.
[17] *Ibid.*, p. 163.
[18] As a matter of fact, we know little enough today.
[19] 'Extract from Mr Dalrymple's memoir relating to the voyage of the
Investigator', Flinders, 'Journal', vol. I, p. 19.

Not all the delay, however, went for lost. Having conducted a thorough search, Flinders made the best of the situation by remaining at Cape Catastrophe to investigate the country. Naturally, wood and water were needed. They always were. As a matter of fact, Thistle had been searching for water when he was lost. Then too, the scientists had not been ashore for some time, and they were expected to take samples and specimens from along the whole coast.

On 24 February Flinders had a report from the scientists of an extensive inlet they had seen to the east. One last search for the bodies of the boat crew was made, and next day Flinders weighed, rounded the cape, and entered Port Lincoln, the finest harbour in South Australia. From 27 February to 4 March Flinders lived ashore, surveying the port. On the last day he took the opportunity of observing a solar eclipse, and then returned immediately to take the ship farther up the inlet.

Essentially Flinders's problem was this: moving from west to east, to keep the shore always in sight on his port hand. And at this juncture it led him to the discovery of Spencer Gulf, come what may, away from the south-facing coastline. His work in Spencer Gulf brought more of the unremitting labour of repetitive triangulation. Yet as he worked his way northward along the west side, for a distance of 180 miles, he became increasingly aware that he might be led into the strait he had been sent to find. The farther he went the keener he became; and we can only imagine his disappointment at seeing the sides of the gulf close in, ending in mud flats covered with water as salt as the sea itself. Here was only a dead end of barrenness, a zero.

But a fact is a fact, and he had discovered this one. So back down the eastern side and out to sea he went, the whole examination having taken some fifteen days.

Spencer Gulf is forty-eight miles across at its mouth. Consequently, when he rounded Cape Catastrophe, Flinders had not seen the great island lying to the east. So, as he left the gulf and turned to port he found himself confronted by an unexpected problem, whether to break off the running survey and make for the island, or follow the shore into what appeared to be yet another great inlet. Caught in a gale, he hurried over to take shelter in the lee of the island. To his surprise he found there such abundance of kangaroo that he quickly decided to lie over replenishing his food stock. Two days passed at killing and butchering on Kangaroo Island. Then, crossing back to the main, the *Investigator* entered the new inlet.

One has the impression of haste here. Beginning off Cape Spencer at the tip of Yorke Peninsula, Flinders spent only six days examining the Gulf of St Vincent. Criss-crossing under adverse winds, he reached the head of the Gulf and once again ended his search for a strait on a mud flat. On 1 April he cleared the gulf, having noted nothing that might suggest the site of the future Adelaide.[20]

Ordinarily Flinders would certainly have devoted days to a thorough examination of Kangaroo Island. But now time was running out. Unknown land lay ahead, winter gales were expected, and food stocks had dwindled. All he could do was chart the north side,[21] and leave the rest to the future. Laying down first, Investigator Strait, then Backstairs Passage,[22] he turned eastward once again, heading for the surprise of the voyage.

3

The meeting of Matthew Flinders and Nicolas Baudin, commanding the French expedition, along the south Australian coast has no parallel in the annals of discovery. The odds against such a coincidence of time and place must be astro-

[20] The Peace of Amiens was signed on 27 March, while Flinders was in the Gulf of St Vincent.

[21] Where he came upon the breeding place of pelicans, about which he rhapsodised so extravagantly in his journal. 'These birds were in great numbers, and many of them too young to fly. From the quantity of scattered bones and skeletons upon the islands, I infer, that the pelicans not only commence their being here, but that they have selected this retreat for the closing scene of their existence. Here, at a distance from man, the great disturber of all, whilst surrounded by his feathered progeny, and in the very same spot where he first emerged from his own shelly prison;—and in this retreat, the aged pelican can quietly resign his small portion of ethereal flame back to the great eternal source of vitality whence it emanated, without having his last moments interrupted, and perhaps without a pang. Requiescant ossa in pace, barbare!' 'Journal', vol. i, p. 187 sq.

[22] Between Kangaroo Island and the mainland immediately east of the Gulf of St Vincent. John Stevens, in his *Oriental Navigator*, called 'Backstairs Passage' an 'insignificant and unpleasant appellation'.

nomical. But even beyond this, the discussions between the two captains, and the later consequences, had about them a quality of weirdness that is hard to believe.

Toward the end of the day on 8 April, one of Flinders's lookouts reported a white pyramidal rock ahead. In a few moments the rock became a ship which Flinders took to be an English sealer or whaler. As a precaution the *Investigator* cleared for action. At about 6 o'clock, having by then identified *Le Géographe*, Captain Baudin, Flinders lowered down the cutter and, together with Brown as interpreter and witness, went on board the Frenchman. Although the crews fraternised as all sailors do from habit, *Investigator* kept her broadside to. The first conversation lasted about an hour. At 7.10 Flinders, after arranging for another meeting and setting night signals, returned to his own ship. At dawn next day he again went over to the *Géographe*. By 8 a.m. he was back again in the *Investigator* and the two ships parted company.[23]

We have a fairly clear notion of the discussions during these two brief conversations. At both meetings Baudin talked about Bass Strait. At the second session Flinders reported in general on his work from Cape Leeuwin eastward, and spoke particularly about Spencer Gulf, the Gulf of St Vincent, and Kangaroo Island. The French were also much interested in the hypothesis of a strait dividing New Holland. Why both meetings took place on board the *Géographe* is not clear. One would think the first visit should have been returned. But what seems queer about the whole affair is that, until near the end of the second meeting Baudin did not know to whom he was speaking. True, he had left France months before Flinders sailed. But then, why were there no formalities? Was there suspicion? All the more reason for introductions. Could Flinders have been mistaken in saying Baudin did not know him? Perhaps.[24]

So much for the incident as it took place at Encounter Bay. Evidently Flinders thought the conversations friendly and tolerably candid, if not particularly useful to himself. But the sequel told another tale.

Nicolas Baudin died in 1803. In 1807, while Flinders was a

[23] Flinders, 'Journal', vol. I, p. 192 sq.
[24] *Ibid.*

prisoner on the Île de France (Mauritius), François Péron, Naturalist to the French expedition, brought out the first volume of the French narrative, *Voyage de Découvertes aux Terres Australes . . .*, over the imprimatur of the imperial government. In that work Péron set down the most extravagant claims imaginable for French discovery along the south coast of New Holland, claims which violated not only demonstrable fact, but even common decency.

Péron recognised the priority of Pieter Nuyts, George Vancouver, and Bruni d'Entrecasteaux, whose discoveries taken together extended eastward from Cape Leeuwin to Nuyts Archipelago (133° 30′ E.). He also recognised George Bass's discoveries as far as Western Port (145° 02′ E.). The remainder of the southern coast, all of the $11\frac{1}{2}°$ of longitude between Nuyts Archipelago and Western Port, he claimed for France. And he named it Terre Napoléon.

But the fact is Flinders had, as we know, surveyed all the coast from Nuyts Archipelago to Encounter Bay; in 1800 Lieutenant Grant had sailed the *Lady Nelson* eastward from Cape Otway through Bass Strait; and nearly two months before the meeting, John Murray had taken the *Lady Nelson* from Port Jackson through Bass Strait to Port Phillip. These discoveries by Flinders, Grant, and Murray reduced legitimate French claims to a maximum of 1° 17′ of longitude—on the order of 150 miles of coastline.

Péron could not possibly plead ignorance of Flinders's work. He had attended the meetings on board the *Géographe*. It is suggested that he had other fish to fry. Else why did he allege, as he did, that in the talks with Baudin, Flinders had maintained *'une grande réserve sur ses opérations particulières'* ?[25] And why did he go out of his way to place such prominent French names upon the charts : for Spencer Gulf, Golfe Bonaparte; for St Vincent Gulf, Golfe Josephine; and for Kangaroo Island, Île Decrès, after the French Minister of Marine ? All that need be said is that Péron found himself unable to discriminate between the morality of science and the more elastic ethos of politics. For a scientist that is enough.

[25] *Voyage de Découvertes aux Terres Australes . . .* (2 vols. and atlas, Paris, 1807–16), vol. I, p. 325.

Flinders first heard of these 'aggressions', as he called them, while he was still a prisoner on Mauritius. Of course he reacted violently. The naked fraud, his own situation, the sequestration of his journals, the official imprimatur upon Péron's claims, all these elements infuriated him. And indeed, even when he wrote his narrative, he still had not cooled off:

'The motive for this aggression I do not pretend to explain. It may have originated in the desire to rival the British nation in the honour of completing the discovery of the globe; or be intended as the fore runner of a claim to the possession of the countries so said to have been first discovered by French navigators. Whatever may have been the object in view, the question, so far as I am concerned, must be left to the judgment of the world; and if succeeding French writers can see and admit the claims of other navigators, as clearly and readily as a late most able man of that nation* has pointed out their own in some other instances, I shall not fear to leave it even to their decision.'

'*M. De Fleurieu.'[26]

François Péron died in 1807, the year in which his book was published. But the issue remained unresolved—at least on paper if not in fact—until 1824, when Louis de Freycinet brought out a new edition of the Voyage de Découvertes.

The critical passage on these claims in Péron's 1807 text had read as follows:

'De ce grand espace [the south coast of Terra Australis], la partie seule qui du Cap Leuwin s'étend aux îles St. Pierre et St. François, étoit connue lors de notre départ d'Europe. Découverte par les Hollandois en 1627, elle avoit été, dans ces derniers temps, visitée par Vancouver et sur-tout par Dentre-casteaux; mais ce dernier navigateur n'ayant pu lui-même s'avancer audelà des îles St. Pierre et St. François, qui forment

---

[26] Flinders, Voyage, vol. 1, p. 193. Flinders might have fared better at the hands of Alexander von Humboldt, who had been officially invited to go as naturalist with Baudin. Humboldt, having at first agreed, then withdrew. Enc. Brit. (11th edn), 'Humboldt'.

la limite orientale de la terre de Nuyts, et les Anglois n'ayant
pas porté vers le Sud leurs recherches plus loin que le port
Western, *il en résultoit que toute la portion comprise entre ce
dernier point et la terre de Nuyts étoit encore inconnue au moment
ou nous arrivions sur ces rivages.* [Italics mine.]'[27]

In Freycinet's 1824 edition the italicised passage reads: 'il
en résultoit que toute la portion comprise entre ce dernier
point et la terre de Nuyts *nous* étoit encore inconnue. . . .'[28]

Thus Grant, Murray, and Flinders remained ignored. But
the course of events had run against Péron, and Freycinet's atlas
carries the names Spencer Gulf, Gulf of St Vincent, and
Kangaroo Island. By then Flinders too was dead.

4

'The entrance to the Murray River is through a narrow
opening in the beach . . . and is ever changing its form and
appearance, according to prevailing winds.' Curling over a wide
bar, 'the surf usually breaks heavily across the entrance except
in the finest weather.' So reads the modern *Australia Pilot*.[29]

Sailing in 'light and unfavourable' winds, and held away
from the shore by tidal currents, Flinders had the misfortune to
miss the entrance to the largest river in all Australia. Here was
the answer to the problem of continental drainage. Its discovery
in 1802 would certainly have altered the economy of Australia
during the first half of the nineteenth century. But miss it he
did, and the useful navigation of the Murray had to await the
overland journeys of Charles Sturt.

By 21 April Flinders had reached Cape Otway, but, driven
off by gales, he steered over to King Island for a look at its north
side. Brown spent a few hours ashore, then, the gales abating,
Flinders picked up the thread again at the cape. He had determined, he said, 'to run over to the high land we had seen on the
north side of Bass' Strait; and to trace as much of the coast from

[27] Vol. I, p. 316.
[28] Vol. II, p. 186, ed. by Louis de Freycinet.
[29] Vol. I, p. 244 sq.

thence eastward, as the state of the weather and our remaining provisions could possibly allow.'[30]

26 April. 'At noon, there was some appearance of an opening round the rocky point, but the water seemed to break across . . . The small opening round the Rocky Point assuming a more important form as we came more abreast, soon after noon bore away to examine it; and finding it led into a large piece of water, at $1^h 30'$ we entered it. . . .'[31]

Thus Port Phillip which, as we know but Flinders did not, had been discovered by Murray only ten weeks before, and which for a time Flinders mistook for Western Port. Anchoring on the eastern side of the bay, he left the ship to Fowler, determined to examine as much of this sheet of water as he possibly could on a three-day excursion. The result was superficial. He approached but did not enter what is now called Outer Geelong Harbour. He probably saw Hobsons Bay, but certainly not from less than ten miles, and so once again he missed a river —the Yarra at Melbourne. He made no attempt to survey the eastern side.

Flinders did, however, form a most favourable opinion of the area. Despite its narrow entrance, he noted that the port was 'capable of receiving and sheltering a larger fleet of ships than ever yet went to sea', and that the surrounding country appeared quite suitable for cattle, or better, sheep. In sum, he had no doubt that a settlement would one day be erected at this place.[32]

A mere week was all he could spare for Port Phillip. On 3 May he weighed, pausing outside the entrance only long enough for Westall to make a sketch for future navigators. At 1 o'clock of the sixth day following, 9 May 1802, H.M. Sloop *Investigator* passed through Sydney Heads and came to anchor.

Flinders placed himself forthwith under the orders of the Governor, Philip Gidley King, and reported that he had performed his survey in five months; that since leaving home he

[30] Flinders, *Voyage*, vol. I, p. 208.
[31] Flinders, 'Journal', vol. I, p. 206 sq.
[32] Flinders, *Voyage*, vol. I, p. 218 sq. The settlement that became Melbourne was made on the Yarra in 1835.

had logged just over 20,000 miles, 6,000 from Cape Leeuwin to Port Jackson; that he had lost his Master at Cape Catastrophe; that he had found no rivers; that he had met Baudin at Encounter Bay. But best of all, that very day, 'there was not a single individual on board who was not upon deck working the ship into harbour'.[33]

[33] *Ibid.*, p. 226.

# CHAPTER SEVEN

# The East Coast

## July–October 1802

1

In conference with Flinders, Governor King now decided to send the *Investigator* north as soon as possible. The plan called for an examination in detail of all the east coast from Hervey Bay, which Flinders had entered in the *Norfolk*, to the southern end of the Great Barrier Reef. In particular, Flinders was to study those irregularities of the coast that Cook had of necessity passed hurriedly by. As Flinders himself expressed it, Cook 'had reaped the harvest of discovery, but the gleanings of the field remained to be gathered.'[1] But the gleaning, especially in the deadly labyrinth of the reefs, could be a time-consuming business. Then there was the passage of Torres Strait, about which so little was known that up to that time every navigator who had made it had added something to the charts. This was to be followed by a survey of the Gulf of Carpentaria, and an investigation of the north and north-west coasts. It was expected that the entire phase might require from ten to twelve months.

What meagre information Flinders had indicated that, under the north-west monsoon, the eastern side of the Gulf of Carpentaria became a lee shore on or about 1 November.[2] This being the case, or at any rate the assumption, he must therefore try to reach the head of the Gulf by that date, and then determine his future course of action.

In 1802, Port Jackson was less than adequate as a supply

---

[1] Flinders, *Voyage*, vol. 1, p. lxxxii sq. It was not proposed that Flinders should repeat Cook's work along the Inner Route to Torres Strait.

[2] Actually. the condition is not so serious as Flinders supposed. Winds can be squally, but they tend to blow off the eastern shore instead of on to it.

depot, and by a fairly wide margin. It offered precious little, for example, by way of boatswains' stores. Sails, cables, anchors, tar, paint and varnish, all had to be imported from England. At so great a distance from his source, a man in Flinders's position was obliged to plan for his third step before he had even begun his second. Therefore, he now sent off a request for fresh stocks of these necessaries.[3] As to food the story was little better. Fresh meat, if any, could be had only at the most exorbitant prices. What vegetables there were came from no market, but from the Governor's garden. Rum was available only from American vessels, at the best prices the Yankees could get and still unload their holds. Flinders bought and loaded fifteen tons of bread, and contracted for both flour and wheat which he placed in stock for future use.[4] On so flimsy a basis was this voyage expected to flourish.

The *Investigator* lay in port for twelve weeks. What held her there was the ever-imperious need for refitment. Rigging, sails, decks, upper works, hull, even masts, had all to be examined, repaired, replaced, cleaned and painted. The ship's crew supplied most of the labour which, in lieu of idleness, explains why Flinders had to inflict corporal punishment at Port Jackson on only five occasions.[5]

The time passed quickly, and not every day was spent in work. For the crew there was leave to go ashore, with perhaps extended time to explore the back country, behind Parramatta. For Flinders there were visits to the Governor, and visits to the ship: on 10 June, by His Excellency; on 22 June, by Captain Baudin; and on 14 July, by Baudin and Lieutenant Governor Paterson. On 4 June, 'Dressed the ship with colours in honour of His Majesty's birthday. At 1 p.m. Fired a royal salute, and afterwards the Commander and officers dined with His Excellency the governor, to celebrate the birthday.'[6] On 5 July Flinders and Fowler sat together on a Court of Vice-Admiralty

---

[3] Flinders to Admiralty, 15 May 1802. P.R.O., Adm. 1/1801.

[4] On 13 June there arrived at Port Jackson the ship *Coromandel*, bringing the provisions Flinders had requested the day he left England.

[5] Flinders, 'Journal', vol. I, p. 226 sqq. One Andrew Robson, a marine, took twelve lashes on 14 May for drunkenness, and twelve more for 'mutinous expressions'. On 15 June he got twelve more for leaving his sentry post.

[6] *Ibid.*, p. 227.

to try the captain of a transport for his execution of fifteen convicts charged with attempted mutiny.[7]

At the Governor's direction, Mr John Aken, chief mate of the Bombay ship *Hercules*, then lying in Port Jackson, was appointed Master to replace Mr Thistle.

Of letter-writing Flinders did surprisingly little during these weeks. Official reports went to the Admiralty. A long, rambling account of the Southern Portion,[8] together with plans for the next stage, was sent to Sir Joseph.[9] A brief note of 1 July informed Alexander Dalrymple of several innovations on the charts.[10] This was all; all, that is, except for two to Ann, both truly heartbreaking.

No letter from Ann awaited his arrival at Port Jackson, and so, on 31 May, he began a letter of his own, thoughtfully jotting down whatever he thought might amuse her. A sketchy paragraph on the voyage thus far; a description of the company she might have enjoyed but for the Admiralty's intervention; pleasant words about Mrs King and Mrs Paterson; the hope that they might be £1,500 richer by the end of the voyage than they were at the beginning; and a most revealing passage on what he chose to call the 'politics of the ship':

'Mr. Fowler agrees better with me than he did earlier in our acquaintance; he does not find it so difficult a task to please me, as he once thought; and I believe he now has the inclination to do it.[11] I wish so much could be said of my brother: the distance between us has widened considerably. He is satisfied with being as much inferior to other officers as I [would] have him superior to them.[12] With my messmates and all the other gentlemen of the ship, with but one exception,[13] every thing goes on smoothly and well. John Franklin approves himself worthy of notice. He is

---

[7] *Ibid.*, p. 231.

[8] As also one from Brown to Banks, B.M., Add. MSS. 32439. 56–8.

[9] B.M., Add. MSS. 32439. 54–5.

[10] S.L.V., 'Flinders Papers'.

[11] N.M.M. 60/017. FLI/25. No hint of this friction appears in any previous documents that have come to my attention. J.D.M.

[12] This sentence on Samuel Ward Flinders is conspicuously omitted from the copy of the letter lodged in S.L.V. For more on this fraternal relationship, see Sidney J. Baker, *My Own Destroyer* (Sydney, 1963), esp. p. 110, and p. 127 sqq.

[13] Perhaps Robert Brown. *Ibid.*, p. 110.

9

capable of learning every thing that we can shew him, and but for a little carelessness, I would not wish to have a son otherwise than he is.'

It was not until some weeks more had passed that news from Ann arrived. There was one letter dated October 1801, and another of 7 January 1802. In the latter she informed him of an illness and of an operation that had been necessary to save her eyesight. This distressing news was already seven months out of date. But what dismayed him even more was her questioning heart. In the face of his leaving her so soon after their marriage, she found herself struggling to believe that he really loved her. His response was filled with pathos.

'My dearest friend, thou adducest my leaving thee to follow the call of my profession, as a poor proof of my affection for thee. Dost thou not know, my beloved, that we could have barely existed in England? That both thou and me must have been debarred of even necessaries; unless we had given up our independence to have procured them from perhaps unwilling friends.[14] It was only upon the certainty of obtaining an employment, the produce of which would be adequate to thy support as well as my own, that I dared to follow the wishes of my heart and press thee to be mine. Heaven knows with what sincerity and warmth of affection I have loved thee,—how anxiously I look forward to the time when I may return to thee, and how earnestly I labour that the delight of our meeting may be no more clouded with the fear of a long parting. Do not then, my beloved, adduce the following of the dictates of necessity as my crime. . . . Let not unavailing sorrow increase thy malady, but look my dear Ann to the happy side. See me engaged, successfully thus far, in the cause of science and followed by the good wishes and approbation of the world.'[15]

Life had not yet worked out. For Ann it was bitter gall. For Matthew? Well, while she could only sit and wait, he at least

[14] Why this is so is not quite clear. After all he might have changed his profession in order to support his wife.
[15] Flinders to Ann, 20 July 1802. N.M.M. 60/017. FLI/25.

had his work, work in which he was supremely happy. But the feeling that in his enthusiasm he had not been quite fair to Ann, continued—and still continues—to insinuate itself. It had always been Ann who paid. Ann always would pay. Ann was a saint.


2


22 July. H.M. Sloop *Investigator*, in company with her tender, *Lady Nelson*, brig, cleared Sydney Heads, turned to port, and began her second expedition. Her first objective was Break Sea Spit, round the end of which lies Hervey Bay, some 800 miles north of Port Jackson. By 27 July she had arrived at Double Island Point at the southern end of Wide Bay, and, coming close inshore, ran nearly the length of Fraser Island at night, guided only by the fires of natives over on the main. The following day Flinders crossed the tail of Break Sea Spit and entered the bay he had explored just three years before. After allowing a day for the scientists to examine the land at Sandy Cape, on 1 August he steered westward across the mouth of Hervey Bay to South Head.

South Head is indeed an insignificant-looking place on the map. But it was in fact just there that Flinders made one of the most important discoveries of his career. In 1770 Cook had stretched across Hervey Bay, and had measured its greatest width at fifty-nine miles. In the *Norfolk* Flinders had thought that too great a distance, but without chronometers he could offer no real proof. This time he remeasured it carefully, and found Cook in error by some sixteen miles. As his track across the bay was nearly due west, it became immediately apparent to Flinders that the longitude of all Cook's positions from South Head to Torres Strait was open to question. This was not all. As one moves toward Torres Strait, this coast trends toward the west, with the result that Cook's error for the longitude became progressively greater. Thus, at Hervey Bay Flinders differed from Cook by sixteen miles, but at Cape York the disparity had grown to thirty-five miles, half a degree in some of the most dangerous water in the world.

There is nothing here that can be fairly charged against Cook.

As a first approximation, without chronometers, Cook's plotting was excellent. But the introduction of time-keepers made Flinders's corrections virtually inevitable, however little he may have relished finding his hero mistaken.

Indentations in the coast beyond Hervey Bay consist generally of shoals and mangrove swamp. Above high spring tides the land is drained by sluggish creeks reaching back into the country a few miles, making islands out of sandbars, each creek ending in a cul-de-sac. Such, for example, is the shoreline around Port Curtis and Keppel Bay. Strictly speaking, Facing and Curtis Islands are islands. They are indeed bodies of land entirely surrounded by water. But their continued existence as such over many centuries cannot be very certain. Clearly the waters separating them from the mainland could not be described as navigable. This was the terrain Flinders now attempted to examine, sometimes from the ship, but often in a boat or on foot. Not infrequently he found it necessary to 'wade some distance in soft mud, and afterwards to cut through a barrier of mangroves, before reaching the solid land'.[16]

These walking excursions were, incidentally, not without risk, as the Master's Mate discovered at Keppel Bay. Entangled in a swamp, the Mate and a sailor passed a night, 'persecuted by clouds of musketoes' [sic] only to fall in at dawn with a party of some twenty-five natives. The affair ended happily enough; but for the Mate, never again.

Next after Keppel Bay in point of discovery came Port Bowen, now Port Clinton. It was much the same as what had gone before. But just beyond its northern end, where the mainland breaks off, there lies a gap in the coast called Strong Tide Passage. At the flood and ebb the stream runs through this gap at five, sometime six, knots. Even for power boats, the passage is described today as 'dangerous at all times, and cannot be recommended to any vessel'.[17] The day Flinders went through it, he nearly lost his boatswain. Having anchored inside, he sent off the cutter to haul the seine. On taking it up again, 'the cutter was upset by the tide, and the boatkeeper thrown out. The boatswain jumping into the gig in order to pick up the

---

[16] Flinders, *Voyage*, vol. II, p. 29.
[17] *Australia Pilot*, vol. IV, p. 89.

boat-keeper, got a thwart hawse of the cutter, and in order to save himself from being washed out of the gig, he thought it necessary to cut the other boat adrift. He then let go and went after with the gig. . . . At daylight the boatswain returned on board having seen nothing of the cutter, but had been near losing himself, being bewildered in the dark by the rapid tides in a strange place.'[18] And Flinders must have thought once again of Mr Thistle disappearing at Cape Catastrophe.[19]

The run through Strong Tide Passage had brought Flinders to Broad Sound, the largest complex of bays and inlets with which he had to deal on this coast. There he erected a tent on shore, and there he spent three weeks surveying the coast or exploring the surrounding country. The abnormal rise of tides there occupied his interest, and led him to advance Broad Sound as a suitable place for future settlement. The climate appealed to him for possible plantations of cotton, sugar, coffee, and tobacco. But his remarks on the subject could not be called enthusiastic.

Actually, the stay in Broad Sound was lengthened beyond the schedule by yet another display of ineptitude on the part of brother Samuel. Having given Fowler charge of the ship, Matthew placed Samuel at the tent with orders to make a continuing series of astronomical observations. He himself then went off on a long surveying excursion. When he returned from this sortie, he found that the chronometers had been allowed to stop. His 'Journal' on the day records only the fact, and decently omits the embroidery. This lapse cost five precious days for re-establishment of the rates.[20] He rewarded his brother with

[18] Flinders, 'Journal', vol. I, p. 276. Two days later, this boatswain, Mr Douglas, evidently shaken, took to the bottle and was 'suspended from his public duty upon deck for fighting with W$^m$ Job, a seaman, and for drunkenness'. Flinders also punished Job with twelve lashes, 'after explaining the heinousness of striking a superior officer'. 'Journal', vol. I, p. 278.

[19] It is interesting to note, by the way, that after passing the Tropic of Capricorn Flinders kept always in mind the possibility of finding debris thrown up on the beach from the wreck of the French ships, *Boussole* and *Astrolabe*, under command of the great Comte de la Pérouse. The search, in the best traditions of the sea, was, however, quite hopeless. La Pérouse had gone down in 1788 at Vanikoro in the Santa Cruz group. The wreckage was not found until 1826.

[20] No chronometer is a perfect timekeeper. This being the case, it is necessary to know not only the difference between the chronometer-reading and true time, but also the rate at which the clock gains or loses. Moreover, since merely resetting

this tedious job, and went off on another excursion. It was too much for Samuel. After four days, being intent upon the observations and the computations involved with them, the lieutenant once again forgot to wind the chronometers, 'to my no less surprize,' wrote Matthew, 'than regret'.[21]

As he reported it, 'I was now at a stand what to do. The necessity of having good rates to our timekeepers before we sailed for Torres Strait and the north coast, made me almost determine to go on shore myself for a few days; but on the other hand, the rapid approach of the northwest monsoon on the north coast [it was now 25 September] and the delays we had already made in the sound and the neighbourhood, finally induced me to go away as fast as possible, with the best rates we could scrape together. . . .'[22]

3

Two days later the *Investigator* left Broad Sound and sheered away from the coast, heading for Torres Strait. For a day or so, Flinders looked about the Percy Isles; but on 4 October, running short of time, he went his way, hoping to find quick passage through the Barrier Reef into the open Pacific. Whether he had decided previously to send the *Lady Nelson* on to the strait independently, or whether a look at the reefs determined him, Flinders now saw the imprudence of attempting to keep company with the little tender. On 6 October, therefore, he wrote a set of instructions for Lieutenant Murray, ordering him to proceed to a rendezvous in Torres Strait. If, at the end of a given time—two months—the *Investigator* had not appeared, Murray was to go through, and make directly for the north-west cape. From there, after examining an opening in the coast laid down by William Dampier, he was to proceed directly to Port Jackson.[23]

the clock can alter the rate, a new rate must be established. Forgetting to wind the chronometers is not recommended.

[21] Flinders, 'Journal', vol. I, p. 302. Trying to make a navigator out of Samuel was an exercise in futility.

[22] *Ibid.*

[23] *Ibid.*, p. 314.

In fact, however, the work of the *Lady Nelson* was already done. Twelve days later, while both ships were still fighting their way out of the reefs, the tender smashed her main keel. Flinders had no choice but to send her back to Sydney, and go it alone.

The week from 5 to 11 October was pure hell. Flinders had not simply stumbled into a trap. A study of Cook's charts had confirmed that he was well inside the Great Barrier Reef. But, pressed for time, he had allowed himself to believe that the quickest solution would be to attack the reefs directly, and try to find his way out among the jutting rocks. This illusion, born of haste, he soon regretted. A few entries in his 'Journal' suffice to indicate the situation in which he instantly found himself:

'6 October. From the high breaking upon the outer reef seen this afternoon, I conceived hopes that there could be no extensive reef to windward [i.e. eastward] of it, and that as soon as we should be able to weather the reefs and shoals near which we tacked at 4 P.M. we should get out into the open sea.'[24]

This optimistic view presently evaporated.

'7 October. The appearances of shoals were very numerous this morning, the shadows of white clouds, ripplings, and smooth places, being scarcely distinguishable from reefs. Our whale-boat, however, enabled us to discriminate, and in a little time I learned to disbelieve all appearances but those where something was above water, or where the water had a tinge of green in it; with all these deductions, however, there still remained a formidable mass of reefs, through which there appeared to be but one small channel.'[25]

Again:

'8 October. The prospect at noon today is still worse than ever; for except to the westward, whence we came, the reefs encircle us all round. . . . The breakers to the eastward denote

[24] *Ibid.*, p. 315.        [25] *Ibid.*, p. 316.

the outside of these reefs to be exposed to the open sea, and are, indeed, the only alleviation to the hopelessness of our present prospect.'[26]

And again:

'9 October. The very different appearance of the shoals at 7 this morning, from what they were when we passed between the same reefs at 3 P.M. yesterday, is almost beyond belief. There was no appearance of any passage this morning. . . .'[27]

To the strain of delay was added the certainty of unremitting danger, perhaps even a species of claustrophobia, all of which wore the commander's temper paper-thin:

'12 October. At daylight it appeared that the ship had driven about two miles to the northeastward [i.e. toward the reefs] . . . This had not been perceived by the watch, a neglect that might have proved fatal to us, and which I am determined not to pardon a second time. The officer of the middle watch is the person to whom I attribute the blame.'[28]

Only the day before he had determined to find a new solution. By turning back to the Percy Isles he could coast northward along the inner edge of the Barrier, where he might reasonably expect to find—sooner or later—a sizeable break in the Barrier itself. It would still be dangerous, but not hopeless.

Four days later, after he had broken free of imminent danger, Flinders took a day to go ashore on the Cumberland Isles. It was a welcome holiday. On the 17th he ordered the *Lady Nelson* back to Sydney, sending with her two letters: one to Governor King,[29] and a very brief note to Ann.[30] Then, setting a north-west

[26] *Ibid.*, p. 317.          [27] *Ibid.*, p. 319.

[28] *Ibid.*, p. 323. The 'Journal' indicates that Robert Fowler had the evening watch, and that he was relieved for the middle watch by, of all people, Samuel Flinders. In his *Voyage*, Matthew, from whatever reason, changed his story: '. . . it was difficult,' he wrote, 'from the circumstance of having occurred at the relief of watch, to discover with whom the culpable inattention lay.' Vol. II, p. 92. On the other hand, one might ask whether the ship would drag her anchor for two miles during the ten minutes or so it may have taken to relieve the watch.

[29] B.M., Add. MSS. 32439. 72–3.

[30] N.M.M. 60/017. FLI/25.

course along the inner edge of the Barrier, he went on to look for a gap. On 20 October, after logging only 500 miles in fourteen days, the *Investigator* broke out into the Pacific:

'Continued our course to the N.E. ward, and at 4 no reefs were in sight.'[31]

His final comment on this harrowing subject reads as follows:

'The commander who proposes to make the experiment, must not, however, be one who throws his ship's head round in a hurry, so soon as breakers are announced from aloft; if he do not feel his nerves strong enough to thread the needle, as it is called, amongst the reefs, whilst he directs the steerage from the mast head, I would strongly recommend him not to approach this part of New South Wales.'[32]

A clear northward run of 600 miles in six days brought the ship to the latitude of Torres Strait. There Flinders hesitated momentarily to inspect an uncharted reef, the Eastern Field; then, turning due west, he began his approach to the Strait.

1 November was only four days away.

[31] Flinders, 'Journal', vol. I, p. 333. This is now called 'Flinders Passage', at 19° 42′ S., 147° 45′ E. on the inner side.
[32] Flinders, *Voyage*, vol. II, p. 104.

# CHAPTER EIGHT

# The North Coast

## October 1802–February 1803

### 1

'A voyage which should have had no other view, than the survey of Torres' Strait and the thorough investigation of the North Coast of Terra Australis, could not have been accused of wanting an object worthy of national consideration.'[1]

As he paused at Pandora Entrance before Torres Strait, Matthew's memory took him back ten years, to the *Providence*, to the days when he had sailed as a midshipman with William Bligh. Then he had thought how great a thing it might someday be to take his own ship through the Strait. In boyish fancy, he saw himself a hero following in the track of Captain Cook. Now at 28 he saw matters in a different light. The transit of Torres Strait had become an intellectual problem, not a feat of heroics. The question was not so much whether he would succeed or fail, but how elegantly he would do it.

'The navigation from the Pacific, or Great Ocean to all parts of India, and to the Cape of Good Hope, would be greatly facilitated, if a passage through the Strait, moderately free from danger, could be discovered; since *five or six weeks* [italics F's] of the usual route, by the north of New Guinea or the more eastern islands, would thereby be saved. Notwithstanding the great obstacles which navigators had encountered in some parts of the Strait, there was still room to hope, that an examination of the whole, made with care and perseverance, would bring

---

[1] Flinders, *Voyage*, vol. I, p. xlviii.

such a passage to light. A survey of it was, therefore, an object much to be desired; not only for the merchants and seamen trading to these parts, but also from the benefits which would certainly accrue therefrom to general navigation and geography.'[2]

A nod to utility, and a bow to the advancement of learning.

History records that Luis Vaez de Torres, a Spaniard, was the first navigator to pass this strait. That was in 1606. History also records that, following their self-interest, the Spanish suppressed the fact, hoping thereby either to gain time on their rivals, or to elude them in flight. In any case, until the time of Cook, for all the rest of Europe knew Torres Strait did not exist, and Terra Australis formed one piece of land with New Guinea. Cook sailed through the Strait in 1770, having come at it by way of the Inner Route along the Queensland coast. Nineteen years later, Bligh went through in the *Bounty* launch. Next came Edward Edwards,[3] sent out to pick up the *Bounty* mutineers and bring them back to England. His ship, the *Pandora*, was wrecked at Murray Island, inside the Strait, in 1791, and Edwards took his crew to Timor, in four of the ship's boats. The following year, Bligh in the *Providence*, and Nathaniel Portlock in the *Assistant*, passed the Strait together on their way home from the second 'breadfruit voyage'. Finally, in 1792, two traders, William Bampton and Matthew Alt, sailed their ships, *Hormuzeer* and *Chesterfield* from the Pacific, past Cape York, into the Timor Sea. Matthew Flinders thus became the ninth commander—the eighth in thirty-two years—to attempt the Strait.

After two weeks or so, backing and filling, anchoring and weighing, getting nowhere, on the Barrier Reef, Flinders was eager and ready to do some surveying once again. Indeed, with less than half of his mission completed he had every right to be eager. But now anxiety intruded, complicating his work, and threatening the elegance of his solution. As he stood off from the Eastern Field he was, as we have seen, deeply concerned about the approaching monsoon. Yet that was not a present

---

[2] *Ibid.*, p. xlvi. For a full discussion of the problem, see *Journals of Captain James Cook*, J. C. Beaglehole, ed., vol. I (Cambridge, 1955), esp. p. cliv sq.

[3] Edward Edwards, Admiral (1742–1815).

danger. As he passed Pandora Entrance, Flinders cut to the south-west, heading for Murray Island. He recalled that in the *Providence* he had seen the natives attack one of Portlock's boats. And he knew, as everyone did, that only nine years before, Bampton and Alt had had to beat off a vicious armed assault from these same islanders. These events prompted him now to take precautions. When the canoes came, the crew were ready, '. . . the marines being under arms, the guns clear, matches lighted, and an officer particularly stationed to watch the motions of each canoe during the whole time that they were about the ship.'[4] This time, to his great relief, the interest of the natives was in trade, not blood; and so the anxiety, if not the vigilance, abated.

Another worry first manifested itself at Halfway Island, well inside the Strait, but before the *Investigator* had reached the most dangerous stage of the passage. On 30 October Flinders was horrified to learn that, although he had been running 'under two topsails and jib only', and although the water was smooth, 'the ship has been leaking at least ten inches (the carpenter's report was 14) of water per hour'.[5] Six inches an hour had been the worst so far. But what made this all the more serious was the suspicion that the leak must be somewhere below the water-line, where there would be no easy remedy. This evidence of decay, so perfectly plain, served only to exacerbate the third, most fearful anxiety of all, submerged coral. Even a strong ship might founder here; for a rotten one there was no hope. Such, then, were the circumstances surrounding the transit of Torres Strait.

It will be recalled that back in Hervey Bay Flinders had first discovered the error of longitude into which Captain Cook had fallen. Having left the coast and sailed north nearly a thousand miles, he had lost Cook's track until now, as he entered the Strait. With Bligh's charts in hand, he began a series of observations to fix, once and for all, the true position of Cape York. By the time the *Investigator* had reached Halfway Island,

---

[4] Flinders, 'Journal', vol. i, p. 342.
[5] *Ibid.*, p. 345. Use of more sail would have tended to heel the ship to one side or the other. The Rossel Current carried her forward as fast as Flinders wished.

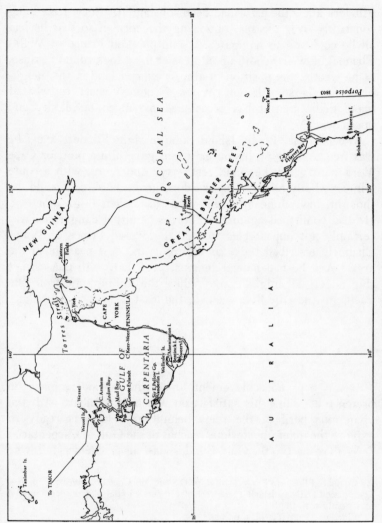

Torres Strait and the Gulf of Carpentaria, 1802–3

Flinders knew the error had been substantial.[6] But a haze hung constantly over the sea, obscuring the horizon so that he had all he could do to navigate. At one point in Prince of Wales Channel he went ashore upon an islet for a look round because, as he wrote, 'the position of almost every island in this neighbourhood is so different in his [Cook's] chart to what I make them, that it has occasioned me much perplexity and uneasiness.'[7]

When at last Booby Island came in sight Flinders knew he was free. Averaging his observations gave him a plot for Cape York with which he could rest easy. And more, with a route 'almost wholly to seek,' he had done in six days—and could, he thought, have done in three—what had taken Bligh nineteen. He had confirmed again that Torres Strait, if dangerous, was certainly not impassable. He had discovered Prince of Wales Channel, described today as affording the best passage in the area.[8] And he had indeed demonstrated that, with due care, a ship under sail might easily reduce the sailing time from the Pacific to India by five weeks at the least.

2

It was a proud achievement, over which Flinders made no pretence at hiding his satisfaction. On 3 November, with the ubiquitous peril of the reefs behind him, he was ready to explore the quiet, mysterious reaches of the Gulf of Carpentaria.

With respect to the Gulf, Flinders saw his problem as follows :

[6] Compare Flinders's *Voyage*, vol. II, p. 116 with the Cook *Journal*, vol. I, p. 384. Cook placed Halfway Island 1° 4' west of Flinders's initial plot. Flinders agreed consistently with Bligh.

[7] Flinders, 'Journal', vol. I, p. 349.

[8] It has been said that Flinders's name appears as an authority for modern Admiralty charts of the area (e.g. 346, 2764, and esp. 445), the implication being that his work was of so high an order of quality that later surveyors have not surpassed it. This is uncritical. Without subtracting a whit from Flinders, it must be pointed out that other factors come into play. All coastlines change constantly, and many are studied continuously. But hydrographic surveying is a costly operation, to be undertaken only if the volume of sea-borne traffic warrants the expenditure of public monies. Thus, if and when the traffic in Torres Strait increases appreciably, Flinders's name will probably disappear from the charts.

'The real form of this gulph remained in as great doubt with geographers, as were the manner how, and time when it acquired its name. The east side of the Gulph had been explored to the latitude of 17°, and many rivers were there marked and named; but how far the representation given of it by the Dutch was faithful,—what were the productions, and what its inhabitants— were, in a great measure, uncertain. Or rather, it was certain, that those early navigators did not possess the means of fixing the position and forms of lands, with any thing like the accuracy of modern science; and that they could have known very little of the productions, or inhabitants. Of the rest of the Gulph no one could say, with any confidence, upon what authority its form had been given in the charts; so that conjecture, being at liberty to appropriate the Gulph of Carpentaria to itself, had made it the entrance to a vast arm of the sea.'[9]

The earliest European examination of the Gulf of Carpentaria occurred in the year 1606, the same in which Vaez de Torres passed the Strait. In that year the Dutch East India Company dispatched the yacht *Duifken* eastward from Bantam to investigate the coast of New Guinea. Having done so, the *Duifken* turned south across the western approaches to Torres Strait, and coasted into the Gulf as far as Cape Keer-Weer ('Turn Again') (13° 57′ S.). She then left the Gulf to return to Banda in the Moluccas. In 1623 another Dutch vessel, the *Pera*, penetrated the Gulf somewhat farther, passing Cape Keer-Weer and going on to the Staaten River (16° 25′ S.) before leaving off to return to Amboina. The first complete circuit of the Gulf appears to have been made by the great Abel Janszoon Tasman in 1644. Tasman left behind no documentation of this, his second voyage to the east, so that it is not certain beyond doubt that it was he who laid down the features of the Gulf. He was known, however, to have been in the area at that time, and would certainly have had that distinction if he followed the instructions given him by the Company.

After Tasman, no European is known to have entered the Gulf for 158 years, that is, until the voyage of the *Investigator*. Improvements in the technique of navigation and cartography

[9] Flinders, *Voyage*, vol. I, p. xlvi sq. That is to say, an arm of the Indian Ocean.

over the century and a half since Tasman placed the seventeenth-century charts under considerable doubt. Flinders therefore advanced south most deliberately. As far as 16° 25′ S. he could rely upon the work of three navigators, whose findings he had before him on an old Dutch chart.[10] Beyond the Staaten River he presumably had but one predecessor and must, therefore, proceed with extreme caution. Sailing only between sunrise and sunset, and going ashore only twice along the entire coast, he took ten days to survey the segment from Booby Island to the head of the Gulf.[11] For the first eight days he sailed with light to moderate breezes in fine weather. On the last two, 12 and 13 November, the breezes remained light, but the sky turned cloudy. There was, however, no sign of the dreaded monsoon, about which he had felt such deep concern even before he left England.

According to his instructions, Flinders was charged with solving the question whether or not New Holland was divided by a hitherto unknown body of water. This clause in his instructions had particular reference to the likelihood of finding an inlet to the interior at the head of the Gulf of Carpentaria. Flinders, however, seems to have had a peculiar genius for missing rivers wherever he went. In the *Norfolk* he had missed the Brisbane. On the south coast he sailed right past the mouth of the Murray; and he neglected to examine the head of Port Phillip, where the Yarra empties into the sea. Now again, the only time he drew away from the shore, in the south-east corner of the Gulf, he missed the Norman, the Bynoe, and the Flinders. And so, having reached the head of the Gulf, he concluded—rightly, but for the wrong reason—that if New Holland was divided, the head of the Gulf was not the place to look for the opening. As the land trended west, and the water became more shallow, he concluded that 'the Gulph would be found to terminate nearly as represented in the old charts, and disappoint the

[10] Private correspondence with Mr R. A. Skelton, of the British Museum, indicates that the 'old Dutch chart' to which Flinders refers (e.g. at vol. II, p. 125 of the *Voyage*) may have been by Van Keulen.

[11] Although the entire Gulf lies within that part of New Holland claimed by Cook, Flinders carefully preserved the Dutch place-names, at least in so far as he could reconcile the features with the old chart. Thus Batavia River, Coen River, Cape Keer-Weer, Nassau River, Staaten River, and Van Diemen River.

PLATE I    *Hawkesbury River*

Seal Island in K.George's Sound taken from the W. dis.g Mw.

Middle Island in the Archipelago of the Recherche taken May.15.1803.at one p.m.

Cliffs distant 5 or 6 miles taken Jan.26.1802 at One p.m.

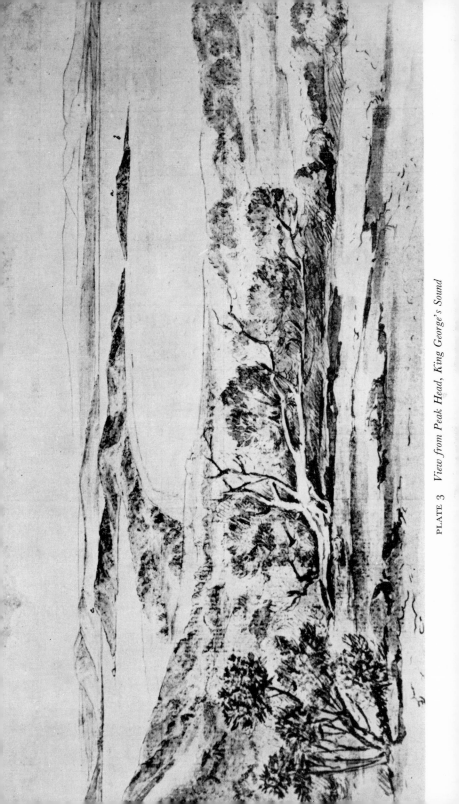

PLATE 3    *View from Peak Head, King George's Sound*

PLATE 5   *Native hut, Keppel Bay*

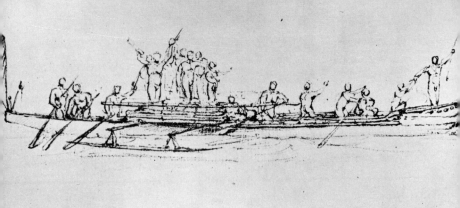

PLATE 6 *Natives, Murray Isles*          PLATE 7 *Native, Shoalwater Bay*

PLATE 8  *Sir Edward Pellew's Group, Gulf of Carpentaria*

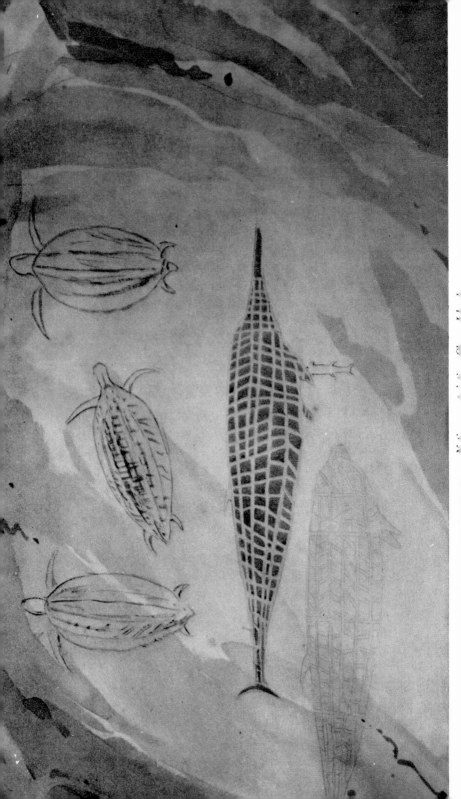

PLATE 10   *Malay Bay*

PLATE 11 *Malay prau, English Company's Islands*

PLATE 12   *Arnhem Land*

hopes formed of a strait or passage leading out at some other part of Terra Australis.'[12]

The most significant fresh discovery made at the head of the Gulf by Flinders had to do with an error in the Dutch chart he carried. Tasman, or whoever made the examination, had failed to notice the water lying behind a hill supposed to be on the mainland. Flinders investigated, and found the hill to be the principal feature of what he later named Bentinck Island.[13] The Dutch failure to approach the shore here warned Flinders of what he might expect farther on.

Of useful products the scientists discovered nothing new in the area, the prevalent woods being eucalyptus, casuarina, and pandanus. Birds and fish of many species seemed to thrive, the latter in such abundance that 'it was rare not to give a meal to all the ship's company from one or two hauls of the seine'.[14]

Actually it was in the field of anthropology that the scientists, chiefly Brown, now began to do some of their best work. As they advanced down the side of the Gulf they had seen many natives who differed in certain respects from those of the south and east coasts. They noted, for instance, that a number of these Australians stood well over six feet; that they used a primitive sort of raft for fishing, instead of the highly sophisticated canoes of the Murray Islanders; that they carried crude spears, but not the bow and arrow; and that many, both men and women, had lost the two upper front teeth.[15]

3

On balance, given the excessive heat and its remoteness, Flinders could make no strong recommendation of the head of the Gulf as a place for future settlement. He was right.

[12] Flinders, *Voyage*, vol. II, p. 132.
[13] After Lord William Bentinck (1774–1839), Governor-General of India, 1827–35. As Governor of Madras from 1803 to 1807, Bentinck had taken special pains to procure Flinders's release from Mauritius in 1805.
[14] Flinders, *Voyage*, vol. II, p. 145.
[15] Removal of the mesial incisors (tooth-avulsion) among the northern tribes was recognised in 1802 as a puberty rite, practised more or less universally across the continent. Regional differences, if any, among the tribes appeared in language, and in the technology of weapons and fishing vessels.

Having now arrived at a convenient halting-place, on 24 November Flinders decided to do what he could to find and repair the leaks in the ship. While he and the scientists set up camp on Sweer's Island, Fowler remained on board to supervise the work of caulking. This was not an unusual procedure at all, particularly in tropical waters. But when Fowler's reports of this superficial survey began to arrive, Flinders saw at once that a complete examination of the ship was an immediate necessity. Whether he then saw his future collapsing before his eyes is not known. But this was a turning-point in his life; and we must let Flinders tell the story of these awful disclosures in his own way:

'Whilst the carpenters have been employed caulking the ship's bends, they have been bringing to me, almost every hour, report after report of rotten parts found in different parts of the ship, timbers, planking, bends, tree-nails &c. until it is become quite alarming. Taking the matter into consideration I determined to have as accurate a statement of the condition of the ship as could be obtained without impeding the progress of our voyage; and accordingly the following order was given out

'To M$^r$. John Aken    Master ⎱ of H.M. sloop
   and M$^r$. Russel Mart Carpenter ⎰ Investigator

'His Majesty's sloop under my command having been very leaky for some time past, I judged it necessary that she should undergo a thorough caulking from the copper upwards to the cells of the ports. In doing this, some of the planks were found to be rotten, and on ripping off some of the worst parts, several timbers &c. were found to be in the same state:—You are, therefore, hereby required and directed to make such an examination into all the material parts of the ship as can be done without delaying the service in which the Investigator is now engaged, and to report to me, from under your hands, your proceedings and observations hereon.

'Further, as I understand that M$^r$. Aken has commanded a ship whose situation was somewhat similar to that of the Investigator, you are therefore directed, in case you should find much decay in the timbers or other material parts, jointly

to state your opinion upon the following heads, and this is to
be done upon due consideration.

1$^{st.}$ Whether or no the ship is fit to encounter bad weather?

2. Whether getting on shore is likely to be attended with
worse consequences to the Investigator than to a sound ship?

3. Whether in case of accident happening, the ship would
bear heaving down; or whether laying her on shore would do
her much injury?

4. How long the ship may be fit to run, with safety to the
crew, provided she is in fine weather and no misfortune of
getting on shore should happen?

In the above examination I recommend to you to take with
you the most experienced of the two carpenters mates, and
to hear his opinion upon such points as you think necessary.

> Given under my hand at anchor in the head of
> the Gulph of Carpentaria this 24 day of November
> 1802
>
> /s/ Matth$^w$. Flinders.'[16]

However unpleasant it may be, by all means, let us hear
the worst of it.

26 November:

'The master and the carpenter having made the examination
into the state of the ship, according to my order of the 24$^{th}$.
this day gave in the following report of their proceedings,
addressed

> To Matthew Flinders, Esq. Commander of
> H.M. sloop Investigator

'Sir

'In obedience to your directions we have taken with us the
oldest carpenters mate of the Investigator, and made as thorough
an examination into the state of the ship as circumstances will
permit, and which we find to be as under—

'Out of ten top timbers on the larboard side near the fore
channel, four are sound, one partly rotten, and five entirely
rotten;

---

[16] Flinders, 'Journal', vol. I, p. 372 sq.

'We have seen but one timber on the larboard quarter, which is entirely rotten;

'On the starboard bow close to the stem, we have seen three timbers which are all rotten :—Under the starboard fore chains we find one of the chain-plate bolts started, in consequence of the timber and inside plank being rotten; and also a preventer eye bolt from the same cause.

'On boring into the second-futtock timbers from the main hold, close under the beams of the lower deck, on the larboard side we find one sound and two rotten, and on the other side one sound and one rotten;

'On boring into one of the second-futtock timbers in the cockpit on each side, we find it to be sound on the starboard, but on the other side rotten : the inside plank on both sides is rotten :— On boring into one timber of a side in the after hold, we found them to be sound. On boring into one timber of a side from the bread room, one is sound, but on the larboard side it is rotten.

'The stem appears to be good, but the stemson is mostly decayed;

'The lower breast hook is decayed within side;

'The transoms, sleepers, stern post, and postson are all sound;

'The ends of the beams we find to be universally in a decaying state;

'The treenails are in general rotten.

'From the specimens which we have seen of the topsides and bends, we expect that the insides of them are rotten fore and aft, but that about one inch of the outside of the greater part is yet quite sound.

'After the above report, and upon due consideration, we give the following answers to the four questions put to us :—

'1st The ship having before made ten inches of water an hour in a common fresh breeze, we judge from that and what we have now seen, that a little labouring would employ two pumps; and that in a strong gale, with much sea running, the ship would hardly escape foundering; so that we think she is totally unfit to encounter much bad weather.

'2nd We have no doubt but that if the ship should get on shore under any unfavourable circumstances, she would immediately go to pieces; but with a soft bottom and smooth water she might touch for a short time without any worse consequences than to another ship, if she did not heel much; but altogether, we judge it to be much more dangerous for her to get aground in her present state than if she was sound.

'3<sup>rd</sup> It is our opinion, that the ship could not bear heaving down on any account; and that laying her on shore might so far strain her as to start the copper and butt ends, which would make her unable to swim without vast repair.

'4<sup>th</sup> Mr. Aken has known several ships of the same kind, and built at the same place as the Investigator, and has always found, that when they began to rot they went on very fast. From the state to which the ship now seems to be advanced, it is our joint opinion, that in twelve months there will scarcely be a sound timber in her; but that if she remains in fine weather and happens no accident, she may run six months longer without much risk.

'We are, Sir,
Your obedient servants
John Aken —master
}
Russel Mart—carpenter
} of the Investigator.[17]

There it was. The Master and the Carpenter, both Warrants of experience, had given him a joint opinion which, under the circumstances, was the best professional judgment he could get. After due consideration, these officers had, for better or worse, set the boundary conditions for Flinders's future action: six months if, but only if, he had fine weather and smooth water. But this was impossible! The ship was out of England only sixteen months on a voyage seriously projected for four years. It was not in Matthew's nature to stare ill-fortune down. Ambitious, industrious, and proud, he took adversity hard. And this was the beginning of tragedy. Until now he had only wondered—and not very much—whether he would be able to complete his mission to the satisfaction of all concerned. The approbation of the world in his performance was what he most cherished. But now he was reduced to a consideration far more

[17] *Ibid.*, p. 375 sq.

elemental than that. From this moment his single concern must be the safety of his crew. All else must be subordinated, and he knew it. Never before had he been so lonely.

In sorrow he made his capitulation to Fate:

'If the condition of the ship is as bad as above stated, it surprises one that something of it should not have been found out before, when the ship was in dock at Sheerness, or when she was caulked at the Cape of Good Hope, or at least at Port Jackson when the barricade was removed:—this is accounted for to me in this manner.—Two years back when the Investigator underwent repair in dock, she could not be a quarter part so bad as she now is; and moreover, that the shipwrights did not examine her with a view to such a voyage as the present, but to common short voyages near home.[18]

'When she was caulked at the Cape, she was not then near so bad as at present; and as nothing was done to her but caulking, and no suspicion entertained of her being rotten, it is no wonder that it was not found out, since it is probable that it might not have been now discovered, if the rottenness of the plank had not begun to affect the outer parts.

'At Port Jackson the barricade was removed and many timbers consequently laid open, but these were what had been let in to support the barricade at the time when the Xenophon (the Investigator was formerly so called) was bought into His Majestys service, and consequently formed no part of the ship in her original construction.

'From this dreadful state of the ship, I find the complete examination of this extensive country, which is one of the nearest objects to my heart, to be greatly impeded if not wholly frustrated. I have hitherto considered, that my business is to make so accurate an examination of the shores of New Holland and New South Wales, that there shall be no necessity for any further navigator to come after me;[19] and with this object always in view, whenever circumstances would allow it, I have ever kept close in with the land that nothing might escape our

---

[18] Certainly the Navy Board knew, because they had provisioned her, that the *Investigator* was ordered to foreign service.
[19] See also, Flinders to Banks, 29 April 1801. M.L.

notice; much closer I believe than navigators have usually thought it necessary or safe to do; for, that we might not be deceived in the distance, I always desired to see the washing of the surf upon the shore, and then it was not from conjecture only that our distance could be fixed at four or five miles, or the assertion made that no opening to which a ship was admissible has escaped us. I do not, however, mean to assert that the whole of the coasts along which we have sailed have been thus minutely examined, for it sometimes happened either from the direction of the wind or the shallowness of the water, that we could not get so near; and at other times that the certain loss of the ship would have been the consequence of approaching so near to a lee shore; but whenever the circumstances were favourable, such was my plan, and it was then always adopted; and with the blessing of God nothing of importance should have been left for future discovery upon any of the shores of this great, and in many points, interesting country; but with a ship which cannot encounter bad weather,—which cannot be repaired if any of the shoals or rocks, with which we are almost continually surrounded, does her bottom any injury,—and which, if we could command constant fine weather and be certain to avoid accident, will not run more than six months;—with such a ship, I do not know how to prosecute so great an undertaking.

'Laying aside the two great questions, our safety and the completion of the voyage, for the present, I have determined to go on in the examination of this gulph, if the north west monsoon does not prove too great an hindrance, and afterwards to act as the rising circumstances shall most seem to require.'[20]

4

One wonders what Flinders might have said if he had known of another letter, written in London, on that very day:

'Sir

I have received and communicated to my Lords Commissioners of the Admty your Letter of the 11th May, acquainting

[20] Flinders, 'Journal', vol. I, p. 376 sq., dated 26 November 1802.

me of your arrival with the ship you command at Sydney Cove, and of the occurrences during your passage from the Cape of Good Hope; And I have their Lordships Commands to acquaint you that they approve of your proceedings, and that the Charts mentioned in your Letter are not yet come to hand.

(signed) Evan Nepean'[21]

The letter itself has little importance, yet with grim irony the coincidence serves to point the lesson Flinders had now learnt: this is not a 'Justice-world'.

The voyage now lived on borrowed time; and it says something about his nerve that Flinders chose to carry the survey forward when he knew that each day would become more precious than the last.

By 1 December the men had finished patching the *Investigator*.[22] She was as ready for sea as she would ever be, which was not saying much. Finding no open water to the west of Bentinck Island, Flinders doubled back around Sweers and made for the south side of what he later called Isle Mornington.[23] Two days later he came to anchor under Bountiful Isle just to the east. There, while he went ashore, the crew set about catching turtle.[24] Seven tons came aboard; and besides this, they took seven tiger sharks (the largest nine feet long) whose livers they cut out and boiled for oil.[25]

After a week in the area Flinders closed again with the mainland to begin his work along the western shore. His chart shows clearly that despite the ship he had lost none of his temerity in

[21] Admiralty to Flinders, 26 November 1802. P.R.O., Adm. 2/822.

[22] On this date Flinders served out tobacco, and broached a cask of American rum, found to have leaked 16 gallons from a defect in the head and in one stave.

[23] After Richard Earl of Mornington, Marquess of Wellesley (1760–1842), Governor-General of India, 1797–1805, to whom Flinders appealed for help in 1804. Mornington Island had not been thoroughly surveyed by 1950. Cf. Admiralty chart No. 445.

[24] *Chelonia mydas*. After much exertion, the crew stowed away forty-six, averaging about 300 lb. each. In one female weighing 459 lb. there were found 1,940 eggs, which led Flinders to comment that 'were it not for the immense destruction made of these animals in the different stages of their existence, and that food must in the end fail, their fecundity is such, that all the tropical seas and shores would scarcely afford room for them in a few years'. *Voyage*, vol. II, p. 155. Evidently Brown had been reading Malthus, whose *Essay on the Principle of Population* had appeared in 1797.

[25] Fowler, 'Journal', vol. II, p. 30.

keeping in with the shore. His purpose was surveying, not sight-seeing. But on 11 December he went too far. Hugging the shore, he suddenly found the water shoaling to $2\frac{3}{4}$ fathoms, and 'before the helm was put down, we felt the ship touch upon a rock, and she hung upon it abaft'. He reacted quickly, and the ship came off. But minutes later, 'touched and hung again'. Still a third touch, and off again, with no apparent damage.[26] Henceforth he must remember the difference between discretion and valour.

This was, in fact, a bad day all round. In the late afternoon, as he anchored for the night, he discovered that 'the timekeepers had stopped, having neglected to be wound up by my assistant astronomer at noon'.[27]

By 14 December he had reached Cape Vanderlin. The Dutch had laid it down as a promontory which Flinders, once again running close, found to be a group of islands having an area of some 800 square miles.[28] This would want some inspection, and so, taking Westall with him in a boat he left the ship on 22 December on an excursion. For once no mishap marred his work, which he completed successfully on Christmas Day.[29] After two weeks among the group Flinders resumed his north-ward course. The north-west monsoon had now set in, tending to keep him away from the shore. But, by following the chart, he managed to discover yet a third time that a Dutch 'cape' could be an island. Hence Maria Island, just outside the Limmen Bight.[30] Finding nothing there to detain him, he pushed on to Groote Eylandt, a prominent feature in the old maps.

Whether Flinders noticed it or not, he had been relatively free of trouble for the past month. The run north had been almost routine, unusually, indeed ominously, dull. 1803—year of awful memory for him—opened serenely. Then on 3 January came the

[26] Flinders, 'Journal', vol. I, p. 391.

[27] That is to say, Samuel. *Ibid.* Matthew does not editorialise in the 'Journal'.

[28] Which he later named the Sir Edward Pellew Group after Admiral Sir Edward Pellew, Viscount Exmouth (1757–1833) who, as Commander in Chief in the East Indies, tried in 1806 to relieve Flinders of his captivity.

[29] In 1923 Commander H. T. Bennett, D.S.O., R.N., resurveyed the Pellew Group, and reported it to lie $8\frac{1}{2}$ miles farther west than Flinders had placed it. In view of the recent stoppage of the chronometers the correction is not implausible.

[30] Here Flinders missed the Roper River, which flows to the sea from over 100 miles inland.

first mischance. Just behind the south-west cape of Groote
Eylandt lies a shoal, extending several miles offshore. As a
precaution he sent a whaleboat out ahead to take soundings as
he followed along. Everything went well until, having completed her work, the boat dropped astern for towing. Suddenly,
without warning, she filled with water. Fowler, who was
watching, said her stern came out.[31] In any event, one of the
two men in the boat kept his grip on the ship's line; but the
other, William Murray, captain of the foretop, being unable to
swim, was dragged along beneath the surface, and quickly
drowned.[32]

Groote Eylandt, with Blue Mud Bay behind it, was the last
area in the Gulf which might in any way have taxed Flinders as
surveyor. But the waters there are neither dangerous nor particularly complex, and the survey, therefore, went off quite
easily. It was just here, however, that experience of native life
and culture became interesting. In Blue Mud Bay, for example,
Brown found no sign of living natives; but he did discover
evidence of the dead : several skeletons, 'standing upright in the
hollow stumps of trees . . . the skulls and bones being smeared or
painted, partly red and partly white. . . .'[33] Here was something
new for Sir Joseph; but even that could not compare with
Chasm Islet, little more than a rock off the north side of Groote
Eylandt. For one thing, Brown discovered a new edible plant,
*Eugenia jambos*, and nutmeg[34] growing in great profusion. But
it was the cave-paintings that caught the eye.

There, wrote Flinders,

'we found some specimens of Indian art in these caverns, consisting of rude drawings of porpoises, turtle, kanguroos, and
a human hand. The porpoises were about two feet long, and

[31] Fowler, 'Journal', vol. II, p. 38.
[32] Flinders, 'Journal', vol. I, p. 415. Both Murray and the other man, William
Job, had recently been flogged for fighting, the latter some time back with Mr
Douglas, Boatswain.
[33] Flinders, *Voyage*, vol. II, p. 183. For further reference to this burial practice,
see A. P. Elkin, *The Australian Aborigines* (Sydney, 1956), chap. 12.
[34] *Myristica insipida*. Writing of them in his 'Journal', Flinders said only that,
although they were looking for bushes, the botanists found that the plants had
grown to trees 30 to 40 feet high, 'and this great alteration in form appears to
have arisen from this local situation.' Vol. I, p. 423. In his *Voyage*, however, he

done with something like red paint—[ochre]—upon the whitish ground of the rock, and variegated with scratches of black, probably of charcoal. . . . [The following day] I gave M$^r$. Westall a boat . . . to visit Cavern [Chasm] Islet, the account I had given of the drawings in the caverns there having excited his curiosity. Besides those already mentioned, M$^r$. Westall found two other drawings, the one representing a kanguroo hunt, and the other the pegging of a turtle. In the first, thirty ill-drawn men were preceded by a rude figure of a kanguroo; the whole apparently done with charcoal. The leader of the chase was made nearly twice as tall as the others, which made me suspect that they have some chieftainship amongst them; for I take the superior magnitude of the leader to be indicative of his consequence only, not seeing how they could otherwise express authority or rank in a distinct manner, since they wear no kind of clothing, and most probably have no variety of weapons.'[35]

Leaving Chasm Islet, Flinders returned again to Blue Mud Bay, and this time found signs aplenty that natives were about. A year ago, in King George Sound, he had issued strict regulations on the subject of conduct toward the 'indians' as he called them. There must be no retaliation, 'orders,' as Seaman Smith put it, 'being so humane towards the Natives that we must put up with everything but heaving Spears'.[36] Now, on 21 January, it came to precisely that.

With these standing instructions to seek a friendly contact, several parties of people had gone ashore about their usual duties. Flinders and Westall, as well as the Master's Mate, William Whitewood, were among them. All went armed, and, having observed that the natives were carrying spears, all were on their guard. Fowler thought that 'these natives appeared to be the most troublesome fellows we have seen since our making

came closer to Darwinian theory: '. . . thus what was a spreading bush above, became, from the necessity of air and light, a tall, slender tree, and showed the admirable power in nature to accommodate itself to local circumstances.' Vol. II, p. 188.

[35] Flinders, 'Journal', vol. I, pp. 423 and 425. See also C. P. Mountford, *Records of the American-Australian Scientific Expedition to Arnhem Land*, vol. I, 'Art, Myth and Symbolism' (Melbourne, 1956).

[36] Smith, 'Journal', p. 12.

New Holland'.[37] About mid-afternoon, shortly after he had returned to the ship with Westall, Flinders heard the sound of musketry ashore. He instantly dispatched the Master with two boatloads of men to help. Aken arrived only to find Mr Whitewood on the ground with four spear-wounds in his body, and a marine brought down at the beach with sunstroke. From the description he received of their behaviour, Flinders concluded not only that the natives had begun the trouble, but that, coming armed, they had planned the attack beforehand. That in turn only confirmed his view that 'the more we seek after, and appear desirous of an interview, the more suspicious they become'.[38]

After finishing his work at Blue Mud Bay, Flinders proceeded northward. On 27 January, Brown spent an anxious night alone on shore, but returned aboard with no harm. By 3 February the *Investigator* had reached Caledon Bay,[39] which was successfully surveyed despite the menaces and mischievous thievery of natives. Again, the most valuable information gained concerned the aboriginal culture. Brown and Flinders both found that the tribal customs of tooth-knocking and circumcision were common from the Gulf of Carpentaria to Port Jackson in the east and King George Sound in the west. They also found the use of arm-ligatures, since confirmed as outward signs of initiation into the tribal mysteries.[40]

These discoveries now came to an end. It was 9 February. Nearly twelve weeks had passed since the Master and the Carpenter had pronounced sentence on the *Investigator*. Of the six months they had given her, nearly three were gone. It behoved Flinders to get along. A few miles more, and he was out of the Gulf.

[37] Fowler, 'Journal', vol. II, p. 43.

[38] Flinders, 'Journal', vol. I, p. 431 sqq. Whitewood recovered, but the marine, Thomas Morgan, died immediately in a delirium.

[39] Named after the second Earl of Caledon, Governor at the Cape of Good Hope, 1807–11. Flinders first called it 'Arnhem South Bay'.

[40] See A. P. Elkin, *The Australian Aborigines* (Sydney, 1956), chap. 7.

# CHAPTER NINE

# Retreat

## February–June 1803

### 1

Beginning at Cape Arnhem, the shoreline to the west presents a broken, indented prospect. In contrast to the Gulf of Carpentaria it is by far the more interesting to the eye and challenging to the surveyor. Bays and coves serrate the coast. Oblong islands stretch in skeins to the north-east, barring a clear, straight run to a ship along the mainland. The area had been seen by the Dutch in the seventeenth century, but their charting of it had been so indifferent that, when he saw it, Flinders decided to do what he could to state the facts correctly.

After carefully fixing the position of Cape Arnhem, he ventured into the shallows extending over to Cape Wilberforce, and forming what he called Melville Bay.[1] Three days were all he could spare for this place, and so, on 16 February, he headed out once again to pursue his course westward. He saw no natives, but from the domesticated dogs running about he assumed he was being watched from the shore.[2] But to his great surprise he presently found that he was not alone upon the sea. Just as he passed Cape Wilberforce and began his run to southward along the inside shore of the English Company's Islands,[3] '. . . saw a canoe full of men under the islands, going to 6 vessels, like hulks, which were lying at anchor off the beach where we had

---

[1] Cape Wilberforce was named after William Wilberforce, the reformer, whom Flinders came to know in later years. Melville Bay, first called Arnhem North Bay, he named after Robert Saunders Dundas, second Viscount Melville (1771–1851), First Lord of the Admiralty at the time Flinders's *Voyage* was published.

[2] Flinders, 'Journal', vol. I, p. 460.

[3] So named after the Hon. East India Company.

intended to anchor . . . shewed our colours and pendant, and the
vessels hoisted white flags. Sent L⁺ Flinders with a boat manned
and armed to learn who the people were'.[4]

Flinders took them at first to be pirates, 'ladrones, who had
secreted themselves here from pursuit'.[5] They turned out, however, to be Bugis, just arrived upon the coast to fish for trepang,
a species of sea-cucumber which they dried and smoked, and
carried north to the Tanimbar Islands to be shipped thence to
China for making soup.[6] As soon as he was sure of their peaceful
intent, Flinders established a friendly intercourse with their
principal captain, one Pobassoo, going aboard his prau, and
inviting the six captains aboard the *Investigator*. With his Malay
cook, Abraham Williams, as interpreter, he learned that these
six praus formed part of a fleet of sixty which worked annually
out of Boni in the Celebes;[7] that the other praus would presently
arrive and all would go on eastward into the Gulf of Carpentaria;
and that the fleet would carry back to Tanimbar about 375 tons
of dried trepang. He learned too that they knew of no rivers
flowing out of the continent to the west; and that they had never
heard of the notorious *upas* poison of the Sunda islands.[8]

Thus was explained the vague signs of visitors he had noticed
along the western shore of the Gulf. The encounter ended as
abruptly as it had begun. After the better part of two days both
sides expressed their eagerness to go their ways, and nothing
further came of the meeting.[9]

Flinders's business was to proceed along the English
Company's Islands, hoping in that way to continue his tracing
of the main coast. There he spent two weeks moving from

[4] Flinders, 'Journal', vol. I, p. 462.

[5] *Ibid.*

[6] Of the genera *Actinopyga* or *Holothuria*, also called bêche-de-mer. Flinders
reported in detail on this chiefly for the benefit of the East India Co. who, he
thought, might be interested in developing the trade. Flinders to Banks, 28 March
1803. B.M., Add. MSS. 32439. 82.

[7] Apparently they had worked along these coasts for centuries. Their story forms
a part of the aboriginal mythology in the area. See C. P. Mountford, *Records of the
American-Australian Scientific Expedition to Arnhem Land* (Melbourne, 1956),
vol. I, p. 95.

[8] Flinders, 'Journal', vol. I, p. 463 sqq. *Upas*, which Flinders called 'ippo', is a
harmless gum tree, *Antiaris toxicaria*.

[9] For his part, Flinders was concerned lest his crew would be unable to stand off
sixty praus in case of attack.

island to island, now in the ship, now in a boat, and often on foot along the beach.[10] And there he found what he thought might be 'a delightful situation to a college of monks, who could bear the heat of the climate, and were impenetrable to the stings of musketoes'.[11] Having completed his charting of the islands, he went into Arnhem Bay, grimly determined to carry the survey as far as he could. The best he could manage was a tour round the bay in his whaleboat. His observations were adequate for charting, but, he wrote, 'the general remarks made in this excursion are few with respect to the bay, and still less of the country, for being lame at this time in both feet, with scorbutic ulcers, I did not leave the water side.'[12]

A man can do so much and no more; and for Flinders the end came on 5 March 1803. This was the last day of surveying he ever did. At the age of twenty-nine he finished not in triumph, but in misery and disappointment, out in the middle of nowhere. As he turned north away from the coast, and passed the Wessel Islands, he recorded his thoughts in the log:

'The winds having blown from the eastward mostly during the last four days, I thought it now time to take into consideration the state of the ship, and the necessity of proceeding to Port Jackson without further delay.

'. . . I calculate, that if we sail immediately for Port Jackson, our arrival will complete very nearly the six months specified in the survey [of the ship by Aken and Mart], and that we shall pass along the south coast and through Bass' Strait, where the worst weather is to be expected, before the hard winter winds have gained their strength. This last is a material object, for should the ship prove no worse than our expectation, a heavy gale would probably founder her, and be the loss of almost the whole produce of our risks and labours, as well as the loss of our lives; and I think it more probable that she will be worse than

[10] On 26 February, 'the water being thick, did not perceive a shoal ahead, and the ship grounded upon it.' After some difficulty and a second touch in soft mud, the ship got clear with no apparent damage. *Ibid.*, p. 474.
[11] Flinders, *Voyage*, vol. II, p. 236. What prompted him to make this gruesome suggestion, apropos of nothing, is a mystery.
[12] Flinders, 'Journal', vol. I, p. 479. This was the first sign of scurvy mentioned in the log.

our expectation, or rather our hope, than that she will prove better.

'To be set against these reasons for sailing away immediately with the present fair wind, the following great objections lie : The present fair wind is also the most favourable for continuing the survey of this interesting coast; for the numerous harbours and places of shelter we have already found in it, the increasing rise of the tides, the greater fertility of the soil and value of its produce, as well as its increasing vicinity to our Indian possessions, all tend to make it a very interesting coast. It may well be said, that to leave such a coast as this without exploring it, when there is a possibility, nay perhaps a probability, that I may never again return to accomplish it, shews but very little of that genuine spirit of discovery which contemns all danger and inconvenience when put in competition with its gratification! Upon the score of duty I might (it may be said) be forgiven, but must never boast of a single spark of that ethereal fire with which the souls of Columbus and of Cook were wont to burn!——I am not indeed such a Quixote in discovery as this, although, since I was able to read Robinson Crusoe, it has been my constant pursuit; but there is another reason remaining in aid of the first,—the debilitated state of my health, as well as of many others in the ship, and a lameness in both feet from incorrigible scorbutic ulcers, render me unable to go about any longer in boats, or to the mast head of the ship; both which are absolutely necessary to any tolerable accuracy in this kind of surveying; and I suppose it is unnecessary to state, that the whole of this important part of our duty rests upon me :—For Port Jackson, then, we now steered away, with a fresh and fair wind.'[13]

These were good and sufficient reasons. But why the elaborate self-justification? Was it for the benefit of the Admiralty? But they would expect him to do no more than his plain duty; and his decision, based upon considerations of common humanity, was completely defensible. Was it for Banks? If so, it ought to have appeared in his letter to Sir Joseph, written at sea on

[13] *Ibid.*, p. 482.

28 March.[14] But it does not. And then, why was it deleted in the published narrative?[15] More than likely he was simply talking to himself, soliloquising, as it were, to keep his conscience in a state of equilibrium. The loneliness spilled out on to the pages of his journal.

It was in any case a cruel decision, for which he alone was responsible. Years later he added a poignant remark:

'The accomplishment of the survey was, in fact, an object so near to my heart, that could I have foreseen the train of ills that were to follow the decay of the Investigator and prevent the survey being resumed,—and had my existence depended upon the expression of a wish, I do not know that it would have received utterance; but Infinite Wisdom has, in infinite mercy, reserved the knowledge of futurity to itself.'[16]

2

Leaving the Wessel Islands behind, the *Investigator* headed nearly due west across the Arafura Sea, bound for Kupang, then a Dutch settlement at the south-west end of Timor. What fame that place had arose from the fact that William Bligh ended his journey in the *Bounty* launch there. Flinders had two objects in putting in at Timor instead of making directly for Port Jackson. One was to see whether he might find a ship there about to leave for Europe. If so, he would send Robert Fowler home in her, with his journal to date, but more importantly, to procure another ship for the survey. The other object had to do with the state of health into which the crew had now fallen.

The sail from Wessel Islands to within sight of Timor took twenty-two days. On 26 March, when he still had a choice whether to go to Kupang or break off to southward, he requested Surgeon Bell to examine the crew and advise him on their fitness to continue without interruption. Bell found twenty-two men showing symptoms of scurvy, 'such as spongy gums and livid

---

[14] Flinders to Banks, B.M., Add. MSS. 32439. 82–3.
[15] Flinders, *Voyage*, vol. II, p. 247 sq. Brown, writing at sea to Banks on 30 March, made no criticism of Flinders's decision. B.M., Add. MSS. 32439. 85–7.
[16] Flinders, *Voyage*, vol. II, p. 248.

sores on the legs'. Of these, only four or five were on the sick list, unable to perform their duties about the ship. To these facts, reported orally, Bell added the following observations, given here *in extenso* in order to convey precisely the problem Flinders faced :

'It is more than nineteen months since we sailed from England, and during this time there has [*sic*] been only two opportunities of receiving the usual port refreshments;—four days at Madeira, and eight at the Cape of Good Hope; and once on His Majesty's birth-day at Port Jackson. During our stay in the latter place, the ships company had it not in their power to procure any animal food, and but few vegetables; what they had, being humanely given to them by the governor. For the last eight months, we have had no refreshments but what chance threw in our way, and fruit and vegetables, the best antiscorbutics, formed no part of what was procured. During this period, the ships company have been exposed to almost incessant fatigue in an oppressively hot climate, as also to an exceedingly deleterious atmosphere since Dec. 16 when the weather became dark and cloudy, with thunder, lightning, and rain. The ill effects of this alteration in the weather, were perceptible in a short time amongst the ships company; a violent diarrhoea being produced, attended frequently with symptoms of fever, which, had it not been for timely remedies and the great attention paid to cleanliness, would soon have generated the worst of dysenteries. The weather and this diarrhoea kept pace till the beginning of March, when both disappeared.'

The report concluded by observing that,

'a body, though in health, may at the same time be losing strength; and consequently be likely to fall under any violent and long-continued exertions. If you should dread such an event, it would be well, if possible, to provide against it by refreshing the ships company, and procuring those articles of provision [rice, sugar, molasses, and peas] of which the ship is deficient, or substitute others in their room.'[17]

[17] P.R.O., Adm. 55/76, 'Journal kept on board His Majestys sloop Investigator . . .', vol. II, p. 8. Hereafter cited as Flinders, 'Journal', vol. II.

With no other choice, on 31 March Flinders entered Kupang.[18]
Having ascertained from an American vessel lying in the harbour
that the Peace of Amiens still obtained, he sent his brother
ashore to pay his respects to the Governor, Mynheer Giesler,
to arrange for a proper salute, and to inform the Governor of
his needs. Amenities were exchanged and memóries of Bligh
revived. But unfortunately little could be done to help Flinders
materially. There was at this time no vessel at Kupang ready
to sail for the Cape, the last one having left only ten days before.
If he were to resume the survey, Flinders must either procure
a suitable ship at Port Jackson, or go himself to London where,
with Sir Joseph's help, he might persuade the Admiralty to
replace the crazy old *Investigator*. Even more unhappily, Kupang
offered little in the way of provisions. There being no commerce
within the town, the residents there subsisted wholly upon
stocks of food brought them from Batavia. What could be had,
including rice enough for two years, was arranged for, and
loading began. Flinders then secured the Governor's permission
for the botanists to do their field-work while he busied himself
making astronomical observations to verify the latitude and
longitude of the place.

In addition to his letter to Banks, referred to above, Flinders
posted four others. In conformity with his instructions—'During your continuance on the service above-mentioned, you are,
by all proper opportunities, to send to our secretary for our
information, accounts of your proceedings . . .'[19]—he sent off a
précis of his operations since leaving Port Jackson, and explaining his present circumstances.[20] The other three letters were
personal. In a passionate letter to Ann he assured her over and
over of his love, studiously omitting any reference to his health.
As an afterthought, he asked her to write to his father, telling
him how things were going, adding bluntly, 'at this time I am
not going to do it'.[21] A letter to his cousin Henrietta Franklin

---

[18] On 27 March, 'Got up the cases of lime juice to be examined: found many
bottles broken'. *Ibid.*, p. 9. Flinders was depending upon this store of lime juice
to serve not only on the run to Port Jackson, but there also, since he knew the
stock in port to be low.  [19] See Appendix.

[20] See copy in Flinders, 'Journal', vol. II, p. 16 sqq.

[21] 28 March and 4 April 1803. S.L.V., 'Flinders Papers'. His father had died the
year before.

said, without alluding to the scurvy, that he and his brother were in 'tolerable health,' whatever that meant.[22] Finally, he wrote to Christopher Smith, late botanist in the *Providence*. He spoke of his hopes to get another ship for the resumption of his survey, and of his ambition for a place on the list of Post Captains.[23] But all these letters, he told Ann, must wait at Kupang, go on to Batavia, to the Cape of Good Hope, to Amsterdam, and finally —if at all—to London.

By 7 April the ship was ready. In the afternoon the Commander and several officers and gentlemen went ashore to dine with the Governor. Returning to the ship, he mustered the crew on deck before securing for sea. Another blow fell: two men were missing, one of them being Williams, his Malay cook. The other was one Mortlake, 'a youth received on board at Port Jackson'.[24] Fowler was immediately sent back to report the deserters to the Governor, who sympathised, but was not very encouraging. Without doubt the two had already disappeared into the back country where they would remain until the ship had sailed. What was their fate in this place of broken hopes no one ever heard. When a check in the morning disclosed no sign of the two, Flinders weighed, saluted the Governor with thirteen guns, and stood out the harbour.

3

The Admiralty instructions for H.M. Sloop *Investigator* enjoined Flinders, when he had completed his survey of the north coast, to 'examine as particularly as circumstances will allow, the bank which extends itself *from the Trial Rocks towards Timor*, in the hope that by ascertaining the depth and nature of the soundings thereon, great advantage may arise to the East-India Company's ships, in case that passage should hereafter be frequented by them'.[25]

---

[22] 2 April 1803. *Ibid.*
[23] 28 March 1803. *Ibid.*
[24] Flinders, 'Journal', vol. II, p. 13. How and where Flinders secured a Malay as a cook does not appear.
[25] See Appendix A.

Trial Rocks had long been a mystery to navigators who sailed these waters. They were named after a ship of the East India Company supposed to have foundered there in the year 1622. The *English Pilot* of 1703 said there were 'wild reports going into Batavia, that they have been seen above 20 leagues in length, but, by most laborious enquiry, could never hear of any person that ever saw them. . . .' Dampier was convinced of their existence, but was never able to verify his belief.[26] Still, the reports persisted throughout the eighteenth century, and any ship sailing the waters south-west of Timor would naturally be on the lookout. Actually that sector of the Indian ocean has a number of hazards scattered about its surface : Corona Shoal, D'Artagnan Shoal, Seringapatam Reef, Scott Reef, and Rowley Shoal. What legend reported might have been any one of these. Even Alexander Dalrymple, Hydrographer to the Admiralty, and Aaron Arrowsmith, chartmaker, disagreed.

As he left Timor, then, Flinders determined to make the effort desired by the Admiralty. He set his course toward Arrowsmith's position, and shortly after began taking frequent soundings—two an hour every day—trying to find some hint of a bank. This search went on for ten days, much of it in foul weather, and all of it without even touching bottom. 'Nothing but sky and water to be seen.'[27] His conclusion : 'That they [i.e. Trial Rocks] exist, does not seem to admit of a doubt, but no bank can extend in a line from thence [Arrowsmith's position] at all near to Timor.'[28] The East India Company's ships would be safe.

By the time he left off the search on 27 April, sickness had already returned to the ship. On 21 April, only two weeks out of Kupang, there were ten cases of dysentery. Flinders, fully alarmed, began his final dash for port. The retreat had become a rout.

The rest of the story is quickly told and awful.

[26] See John Stevens, *Oriental Navigator* . . . (London, 1816), p. 69 sq.

[27] Flinders, 'Journal', vol. II, p. 35.

[28] Flinders, *Voyage*, vol. II, p. 263. In the Introduction to the *Journals of Captain James Cook* (Cambridge, 1955), Professor Beaglehole gives it as his opinion that the *Trial* was 'carried by the westerly current on to the reefs near Barrow or Trinonville Island, not far north of North-West Cape'. p. liv. The modern Admiralty chart (2759a) indicates Tryal Rocks [*sic*] at 20° 10′ S., 115° 10′ E.

Covering as much as 137 miles in one day, the ship reached Cape Leeuwin on 13 May. Four days later, the first to die was Mr Charles Douglas, Boatswain, slated for court martial at Port Jackson. 'His complaints were fever and dysentery, both of which have unfortunately too much ground in the ship at this time, there being still 14 men in the sick list, mostly from these dreadful disorders.'[29] The next to go was William Hillier, quartermaster, 'a quiet, good man,' who had suffered, probably from tuberculosis, almost since leaving England. He died on 20 May, just west of King George Sound, and Flinders named Point Hillier after him. On 25 May, off Spencer Gulf, 'departed this life James Greenhalgh, serjeant of marines, of a dysentery. He was the most deserving man in his situation that I ever saw, or perhaps ever shall see.'[30]

There were now fifteen on the sick list, and three days later the number had risen to eighteen, three or four dangerously ill. On 31 May, Flinders was able to record that, 'fortunately, the officers, though far from being in good health, are the healthiest part of the ships company'.[31] At least he had that consolation, for he had now reached the more boisterous waters of Bass Strait where, in the winds of late autumn, standing the watches demanded all the men there were, even in a healthy ship.

At Timor the air-temperature had varied only slightly in the mid-eighties. By now it had dropped to the low sixties, and Flinders kept the galley fires burning all night, to preserve the sick from chill. Even this protection came too late for another quartermaster, John Draper, and for Thomas Smith, seaman, who was buried at sea just outside Sydney Heads.

At last, on 8 June, 5,000 miles and two months to the day out of Timor, the *Investigator* came to anchor at Port Jackson: 'Hoisted out the whale boat and the Commander went on shore to wait upon His Excellency the governor.'[32]

---

[29] Flinders, 'Journal', vol. II, p. 48. This day, incidentally, the Peace of Amiens was broken, and Britain and France were once again at war.
[30] *Ibid.*, p. 53.
[31] *Ibid.*, p. 57.
[32] *Ibid.*, p. 61.

# PART III

# Frustration and Defeat

## 1803-1810

# CHAPTER TEN

# Upon a Small Uncertainty

## June-August 1803

1

As he hobbled painfully into town, Flinders's path from the wharf to Government House seemed as long as it was melancholy. More than naval protocol urged him along. Knowing nothing of the harassed Governor's state of mind, he had now to press King into consideration of fresh difficulties. One, the care of the sick and dying, was an emergency, demanding instant attention. The other, continuance of the survey, if less immediate, was far more complex.

The greeting over, King at once put the sick under the care of the colonial surgeon, who directed the removal of eleven of them to hospital ashore. Only Peter Good, the Gardener, being too ill to be moved, remained on board.[1] A vast improvement in commissary stores at Sydney had taken place since July of 1802. Fresh provisions, both meat and vegetables, were available, and at prices much below what Flinders was willing to pay to save his men. With these, and a supply of sound wine, the deadly tolling of the town bell ended. For Good, as for three others,[2] it was too late. But the last of the four who were mortally ill died on 26 June; the rest came slowly but surely back to health.

Discussions on the future of the mission opened immediately. The central problem, and the first to be attacked, was the present plight of H.M. Sloop *Investigator*. For the moment, Flinders's

---

[1] P.R.O., Adm. 55/78, 'Investigator 1803, Log book No. 3', p. 2. Hereafter cited as Flinders, 'Journal', vol. III.

[2] In addition to Good, Oloff Wastream, seaman; Robert Chapman, marine; and John Simmonds, seaman.

judgment in aborting the voyage stood in the balance. He had not long to wait. On 11 June, 'the carpenters began ripping off one plank all round the ship in order to her being surveyed, agreeable to an application made to His Excellency the senior officer.'[3]

14 June. 'Came on board the Commander of H.M.S. Porpoise,— the Commander of the hon. E.I.C. ship Bridgewater, and the master builder to the colony. On examining into the state of the ship they found out of 98 timbers on one side, only 11 to be sound; out of 89 timbers on the other side, only 5 were sound, and these timbers were all in the after part of the ship, those forward being almost altogether rotten.—The stemson was decayed, and the plank so far gone as to require shifting, even had the timbers been sound.'[4]

If King had any doubts, they now evaporated. For the better part of a year Flinders had been riding a jaded hulk, and the wonder of it was that he and his crew had survived at all. After only a few hours on board the surveyors reported :

'. . . The above being the state of the Investigator thus far, we think it altogether unnecessary to make any further examination, being unanimously of opinion that she is not worth repairing in any country, and that it is impossible in this country, to put her in a fit state for going to sea.'[5]

The deplorable state of affairs had now become official fact. But now what? What were the open choices?

Pestered as he perpetually was with colonial matters, it was perhaps a welcome change for King to be dealing with a significant problem connected with the sea. Here was something more in his line. But the choices were not very promising. A survey

---

[3] Flinders, 'Journal', vol. III, p. 2.

[4] *Ibid.*, p. 3. See P.R.O., Adm. 1/2020 for all official documents dealing with this transitional phase.

[5] *Ibid.* Actually, the ship was repaired at Sydney and sailed back to Plymouth in 1805. In 1810, being little more than a wreck, she was sold out of the navy and demolished. It may be asked, if she could sail home in 1805, why could she not have done so in 1803. The answer must be that in the judgment of those in authority at Sydney in 1803, the thing was impossible. There is some evidence that this question occurred to Banks.

of the armed vessel *Porpoise* revealed that in her present state
she could not be trusted to carry out the *Investigator's* mission.
But Flinders was free to wait until she was if he cared. The
privately owned *Rolla* could be bought into the service, but
only at a very high price, £11,550, more than the Government
wished to pay. King suggested taking the *Lady Nelson* back
out, along with the colonial schooner, *Francis*, in which Flinders
had sailed to Bass Strait a few years before. But this was
inadequate. Or, Flinders might wait for the Governor's own
ship, *Buffalo*, to return from India, however unsuited for surveying she might be. Alternatively King advanced the use of
the *Porpoise*, not for surveying, but to return Flinders to England
where he might solicit a new ship. All of these choices involved
delay of months, and none came even close to a real solution.

In all this mess the Governor could not have been more
energetic or more co-operative in Flinders's cause. But nothing
else offered. In the event Flinders chose wisely. He would go
in the *Porpoise* back to England, where he could perhaps start
fresh with a vessel, if not new, at least more suited to his
purpose. Once this decision had been made, work could proceed
on the *Porpoise*, and Flinders and the men could begin recruiting
their health.

Now again, as at each period in port, it was a time for letter-
writing. Matthew and brother Samuel had especial cause. They
learned by the latest post that their father had died. Matthew
therefore wrote to his stepmother a letter which, in view of
what had gone before, was a model of contrition: 'The death of
so kind a father and who was so excellent a man is a heavy
blow and strikes deep into my heart . . . I had laid such a plan of
comfort for him as would have tended to make his latter days
the most delightful of his life . . . Oh, my dearest, kindest father,
how much I loved and reverenced you, you cannot now know.'[6]
Another letter to Ann spoke briefly of his health, and that of
the other officers and gentlemen. And of course more on his
father.[7] He wrote to Banks, but the letter was never sent.[8] One

---

[6] Flinders to 'Mother', 10 June 1803. S.L.V. 'Flinders Papers'. When this
letter reached home is not known. It contains a postscript dated Isle of France,
25 August 1804.

[7] Flinders to Ann, 25 June 1803; cont'd. 13 July 1804. N.M.M., FLI/25.

[8] Flinders to Banks, 20 June 1803. S.L.V., 'Flinders Papers'.

to James Wiles, late of the *Providence*,[9] finally left Mauritius in 1806. Lastly, he deposited with King a letter, chatty in a detached way, addressed to George Bass.[10] This letter, of course, was never received : Bass had left on his final voyage five months before.

It was sad but inevitable that the old crew of the *Investigator* had now to be dispersed. Days and weeks of training, work, hardship, and latterly of a common experience of death, had bound them together as a team. They could have gone anywhere; and their work was unfinished. The *Porpoise* was far too small to take them all home. Even though a goodly nucleus did shift their gear, the ship's company of H.M. Sloop *Investigator* was no more.

King gave Robert Fowler command of the *Porpoise*, with orders to accept certain directions relating to the survey of Torres Strait from Matthew Flinders, passenger.[11] Other officers, and some of the *Investigator's* men, went on as supernumeraries : Lieutenant Samuel Flinders; John Aken, Master; Edward Charrington, Boatswain; Russel Mart, Carpenter; Midshipmen Sinclair, Franklin, T. Bell and Lound; Denis Lacy, Master's Mate, and John Olive, Clerk.[12] Only Robert Colpits, Gunner, stayed behind, under orders from King to take charge of the *Investigator's* commissary stores.

Of the scientific gentlemen, only Westall decided at once to return to England.[13] John Allen had made up his mind to remain

[9] Flinders to Wiles, 2 July 1803. *Ibid.*

[10] Flinders to Bass, undated. *Ibid.*

[11] Just why King decided to place the junior officer in command is not made clear. Superficially it would seem an extremely awkward arrangement; and indeed it very soon came to a test. Again, see also P.R.O., Adm. 1/2020.

[12] Flinders, 'Journal', vol. III, p. 22 sq.

[13] On 6 August 1803, Brown wrote a letter to Banks, giving a general résumé of the state of his work, his reasons for remaining at Sydney, and a report on the condition of his specimens. B.M., Add. MSS. 32439. 104v.–108v. In this last connection, Brown saw fit to implicate Flinders in a dispute over the packing of specimens in puncheons :

'In representing the necessity of these articles to Capn. Flinders I have always expressed myself with moderation, convinced that any intemperate language on my part would be much more likely to injure than advance my cause : I must say however that the importance attach'd to the preservation of the collection seem'd to me to be very small. A few words from you would I am persuaded set Capn. Flinders right in this matter, for upon the whole I am inclin'd to impute his

at Sydney, but then concluded he could not afford the financial outlay. Brown and Bauer agreed that their mission would profit more by staying where they were to continue their field work and finish their descriptive taxonomy and drawings. In this both Flinders and King concurred; and among them it was agreed that if, at the end of eighteen months after the *Porpoise* had sailed, Flinders had not returned with another ship, the two, still under Admiralty orders, would then take the first available passage home.[14]

Of especial cargo, three items went aboard with Flinders: first, his charts and journals to date, which, following instructions, he would in due course hand over to Evan Nepean; second, Westall's drawings, intended for later publication; and third, a selection of Brown's specimens, including plants, both live in a greenhouse and dried in puncheons, and seeds in marked boxes, for His Majesty's gardens at Kew.

By 9 August last farewells were said ashore and all was ready for sea. Next morning, together with Hon. East India Company's extra ship *Bridgewater*, E. H. Palmer, and the ship *Cato*, John Park, the *Porpoise* weighed and sailed down the harbour with His Excellency aboard. Just inside the Heads, King left the ship, and the three vessels departed.

2

One should suppose that by this time Flinders had had about all the ill luck a man might reasonably expect in the course of two years. Whatever blessings he could count had, at the very least, been offset by misfortunes. But this was by no means the end of it. On the contrary.

The little flotilla stood off to the north-east, intending to pass outside the Great Barrier Reef on the way to Torres Strait. For the first day or so progress was slow; then, on the fourth

conduct respecting the collection more to his total inexperience in these matters than to any other cause.'

Whatever the facts on either side, Brown could be both righteous and combative. Moreover, he was walking a fine line, as his instructions from the Admiralty enjoined both subordination to Flinders and good humour in general.

[14] Flinders, 'Journal', vol. III, p. 19 sqq.

day out, with a more favourable wind, they logged well over a hundred miles, and on the fifth, 160. Seven days' sail took them 745 miles, to a parallel just north of the Tropic of Capricorn.

For an account of the happenings that occurred on the eighth day out of Port Jackson, we must turn to Flinders himself.[15]

17 August 1803 :

'Fresh breezes and cloudy w$^r$ On the Cato making signal for seeing land, hauled up at 2$^h$16 for a dry sand bank bearing S.b.W. ¼ W. At 3 hove to and found no bottom at 80 $^{fms}$ the bank S.S.E. 5 or 6 miles. Made sail after the convoy and at dusk came up with them. *Made signal that we should run under easy working sail during the night.* [Italics mine.] Reefed the topsails and placed a warrant officer at the lookout.[16] At 9½$^h$ breakers were seen ahead, we were then running under the topsails. Hauled to the wind on the starboard tack, and tried to stay, but the ship not coming round, took upon a reef, and coming broad side to, beat up it and the foremast soon went over the side. Not being able to get a gun fired or a light shewn through the confusion that took place and the spray that was flying over the ship, all the people set up a great shout to warn the two ships. They took different tacks [i.e. from each other] and in crossing would have touched each other and gone upon the reef together, but the Cato kept away a little, and from that and missing stays when she tried to tack, she struck a little to the N.W. of us: the Bridgewater cleared the reef standing to the S.S.W.

'After the first flurry of confusion had a little subsided, the small gig and the cutter were got out to leeward, but the latter

---

[15] *Ibid.*, p. 32 sqq. This account was evidently written almost immediately after the shipwreck, since the pagination of the log continues without interruption. Its simplicity amidst the drama speaks far more eloquently than his biographer could possibly contrive to do. Two other versions of the same events, Fowler's and Smith's, do not differ materially as to the facts. Fowler's is less full, but more technical; and Smith's is less technical, if perhaps more moving in the absolute artlessness of this common sailor. A smooth draft by Flinders was given to King upon arrival at Port Jackson. See B.M., Add. MSS. 32439. 127 sqq.

[16] It must be remembered that here Flinders was only describing the actions of Lieutenant Fowler, commander of the *Porpoise*. With or without Flinders's advice, the decision to remain under sail during the night was Fowler's responsibility. Flinders had gone below for the night.

was stove and filled with water. In this state the eyes of every-one were fixed on the Bridgewater, to whom only we could look with any prospect of being saved, and as we saw her in safety, we did not doubt but that she would keep in sight and send her boats to us in the morning. I now spoke to Lt. Fowler, the Commander of the ship, and told him that I should get my charts, log, and bearing books into the small boat, and try to get on board the Bridgewater, where I would take the necessary steps for getting the people out as soon as possible. I observed that the breaking water did not reach any distance to leeward of us, and therefore on getting into the boat,[17] with the six men that were in her, we let her go before the surf and got through with the boat nearly full of water, but without being swamped. We found the smooth water to be upon a coral reef, and just deep enough to float the boat. After rowing with two oars [mis-matched] towards the Bridgewaters light for a short time, I saw that unless she tacked it was impossible for us to come near her; and as by her light we saw she kept standing on, I deter-mined to get back to the wreck leaving my charts &c. in the boat, but the surf ran too high for this and therefore we kept rowing gently all night under the lee of the breakers. The cutter having got a little cleared of the water, had shoved off from alongside with eight or nine people in her, and I desired her to keep with us near the ship till morning.[18] During the night several blue lights were burnt, which some on board saw the Bridgewater answer by shewing a light, whilst others thought it to be only a general light on board her which was still visible. It was last seen at 2 in the morning.

'At daylight, we rowed up and I waded on board, the boat not being able to get to the ship from the fall of tide; and the ship had driven much further up the reef. What we had taken for breakers to leeward during the night, proved now to be a dry white sand bank,[19] sufficient to receive every body and all the provisions we might be able to get out of the ship; and as a still further satisfaction the Bridgewater was soon after seen stand-ing towards us. On the other hand, the Cato having heeled

[17] 'I jumped over-board and swam to her . . . .' Flinders, *Voyage*, vol. II, p. 301.
[18] To perform rescue service in the event of the *Porpoise* beginning to break up.
[19] Presently called 'Wreck Reef'.

down to windward, got filled by the surf immediately and her decks were broken up. Her people were now clinging to the upper gunwhale, all together in the fore chains, afraid to venture through the surf which was of greater extent there than abreast of the Porpoise; and it was impossible for a boat to get at them. The Porpoise very fortunately, heeled to leeward towards the reef, presenting her bottom to the surf, so that no water came into her but from the mere rise of tide through the leaks in the inner bilge.

'A raft had been constructed during the night upon which the people might have got to the reef had the ship split, but at present it was found impossible to get it overboard clear of the wreck of the masts (for the other two had gone over during the night) and therefore the spars were cut asunder. Every body was now set to work to get up provisions and water to be landed upon the sand bank, where I went with the small boat to go off to the Bridgewater so soon as she came near, in order to get her to an anchor, if possible, to leeward of the reef, in which situation she might take every body on board with what else might be saved. On landing I hoisted two handkerchiefs up to a tall oar to attract her notice; but about 10 o'clock it appeared she had gone upon the other tack, not being able, probably, to weather the reef, and she was not seen any more this day. Whether the Bridgewater saw the wrecks or the bank we cannot tell, but her courses, if not the hull, were visible from both the Porpoise and Cato.

'By noon, a cask of flour, another of beef and pork, some rice, spirits, and a cask of water were landed; and as the tide fell the Cato's people quitted her and got through the surf to the small boat which waited to receive them: three young lads were missing, being most probably drowned in attempting to get to the reef.[20] At low water, which happened about two o'clock, the reef was dry close to the ship, and every body was employed sending provisions, water, and some other stores, and getting their own clothes upon the reef, from which they were taken by the boats and brought to the dry bank; for round the bank the water is deeper.

[20] Fowler and Smith said a man and two boys, one of whom had been shipwrecked every time he went to sea, and called himself a Jonah.

'The wind continued to blow fresh from the eastward, with light squalls at times. Our anxiety and expectation to see the Bridgewater made some fancy that she was seen in the evening, but I believe it was not so.

'Before dark, every body had got some clothes and other necessaries on shore; and 4 or 5 hogsheads of water and some pigs and sheep were landed, and every person, with the Cato's people got on shore. These last had left their ship naked, but having got to the Porpoise, L⁺ Fowler had clothed four or five in lieutenants uniforms, and much promotion of a similar kind had also taken place amongst our own people.

'Those who had saved great coats or blankets sharing with those who had none, we laid down to sleep with some little comfort;[21] and except a few of the Catos men who were bruised on the reef I believe there was not a sorrowing heart amongst us. Spars and other pieces of the wreck served for fire wood to warm us through the night. In the day the weather is sufficiently warm, but the nights are very cold to people with wet clothes on.'

'I will leave the reader to Guess our Situation,' wrote Seaman Smith, 'between the Catoes Ships Compʸ & ours Consisting of upwards of 90 men, upon a Small Uncertainty 150 miles from the Nearest land & upwᵈˢ of 900 from the Nearest Port.'[22]

The three accounts that have survived are unanimous in reflecting the very high morale maintained by the castaways. There was, as there always is, an element of self-preservation in this. But the basic ingredient is confidence in the officers, and that was not lacking in the present case.

The first and only hint of depression came with the realisation that, after the first day, they had seen the last of the *Bridgewater*. The men gave way to resentment and contempt at Captain Palmer's inhumanity—as who would not—but Flinders put it down to Palmer's 'fear of an unacquaintance with reefs'.[23]

He was too generous. In later times someone brought to Flinders's attention a copy of the Calcutta paper, *Orphan*,

[21] Having been now perhaps forty hours without sleep, but with much exertion.
[22] M.L. Samuel Smith, 'Journal', p. 44 sqq.
[23] Flinders, 'Journal', vol. III, p. 35.

3 February 1804, in which Palmer's account of the incident appeared.[24] The account was, under the circumstances, plausible enough in what it said. Apprehension there was, and justly so. Besides which, the *Bridgewater* had drifted out of sight of the reef, and having done so, on account of contrary winds could not return. So be it. But what Palmer omitted to say—because he had omitted to act—was that he had made not the slightest effort to lower away a boat at any time to go and investigate. Nor had he, even with contrary winds, tried to make a wide circuit back to the area after daybreak on 18 August.

The *Bridgewater* made her way to India, where Palmer filed his report. This document was taken ashore by a Mr Williams, third mate of the *Bridgewater*, who, knowing Palmer to have been at fault, delivered it and promptly quitted the ship, forfeiting both wages and part of his clothes. Williams's journal eventually came to Flinders's hand, and the truth was out. The English language calls Palmer's conduct pusillanimous, and so must we.[25]

3

Directly they had recovered themselves, a great bustle began among the men on the reef. While parties finished unloading the *Porpoise*, others raised a flag-staff on which they put a large blue ensign with the union downward. Still others went off fishing, and some raised tents. Brown's plants, of course, were gone; and some of Westall's drawings suffered.[26] But Flinders— for once in his life—was lucky. Except for a few loose papers and the charts of the west side of the Gulf of Carpentaria and the north coast, on which he had been working in the afternoon before the wreck, the logs, charts, and bearing books were all saved.

[24] Reproduced in Flinders, *Voyage*, vol. ii, p. 307 sq.
[25] Flinders published Williams's version in the *Voyage*, vol. ii, p. 308. The *Bridgewater* sailed shortly thereafter from Bombay for Europe, and disappeared en route with all hands.
[26] For an account of Westall's losses, see *Drawings by William Westall* . . ., ed. by T. M. Perry and Donald H. Simpson (London, 1962), p. 17. Many of these drawings are now in the possession of the Royal Commonwealth Society. Apparently not many were lost, though quite a number were damaged by water.

Obviously, the principal concern of all on the reef was how and when they would escape. Therefore, as soon as it became apparent that no help was to be expected of Palmer, Flinders, being the senior officer present, called together his juniors, along with Captain Park, and offered a plan. The largest cutter would be repaired and fitted for the journey back to Port Jackson where, with King's assistance, other vessels would be dispatched to bring off the people and what stores could be salvaged. Accordingly, on 23 August the carpenters went to work on the cutter, and in two days had readied her for sea. Command at the reef passed to Robert Fowler,[27] who was given instructions to prepare the means for removing the men if at the end of two months no help had come from Port Jackson.

Having taken all necessary decisions, packed the charts and journals for later retrieval, stocked the cutter with food for three weeks, and christened the cutter 'Hope', Flinders set out on 26 August. With him went Park, the second mate of the *Cato*, the Boatswain, Charrington, and ten seamen: 'At $8\frac{1}{2}^h$ A.M. We left Wreck-Reef bank, and returned three cheers to our ship mates remaining behind.'[28]

On a south-westerly heading, Flinders came up with the land in three days. On the fourth day Cape Moreton came in sight, and there Flinders decided to land for water. 31 August was spent by the time the casks had been filled. But the next day the coasting south began. For seven days and seven nights it continued until, on 6 September, 'bore away to search for shelter along the shore, and finding a shallow cove sheltered by a reef of rocks, hauled the boat up there, and took up our quarters on shore for the first night since leaving the wreck.'[29] Two days later, a fortnight on the way, and scarcely a month after departing thence, Flinders passed once again through Sydney Heads. Of his visit to King he later wrote:

'I proceeded immediately to the town of Sydney, and went with captain Park to wait upon His Excellency governor King

[27] Though not until Fowler protested at Flinders's decision to place his brother, who was junior to Fowler, in charge.
[28] Flinders, 'Journal', vol. III, p. 38.
[29] *Ibid.*, p. 44.

whom we found at dinner with his family. A razor had not passed over our faces from the time of the shipwreck, and the surprise of the governor was not little at seeing two persons thus appear whom he supposed to be many hundred leagues on their way to England; but so soon as he was convinced of the truth of the vision before him, and learned the melancholy cause, an involuntary tear started from the eye of friendship and compassion, and we were received in the most affectionate manner.'[30]

There was much planning, and even more industry, to be done before the rescue operation could begin. The resources of the colony, while adequate, were barely so; and improvisation, even for an emergency, took time. As it turned out, Flinders, impatient though he certainly was, was compelled to wait for two weeks before he could be on his way.

Meanwhile, back upon the 'Small Uncertainty,' the men had settled down to wait. Perhaps not exactly 'settled down'.

'. . . from this time our hands are Imploy'd, some about our new Boat, whose Keel is laid down 32 feet, others Imployd in getting any thing servisible from the Wreck; our Gunns and Carriadges we got from the Wreck & placed them in A Half Moon Form, close to our Flag Staf, our Ensign being Dayly hoisted Union downward our Boats sometimes is Imploy'd in going to An Island about 10 Miles Distant; & sometimes caught Turtle & Fish; this Island was in general Sand Except on the Highest part it produced Sea Spinage, Very plentifully stock'd with Birds & Eggs : in this Manner the hands are Imploy'd, & the Month of October is set in, still no Acc^t of our Capt^ns success our Boat likewise ready for Launching the rigging also Fitted over her Mast head, & had the appearance of A rakish schooner; on the 4^th of Oct^r we Lunch'd her & gave her the Name of Hope, on the 7^th we loaded her with Wood in order to take it over to the Island before Mention'd, to make Charcoal, for our Smith, to make the Iron Work for the next Boat, which we Intend to build Directly, she Accordingly Sail'd.[31]

Their vigil was nearly over.

[30] Flinders, *Voyage*, vol. ii, p. 321 sq.        [31] Smith, 'Journal', *loc. cit.*

CHAPTER ELEVEN

# The Little Sea Boat

## August–December 1803

1

For a brief time at least life had a double purpose. The full
resources of the colony must be pressed into the rescue of the
men on the reef. Of that there was, of course, no question. At
the same time, Flinders's unshakeable resolve to reach England,
find a ship, and return to the real business at hand, never left
his mind for even an instant. The question was whether the
first must necessarily interfere with the second, or whether
some way might not be found to achieve both purposes without
breaking stride. The answer depended upon King. It would tax
his colony.

The ship *Rolla*, privately owned, was even then preparing to
leave Port Jackson for Canton, where she would join the China
Fleet for the passage to India. King therefore entered upon an
engagement with her commander to pick up those at the reef
who desired to take that way home. For those who preferred
returning to Sydney, the colonial schooner *Francis* should be
made available. As for Flinders, it was agreed that the delay of
the China route should best be avoided, that he should go
directly to England in the schooner *Cumberland*.[1]

So far as anyone could see, this arrangement had but one
disadvantage : the size of the *Cumberland*, 'something less than
a Gravesend passage boat, being only of twenty-nine tons
burthen'. No record survives of her dimensions; but from the
fact that from the main deck the height of a man's eye above
the water was only ten feet, it seems clear enough that she was

[1] P.R.O., Adm. 1/2020 contains all official orders for effecting disposition of
officers and men.

167

not built for ocean travel.[2] Yet, assured that she was a 'good little sea boat,' even her size was not Flinders's principal objection. '. . . it was the quickness of her motion and the want of convenience, which would prevent the charts and journal of my voyage from being prepared on the passage, and render the whole so much time lost to this important object.'[3]

Notwithstanding, Flinders accepted the *Cumberland* as the least evil, knowing that at every convenient opportunity along the way he must stop for food and water. This meant anchoring and going ashore at Kupang, then in Dutch hands; possibly at Mauritius, a French colony; the Cape of Good Hope, by the Peace of Amiens a Dutch possession; St Helena; and some one of the Western Isles. As discussion proceeded, King urged Flinders to avoid, if possible, going into Mauritius, both on account of its notoriety for hurricanes, and because he hoped to shun communication with the French. In the end, however, he agreed to leave the matter to Flinders's decision, and provided two letters addressed to General Magallon, the Governor-General.

Within a few days both the *Rolla* and the *Francis* were ready to go. But the *Cumberland*, then on colonial duty up the Hawkesbury, day after day failed to appear. When he could stand the agonising delay no longer, Flinders took the cutter 'Hope' to Broken Bay to fetch her out. That was on 16 September. Four days later, when all provisions—livestock, wine, even fresh vegetables—were aboard, the miniature convoy left.

But one unwitting disservice King had done. France and England had been at war when the *Investigator* left home and Flinders had prudently requested specific instructions as to his conduct *vis-à-vis* the enemy. In reply he had been ordered to act in all respects towards the French 'as if the two countries were not at war . . . and not to take letters or packets other than such as you may receive from this office, or the office of His Majesty's secretary of state [for the colonies].'[4] Then had come peace, peace which for all anyone at Port Jackson knew still endured as Flinders was preparing to leave for home.

---

[2] Flinders, *Voyage*, vol. II, p. 346. Her length on deck may have been about 50 feet, and her beam, 15 feet.

[3] *Ibid.*, p. 323.        [4] Flinders, 'Journal', vol. I, p. 21.

King, anxious to keep in touch, gave Flinders several dispatches, one for the Admiralty and one for the Colonial Secretary. Under the circumstances perhaps neither King nor Flinders was at fault. But to send or carry these papers against instructions could not be called judicious.

At any rate, then, the three little vessels departed in company on 20 September. For the first week they made good distance together, one day as much as 117 miles. Then the wind came round into the north-east, and for the remainder of the journey they averaged less than fifty miles a day. The *Francis* seemed always to hang back. At last, on 7 October, just six weeks to the day after leaving the reef, 'saw two boats, and soon after the flag staff on the further Wreck Reef Bank . . . Answered the cheers of the boat and the people on the bank, from whence also a salute of guns was fired on my going ashore.'[5]

By the time he arrived at the reef Flinders had worked out a plan for dividing the men. First he selected those he wanted with him in the *Cumberland*: Aken, Master; Charrington, Boatswain; Elder, Master at Arms; Olive, Clerk; and seven ratings. These he asked to go if, after seeing the schooner and thinking it over for a night, they chose to follow him. Only John Olive declined. Others, including Fowler, brother Samuel, and John Franklin were to go to Canton, thence to England as conveniently as they could. The rest, that is those left from the *Porpoise* and the *Cato*, who desired to be separated from the service, were to return to Sydney in either the *Francis* or the newly made schooner, *Resource*. Within three days all stores were loaded, all water transferred, and the last man on board. Then, on 11 October, 'at $10^h$ 40' hove to for the Rolla's boat and went on board to take leave of my former officers and people. . . . Returned on board from the Rolla, and returned their three

<hr />

[5] *Ibid.*, vol. III, p. 58. In his narrative Flinders wrote of his brother's reaction at the moment. The lieutenant was in his tent, 'calculating some lunar distances, when one of the young gentlemen ran to him, calling, "Sir, Sir! A ship and two schooners in sight!" After a little consideration Mr Flinders said he supposed it was his brother come back, and asked if the vessels were near? He was answered, not yet; upon which he desired to be informed when they should reach the anchorage, and very calmly resumed his calculations: such,' Matthew added, 'are the varied effects produced by the same circumstance upon different minds. When the desired report was made, he ordered the salute to be fired, and took part in the general satisfaction.' Flinders, *Voyage*, vol. II, p. 328.

cheers. At 25' past noon, bore away upon our course towards Torres Strait.'[6]

Thus disappeared from Matthew Flinders's life a party of good men. Samuel reappears only briefly in his elder brother's life-work. His career was not fortunate. Fowler is next heard from on board the *Earl Camden*, Nathaniel Dance, busily assisting the Commodore at the Battle of Pulo-Aur, the monstrous bluff the China Fleet began and finished against the French Admiral Linois in February 1804. Fowler ended his career a Post Captain. Among them all, only one other ever made a name for himself: John Franklin.

2

Generally speaking, it is not possible to sail a vessel eastward through Torres Strait. Except during the summer months (when the north-west monsoon is blowing) both the tidal stream running strongly towards the west, and the south-east trades forbid. This being the case, Flinders had had to be satisfied with his work on the first pass through. There could be no going back to seek a different channel, or have another look round. Now, however, he had a second chance—not that his passage in the *Investigator* was unreliable: he simply hoped to learn more.

In ten days from Wreck Reef, that is, on 21 October, the *Cumberland* reached Pandora's Entrance. Having previously gone through on the north side, Flinders now moved over to the south and proved the Entrance clear. Danger to his little crew from native attack induced him to steer well off the Murray Islands, which he passed the following day. On 23 October he anchored off Halfway Island. Next day, keeping still to the south of his former track, he sailed between Wednesday and Horn Islands,[7] re-entered Prince of Wales Channel, and went on out into the Gulf. Three days—even as he had once said— were all he needed to run the Strait.

Making all sail in fine weather, he crossed the mouth of the

---

[6] Flinders, 'Journal', vol. III, p. 61.
[7] A slot now called Flinders Passage.

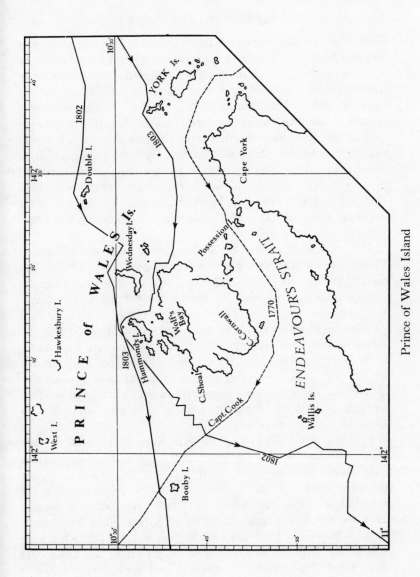

Prince of Wales Island

Gulf in three days. As, in the *Investigator*, he had run inside the English Company's Islands, so now he steered round them to see how far they extended offshore. Unfortunately, 'on searching for my rough charts of C. Arnhem, and the neighbourhood, in order to make all the additions to them that circumstances will permit, I have the extreme mortification to find that they were lost in the Porpoise, together with the fair chart which I was making from them. By help of my bearing book I am enabled to fix the same letters to the isles, that they bore in those charts; but the minute accuracy of form in the coasts and islands, which cost me so much labour and anxiety to obtain is forever lost: the chart *may* [his italics] be made again from the log and bearings, but never correctly.'[8]

He hurried on. When, on 10 November he reached Kupang, Flinders found little change. The former governor, Giesler, had died; but that apart, the depressed little village remained as depressed as ever. Beyond the need for water and a few provisions, he had no reason to stay—except the *Cumberland* had now begun to leak well above the worst expectations he had had when he left Port Jackson. One of the two pumps was nearly gone from overworking; the town offered no facilities for repair, and indeed not even pitch with which to stop the leaks. Therefore, being not only eager to reach England, but anxious as well to avoid the imminent monsoon, Flinders determined to clear out as soon as possible.[9]

Leaky as ever, the *Cumberland* quit Kupang on 14 November on a course set for the Cape of Good Hope. For several days a long swell from the south-west kept her to the north of her intended track. On 20 November, with thunderstorms and a jumbled sea, Flinders noted what was 'apparently a contest between the North and S.E. winds'.[10] Again, on 24 November, 'a high sea rising from the southward,' and one pump working constantly. Still his determination to go on to the Cape held firm. On 27 November, '. . . the last fresh meat served today to the people'.[11]

[8] Flinders, 'Journal', vol. III, p. 73.
[9] But not before he heard that Baudin had arrived at Kupang half a year ago, and had sailed in June for the Gulf of Carpentaria.
[10] Flinders, 'Journal', vol. III, p. 87.
[11] *Ibid.*, p. 91.

By 3 December, being then nearly due east of Mauritius, Flinders knew the time for decision had come. As he saw it:

'From the length of the passage between Timor and the Cape of Good Hope, and the small size of the Cumberland, it had been determined at Port Jackson that we should put in at the Isle Mauritius on the way, both to take in water and refreshments as well as that if the Cumberland should be found incapable or inconvenient to perform the whole passage to England, the Isle Mauritius was likely to be the place where the Cumberland might be freighted back to Port Jackson or sold to the greatest advantage. This intention was laid aside from the report of a Mauritius trader, then at Port Jackson, that ships usually avoided the island during the months of November and December, from the gusts of wind and bad weather that prevailed in those months.

'On considering that the reporter might have an interest in keeping the Port Jackson people ignorant of the first prices of the goods which he had bought and might in future bring to sell them; and that the deviation from our course to the Cape was no more than 200 miles, I determined to put in at the Isle Mauritius, being induced by the following reasons—

'The upper works of the schooner have become so leaky as to require a spell of from five to ten minutes in every hour to keep her free at this time; and as our pump geer [sic] is getting bad, being partly worn out, it was to be feared that if we should meet any unfavourable wind off the Cape to raise much sea and make the schooner heel, that we should hardly get round safe; one principal reason, therefore, for touching at Mauritius is to get the upper works caulked.

'To complete again with wood and water and to procure a small supply of spirits constitute the second reason. Of this last article we have been at a short allowance since leaving Timor, 22 gallons being all that could be got there.

'My third principal reason is the possibility of finding a homeward bound ship there, in which I might obtain a more expeditious and convenient passage to England than can be expected in so small a vessel as the Cumberland; for her greatest rate of sailing, after all our schemes in trimming her, is only seven knots, and in a strong breeze with much sea she must always lie to, however fair the wind may be;—add to which, it is impossible to go on in completing my charts and accounts of New Holland while on board her, for it is only in the finest weather that I can do more than write the daily log. It would be more advantageous to get a passage from Mauritius than any port further on, from the much greater probability of being able to get the schooner sent back to Port Jackson from thence, or otherwise of selling her to greater advantage.

'Besides these, there are several subordinate reasons of much less consequence, such as—

'—Delivering governor Kings letters to General Magallon the governor, which were otherwise to be sent from the Cape.

'—Learning some further intelligence on the Geographe and Naturaliste.

'—*Acquiring a knowledge of the periodical winds and weather there;—of the port and the present state of the French colony; and how far it or its dependencies in Madagascar may be useful to Port Jackson* [italics mine]; as also whether it may not be a convenient place for me to touch at during some part of my future expected voyage.

'—the possibility of another war having taken place; in which case, by touching at this French colony, for which I have a passport, the necessity of stopping at the Dutch settlement at the Cape, for which I have no passport, would be avoided; for I could take in a sufficiency at Mauritius to carry us on to St. Helena.'[12]

And so, 'on the 6th in the evening, altered the course half a point for that island, to the satisfaction of the people'.[13]

---

[12] *Ibid.*, p. 94 sq. In after years, even without this third volume of his journal, Flinders was able to reproduce these reasons substantially as he had written them at the time. Cf. *Voyage*, vol. II, p. 351 sq.

[13] *Ibid.*, vol. II, p. 351.

# CHAPTER TWELVE

# His Excellency's Prisoner

## December 1803–March 1804

### 1

No one, probably least of all those lonely men commanding imperial outposts on both sides, really expected the Peace of Amiens to last through 1803. It was like the eye of a hurricane, quiescent and subsided; but while Napoleon lived, men knew that more must come. Early in the year preparations and alarms spread far beyond the bounds of Europe, into the Eastern Seas. The actual outbreak came, as we have seen, on 18 May.

Word of renewed hostilities reached India's Malabar Coast on 6 September. From there it arrived at the Île de France on 21 September, just four days after Flinders left Port Jackson in the *Cumberland*. At that moment Governor King had no inkling of these events. But the fact is, from the time he left Timor, Flinders was in all innocence in a war-zone, heading for trouble.

The last eleven days to Mauritius were exhilarating. The haven ahead lay friendly and safe, a mere 1,500 miles away, no great distance even for the tiny schooner. Thus the log, day after day: 'A considerable following sea from E.S.E.; as much as it is altogether safe for us to run before . . . Sea rising from the S.E. and running long and high . . . Fresh trade wind and fine weather, with a following sea . . . A sea following from E.S.E.'[1]

9 December. 'At 6 saw a strange sail to the N.E. ward and hauled up towards her; but afterwards edged away more, and at dusk shewed a light. She was a tall ship with all sail set, steering about W.S.W.: we saw no more of her, and I think she tried to avoid us.'[2]

---

[1] Flinders, 'Journal', vol. III, p. 96 sqq.
[2] *Ibid.*, p. 98.

12 December. 'At this time there are two people on board
besides myself affected with a bilious remitting fever, such as is
usually thought to be generated by the miasma of marshes or
swamps. I attribute this mostly to the late wet and sultry
weather, and from not being able to keep our sleeping and
messing places so well aired and so clean as we might do if we
were not so much lumbered or were in a larger vessel. Having
no medical man on board, our getting to port receives an
additional object to hasten it.'[3]

At daylight of 15 December the south-east end of the Île de
France came in sight. Flinders kept on, and in mid-morning saw
a flag on shore.[4] He showed his colours, and at 11.30 'a small
schooner came out of a small creek and stood towards us for a
time, then steered along shore'.[5]

The *Cumberland* followed the Frenchman into the Baie du Cap.

'On steering into this small reef harbour at the S.W. part of the
island, we observed that the men left the schooner that came in
before us, and ascended the steep hills with much expedition,
each carrying something; and others were gathering at the top
with musquets. They refused to come off to us, or otherwise I
had not intended to hoist out a boat, meaning to sail as soon as I
could get some one to shew me the port on the N.W. side of
the island. In conclusion, we learned that there was war between
England and France which accounted [for] these strange
appearances.

'I began now to consider that my passport did not actually
extend further than the Investigator, and how far the French
might be indulgent enough to take the *intention* in preference
to the *letter* of the passport, I was doubtful. I applied to the
officer that came on board to have a few casks of water filled,
intending privately, to get under weigh indeed in the morning
with the other schooner, but instead of going to Port N.W.
[Port Louis] with her, to make sail for the Cape as fast as I

[3] *Ibid.*, p. 100.
[4] He had travelled 6,797 miles in 68 days from Wreck Reef.
[5] Flinders, 'Journal', vol. iii, p. 101. Since the French officers presently communicated their version of the facts to Decaen, it is important to have before us
what Flinders wrote at the moment, and not what he published years later from
memory.

could; but on inquiry I found the Dutch and French had possession of the Cape, and as we could not go so far as S$^t$ Helena without refitting or without more wood and water, I was under the necessity of putting a good face upon it.

'The French commandant of this neighbourhood came afterwards on board with other officers and examined my passport and commission particularly, and requested to send them to the Port N.W. for the governor's inspection; but I objected to parting with these, upon which they offered me horses to go by land, and a pilot to take the schooner round. Finding it was better to accept of one of these I agreed to the latter and went on shore with the officers accordingly.

'The second officer in command and who came first on board, entertained me very politely, but after breakfast in the morning I found we could not set off without permission from the commandant, which was expected, but I chose to remain on board, saying that on the following morning I should go round, if no definite regulation was settled before. I found the pilot on board in expectation of an order to go out with us.

'Mons. Dunienville, the major of this district of Savanne, did not let his hospitality rest here, and with giving us a quantity of tamarinds and bananas; but pressed me to dine at his house where he invited several of the neighbouring gentlemen; and at this time the commandant had consented that I should go round in the schooner, as I first wished; and our friendly party, ladies and all, attended me to the shore and sent off a basket of mangos with other refreshments. Monsieur le Citoyen Dunienville and his lady seem to be indeed amiable people.'[6]

Late in the afternoon of 16 December the *Cumberland* got under way. At four the following afternoon she anchored off Port Louis.[7]

2

As Flinders entered the port he was confronted by an imponderable situation. Not one, but two important circumstances had irrevocably changed. With the outbreak of hostilities

[6] *Ibid.*, p. 102 sq.  [7] Here ends Flinders's Journal.

he found himself cast once again as an enemy. Yet he hoped, indeed expected, that the French governor here, General Magallon de la Morlière, would treat him for what he really was, a disinterested neutral. Was there not historical precedent in the cases of both Cook and Vancouver? He had already learned, however, that Magallon, an officer of the Republican régime, had been relieved, and now commanded at the island of Bourbon. The man he would actually meet was one General Charles-Mathieu-Isidore Decaen (1769-1832), an ardent Bona-partist. Yet even in perplexity and confusion he found no cause for alarm.

It was already late afternoon when he stepped ashore in dress uniform, and walked anxiously through the town to Government House, escorted by an officer and an interpreter. The Captain-General was at dinner and could not be disturbed. Two hours passed before Decaen was ready to deal with the case. The general's briefing by his officers took another half hour, and then Flinders was led into the room. There he saw two men, 'the one, a shortish thick man in a laced round jacket, the other a genteel-looking man whose blood seemed to circulate more tranquilly'.[8] The first was General Decaen who, according to Flinders, 'fixed his eye sternly upon me, and without saluta-tion or preface demanded my passport, my commission!' A few questions followed, directed in the main at the implausibility of anyone's sailing from Sydney to Port Louis in a twenty-nine ton vessel. These were answered so matter of factly that to Decaen's mind the whole thing seemed absurd. His Latin temper exploded: 'Vous m'en imposez, monsieur! It is not probable that the governor of New South Wales should send away the commander of an expedition on discovery in so small a vessel!'[9] In a sense, of course, he was right. Decaen, who had experience as an intelligence officer—and an able one at that— saw at once the possibility that Flinders might be an agent. The story made no sense.

On the other hand, it seems quite unlikely that Flinders, whose

[8] Flinders, *Voyage*, vol. II, p. 360.

[9] *Ibid.*, p. 360 sq. Among the dispatches Flinders carried for King was a letter to Sir Evan Nepean at the Admiralty explaining his disposition of Flinders and the crew of the *Porpoise*. Even though it was signed by King, Decaen either disbelieved it, or simply ignored it when he saw it.

hands in the matter were so entirely clean, had yet formed the
faintest notion of what Decaen was talking about.

Decaen now wished to see more papers : charts, journals,
orders, letters—anything at all connected with the voyage.
Dismissing Flinders, he directed his officers to repair immediately to the *Cumberland* to fetch them. Flinders packed these
documents in a trunk, which was then sealed. Incensed, he
begged to be excused : '. . . the captain-general's conduct must
alter very much before I should pay him a second visit, or even
set my foot on shore again.'[10] This line, however, was inadmis-
sible. The Captain-General had ordered Flinders's removal to
lodgings ashore. He was, in fact, under arrest. Not only he, but
Mr Aken, Master, with him. In agitated disbelief, but in no
position to resist, the two put some clothes together, and at
one o'clock in the morning left the *Cumberland*. Thus the first
day in enemy hands.

The Café Marengo, much run down and very dirty, swarmed
with insects. A room on the upper floor of this tavern, with a
sentinel stationed outside their door, was just the thing for these
English imposters. There were beds, but, as Flinders put it,
'between the musketoes above and the bugs below, and the
novelty of our situation, it was daybreak before either of us
dropped asleep.'[11]

At six, two grenadiers entered. One posted the other as a
guard inside the room, and left. Breakfast arrived at eight,
dinner, consisting of good bread, fresh meat, fruit and vegetables, at noon. And the guard continued his pacing to and fro
all the while.

At one o'clock Flinders was called for by one of the General's
aides, taken again to Government House, and given a second
interrogation :

Why had he come to the Île de France in the *Cumberland*,
using a passport made out for the *Investigator* ? Where were the
officers and scientists of the *Investigator* ? Had he any knowledge
of the war before he arrived ? Why had he used cartel colours,
and why had he chased a vessel into the Baie du Cap ? Why had
he come round to Port Louis, and on whose authority ?

His answers were taken down, placed with his other papers,

[10] *Ibid.*, p. 361.                    [11] *Ibid.*, p. 362.

and delivered to Decaen. Presently, much to his surprise, an orderly returned with an invitation to Flinders to join the General at dinner. Whatever may have been Decaen's motives in taking this step, they were unfathomable to his intended guest, and must remain so to us. Flinders thought he saw a trick. But in any case, still regarding Decaen's previous behaviour as insulting to a British officer—he had in effect been called a liar —Flinders curtly declined: '. . . under my present situation and treatment it was impossible; when they should be changed, —when I should be set at liberty, if His Excellency thought proper to invite me, I should be flattered by it, and accept his invitation with pleasure.'[12]

More than likely Decaen's gesture concealed no deep, ulterior motive. After all, he had other ways of extracting information if he wished to use them. This was a dangerous snub.

Sir Winston Churchill, who had reason to know, put it thus : 'The position of a prisoner of war is painful and humiliating . . . All military pride, all independence of spirit must be put aside. These may be carried to the grave, but not into captivity.'[13]

Nothing further transpired that day, or the next. On 20 December word came to him of serious disorders on board the *Cumberland*, where the crew still lodged; that the men had taken spirits out of the Commander's cabin and had gone ashore without leave, much as they pleased. Flinders made representations accordingly and requested that Aken be placed in charge. The request was denied, but Decaen ordered that a strict guard be placed over the crew.

By next day Decaen had had time to study Flinders's papers, and had found that passage near the end of volume III of the Journal, giving among the 'subordinate' reasons for running in to Mauritius :

'—Acquiring a knowledge of the periodical winds and weather there;—of the port and the present state of the French colony; and how far it or its dependencies in Madagascar may be useful to Port Jackson. . . .'[14]

---

[12] *Ibid.*, p. 363.
[13] Winston S. Churchill, *London to Ladysmith* (New York, 1900), p. 96.
[14] Flinders, 'Journal', vol. III, p. 95.

More than any other single factor, that one sentence killed Flinders's case. It was evidence. Despite all protestations of innocence, all reference to the freedom accorded the late Captain Baudin at Port Jackson, all chronicles of exploration, Decaen now saw nothing but espionage. Everything else was mere façade. He therefore charged Flinders explicitly with violating his neutrality, and probably about this time determined to hold him in custody permanently, or until orders for disposition of the case should come from Paris.[15]

To a partisan of Matthew Flinders Decaen's action appears high-handed, arbitrary, unjust, and unwarranted. To be sure, detention for six and a half years without formal proceedings comes close to being all of these, and inhumane besides. But the arrest as such was none of them. Consider Decaen's position. A state of war existed. He and he alone was responsible for executing French policy in all the area east of the Cape of Good Hope. So far as this theatre of war was concerned—and it was deeply involved—only one man, Denis Decrès, Minister of Marine and Colonies, stood between Decaen and Bonaparte. Any mistake at the Île de France would be known immediately at the summit of the French hierarchy. Now he saw a brazen attempt to penetrate his capital; and it had come only a few months after François Péron, Naturalist in Baudin's expedition, had handed him a *mémoire politique* alleging a British intention to use Port Jackson as a base from which to attack Spanish colonies in South America. It was too much to ask Decaen to ignore this circumstantial evidence. The bill of particulars he could write against Flinders would more than justify detention. It was his duty to be suspicious; and he needed no such minor irrelevancy as a refusal to dine for an excuse.

History, of course, has proved the Captain-General's suspicions unfounded. Flinders was not in fact a spy. Doubtless his

[15] An interesting study of the present case from the legal point of view appeared some years ago in connection with discussions then being held of the position of scientific missions in time of war : A. Auzoux, 'L'Arrestation du capitaine Flinders, 1803–1810', *Revue d'histoire diplomatique*, An. 26 (1912), pp. 481–515. M. Auzoux concludes : 'En réalité, Decaen sacrifia, à l'intérêt supérieur de son pays, celui d'un individu, douloureux conflit que angoissera toujours l'homme d'honneur appelé à le trancher, en dépit des congrès et des conventions.' p. 496. As to Péron's allegations, Auzoux remarks : 'Les aveux de Péron n'etaient pas faits pour lui inspirer une confiance illimitée dans la neutralité des missions scientifiques.' p. 487.

information on Mauritius could have been used against the French; but even without it the British were so well informed that even Napoleon could not understand why they had not already taken it.[16]

So much for the rationale. On the side of personality, again Flinders was unfortunate. French colonials on the Île de France detested Charles Decaen. And why not? Time had passed them by; their *ancien régime* was gone, and in its place had come this exiled upstart, ruthless, impetuous, ambitious and now harassed. In contrasting him with the French Admiral Durand de Linois, Professor Parkinson has described Decaen as having 'ability without reputation'.[17] If clash of personalities came into play at all, as indeed it must have done, that is about all we need to know about Decaen. As for Flinders, had he not once told Christopher Smith that 'the honour of being an honest man and ranked as a gentleman', which latter he certainly was not, 'is sufficient for me'?[18] They were two of a kind. There is no evidence whatever that these men hated each other on sight. But with no common bond, as for instance social rank, they deviated further from one another with every hour that passed.[19]

---

[16] C. N. Parkinson, *War in the Eastern Seas, 1793–1815* (London, 1954), p. 310. A sample of colonial opinion regarding Decaen may be seen in *Arch. Col. Île de France*, 'Correspondance Générale', vol. 13, p. 263, in the Archives Nationales. The words 'Jacobin' and 'parvenu' are not spared.

[17] Parkinson, *op. cit.*, p. 193.

[18] Flinders to Smith, 14 February 1800. N.M.M. 60/017. FLI/4.

[19] On 21 December Flinders wrote a letter to Decaen (*Voyage*, vol. II, p. 368 sqq.) in which he pressed his views zealously. It was unavailing, and in fact merely irritated the General. Years later, Flinders not only published this letter, but explained the tone he had used in writing it:

'The lapse of several years,' he wrote, 'has enabled me to consider the transactions of this period under different views, to regard them with almost the coolness of an uninterested observer; and I see the possibility that a dispassionate reader may accuse me of taking too high a position, and using too warm a style,—in rather giving way to the dictates of feeling than dwelling upon the proofs of my innocence; perhaps also, he may accuse me of vanity, in seeking to enhance my own zeal and claims. Without attempting to controvert these censures, I beg him to consider all the circumstances of my situation: my voyage, shipwreck, and anxiety to pursue the steps of our celebrated navigators. Let him suppose himself to have executed so much of the same task, escaped the same dangers; and under the influence of powerful motives to reach England with expedition, to be arrested on the way, his misfortunes either not heeded or converted into proofs of delinquency, and himself treated as a spy; and this is done by the representative of a government which had promised assistance and protection, and moreover owed him a return for the kind

The seventh day of detention was most distressing. Summer had begun, which in Port Louis meant that daytime temperatures would be in the 90s for the next four months. Incarceration in the middle of the town amounted to cruelty; and for a man in poor health, suffering from scurvy, conditions quickly became unbearable. Flinders therefore requested a surgeon to attend to his scorbutic ulcers.

But that was not all. He requested also permission to write to the Admiralty, his family, and friends. In answer he was told that the General had no objection to his writing to whom he pleased, but the letters must be sent unsealed to the town major, who would then make what disposition of them he saw fit. For what it was worth, this at least clarified for Flinders the seriousness of his position. It was a bitter blow.

As for the scurvy, on Christmas Eve the surgeon paid a visit, and recommended a strict diet of lemonade and vegetables. The General could do no less.

Christmas Day Flinders spent drafting a memoir for Decaen. Without reciting again any of the well-known details of his past activities, he launched straightaway into a denial of guilt. Admitting for the sake of debate that he could have spied, he contended vigorously that he had come to Port Louis for no such purpose. He was not, as 'you told me impetuously', an imposter.[20] On the whole, this letter was, so to say, less intemperate than its predecessor of four days earlier. That same evening he received a response, short and to the point: '. . . until *the general opinion judges of your faults or mine* [italics Decaen's] [you are] to cease all correspondence tending to demonstrate the justice of your cause; since you know so little how to preserve the rules of decorum'.[21]

Flinders never became exactly docile in confinement; but by the year's end his passion had cooled. Either he grew enervated in the tropical heat, or he realised the uselessness of protest.

---

treatment recently experienced by Frenchmen in the port from whence he came. Let him suppose himself writing to his oppressor with these various recollections crowding on his imagination; and the allowances he would then desire for himself, I request of him to make for me.' (*Ibid.*, p. 370 sq.)

Common decency compels us to make the allowances that Decaen could not.

[20] *Ibid.*, p. 372 sqq.
[21] *Ibid.*, p. 375.

Perhaps both. In any event, a few days after Christmas he showed signs of accommodating his mind to his misfortune. On 27 December he asked for his printed books from the schooner, private letters and papers out of the sealed trunk, and several charts and other hydrographic records. Some of the books came up promptly, and next day he was allowed to go to Government House to select the papers and journals he needed. It was there he learned that Decaen had confiscated the third volume of his journal—that containing the damaging statements. It was a loss he could never repair, and he never saw the volume again. Gone too were the dispatches he had been carrying to London for King.

On New Year's Day he began working on his charts of the Gulf of Carpentaria. This, together with his books, tended to ease his mind. But time hung heavily on his hands, cooped up as he was in this dirty little tavern. Again he concerned himself with his men, once a week sending them a basket of fruit and vegetables from the town market. From Aken, who had more freedom, he learned that the *Cumberland* and her stores had begun to deteriorate noticeably. He could do nothing to save her, and, reading this as yet another sign of Decaen's determination to hold him, on 3 February he wrote a note asking the Captain-General for an interview. This request was refused, and so Flinders wrote a letter containing, as he said, the following propositions:

'1st. If your Excellency will permit me to depart with my vessel, papers, &c., I will pledge my honour not to give any information of the Isle of France or any thing belonging to it, for a limited time, if it be thought that I can have gained any information; or if judged necessary, any other restrictions can be laid upon me. If this will not be complied with, I request,

'2nd, to be sent to France.

'3rd. But if it be indispensable to detain me here, I request that my officer [Aken] and people may be permitted to depart in the schooner; as well for the purpose of informing the British Admiralty where I am, as to relieve our families and friends from the report which will be spread of the total loss of the Porpoise and Cato, with all on board. Mr. Aken can be laid under what restrictions may be deemed requisite; and my honour shall be a security that nothing shall be transmitted by me, but what passes under the inspection of the officer who may be appointed for that purpose.'[22]

With the war on his doorstep Decaen was in no mood to treat. He took no more notice of this letter than of another Flinders wrote a week or so later, asking for more of his books. Perhaps he noticed a none too subtle alteration Flinders had made in the formal closing of his letters. Whereas the first several had ended, 'Your Excellency's obedient servant,' now it was 'Your Excellency's prisoner'. The change would not endear him to the General. But then it was not intended to.

By 1 March Port Louis had got Flinders down. The oppressive heat, the continuance of his scurvy, and the infernal plague of insects, none of these had improved. To make matters worse, he had run out of money—what little he had brought ashore— so that he could no longer have his laundry done. And new money, against bills drawn on London, could be had only at 30 per cent discount.

In this melancholy state he inquired of an aide what he, the aide, thought were the prospects for release. The aide thought Flinders would be a prisoner so long as the war lasted; but that sooner or later he would probably be moved to a more salubrious climate. Even years later Flinders acknowledged surprise at this opinion. Not that he was a stupid man: far from it. Nor had he any reason to suppose that Decaen's attitude toward him would soften. He simply refused to believe that the French government, that is to say, Bonaparte, well known as a patron of science, would sanction such treatment of a scientist as this. Thus, why should Decaen take the risk of official displeasure? But the aide was right.

Within the week a visit from Captain Bergeret, of the French Marine, brought him word that very probably he would soon be moved to better quarters. And so it turned out. On 23 March the crew of the *Cumberland* were brought ashore and sent to the eastern side of the island. On the last day of March, 105 days after his arrest, Flinders was removed to a house about a mile

[22] *Ibid.*, p. 382 sq.

away used by the government to house other British prisoners of rank.

From one point of view at least—if it were much consolation —the worst was over. Without due process, or indeed any process of law, Decaen had had his revenge; Flinders had been made to pay for breaking the 'rules of decorum'.

# CHAPTER THIRTEEN

# The Consuming Years

## 1804-1810

1

On 30 April 1803 the government of the United States of America purchased the Louisiana Territory from France for 60,000,000 francs. Three weeks later, with the outbreak of war, there began a long crescendo of anguish for Europe. The awesome genius of Napoleon had raised the stakes of fortune until only one goal remained : the conquest of England.

At the age of thirty-five Bonaparte opened this deadly game. On 14 May 1804 he had himself proclaimed Emperor. On 21 October 1805 his dream of invading England came to an end by Nelson's hand off Cape Trafalgar. But less than two months later he crushed Austria and Russia at Austerlitz. Prussian resistance collapsed at Jena on 14 October 1806. With Europe under control, but deprived of his fleet, Napoleon now determined upon the economic strangulation of Britain. Reasoning that England must export or die, he devised and decreed in 1806 an embargo on all goods entering Europe from Britain. By the Treaty of Tilsit, July 1807, Russia entered this Continental System. The invasion of Spain and Portugal in 1808 was intended to close the last European ports through which Britain still traded freely. But this was a mistake. The Peninsular War that followed lasted for six years, and worse, brought Napoleon face to face with a general who, loathing war, was nevertheless his superior in the field : Sir Arthur Wellesley, future Duke of Wellington.

Across the Channel, English politics, remarkable only for ineptitude, presented a sombre contrast to Napoleon's success. In 1804, Pitt's second administration replaced the feeble government of Addington, and renewed the former vigour of the whole nation. But at forty-five, his stamina gone, Pitt was already an old man. When, at the moment of Austerlitz, his friend Henry Dundas, First Lord of the Admiralty, stood impeached by the House for financial mismanagement, Pitt's health gave way. He died in office in January 1806.

Grenville's Ministry of All the Talents which succeeded him failed for two years to effect the slightest derangement of Napoleon's plans, its one achievement being the abolition of the slave trade. This coalition fell in 1807, and was followed by a government headed nominally by the Duke of Portland. Here was an improvement—almost anything would have been—but it too ended quickly when in 1809 a smouldering quarrel between Canning at the Foreign Office and Castlereagh at the War Office erupted into a common duel. In the event, Spencer Perceval moved from the Exchequer to become Prime Minister. His administration, the fourth in five years, lasted until 1812.

On the other side of the world the commerce war moved likewise towards a climax. There the French strategy was to sever the trade route between Canton and Bombay if possible, or to harass it if not. It will be recalled that news of hostilities had reached India in September 1803; and that in February following, Admiral Linois lost, as he should not have done, the Battle of Pulo-Aur in which Lieutenant Fowler distinguished himself.

In June of the same year, Admiral Peter Rainier, Commander in Chief of British forces in the East, ordered a blockade of Mauritius, a manoeuvre which, if not instantly successful, at least began to counter the French *guerre de course*. The capture of the Cape of Good Hope by the British in January 1806 left Mauritius the sole French naval base in the East, exposed it to tighter blockade, and rendered its eventual capture more or less inevitable. By 1806 Mauritius was short of grain; and in 1808 it was in acute danger of famine. The net was drawn tighter. In September 1809 a commando-type raid struck the neighbouring island of Bourbon. Finally, on 3 December 1810, General Decaen capitulated.

Thus in broad brush the chronicle of Europe during the years of Flinders's captivity. What news the prisoner had of these events came to him in bits and pieces, months out of date, largely from his French friends on the island. Yet, however eager he may have been for it, his private world was and continued so detached that the intelligence made scarcely any difference. It was just as well : there was little enough to bring him cheer.

2

The island of Mauritius is fertile, moody, and beautiful. Lying three degrees within the tropics, it has on its east coast an annual rainfall of 145 inches. Mountains reaching in some places an elevation of 2,700 feet cover the island. It is notorious for the violent hurricanes which sweep across it, filling the watercourses to overflowing, ruining the coffee and sugar plantations. Even so, the uplands, and especially the central plateau, have always been pleasant, picturesque and productive, offering welcome relief from the sweltering heat of Port Louis.

By the turn of the nineteenth century the island had become completely self-supporting except for grain. Maize, vegetables, poultry, goats, and hogs formed the basis of the local economy. With a large slave population to supply labour, ebony and coffee (for America) offered the frugal planter a profit estimated by Flinders at twenty per cent.[1]

These qualities apart, however, the principal characteristic of Mauritius in the days of sail was its remoteness : 600 miles from Madagascar, 1,500 from Bombay, 2,900 from Capetown, and, by way of the Cape, 9,000 miles from London, if and when there were ships and favourable winds to take them to any of these places. This being the case, Mauritius was at that time a world by itself, so far isolated that its colonials had come close to forming a sub-culture, French to the bone, but so conservative in outlook as to be an anachronism. It was indeed so remote that Napoleon, aware that he could never really control it, laughed about it and simply wrote it off. There Matthew Flinders languished.

[1] Flinders, *Voyage*, vol. ii, p. 436. This prospect led him to invest a considerable sum after his return to England. See next chapter.

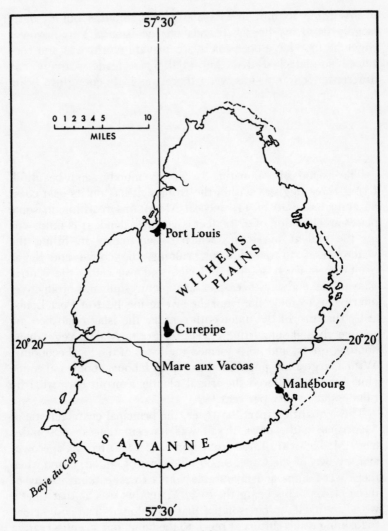

Mauritius

The remoteness from home, from Ann, borne in upon him day after day, every day for six and a half years, created a psychological burden which at times made his life almost insupportable. Nor was this all. For one thing, each month of detention subtracted just that much from his chances of ever completing the survey of Australia. The resulting attrition of his hopes spawned in him an implacable, at times unreasoning bitterness against Decaen. Sunk in melancholy for weeks on end, Flinders came soon to focus all his feelings upon the General. This was perhaps natural and understandable. It was also quite useless.

Then too, his sudden translation from a life of ceaseless action to one of sedentary inaction brought the special problem of combating boredom. Over the course of his detention he was to undertake a number of projects, most of them scholarly, productively related to his profession; others only 'busy work'; but all of them of therapeutic value.

To these profound troubles were added others of a more transient character. By the end of December 1803, scurvy had taken its toll. While we have no clinical information on how far his case had advanced, it is known that in March 1804 a walk of only a mile left him completely exhausted.[2] It is safe to assume that he had also reached the stage where the disease itself induces mental depression.

Finally, he was a stranger. Even worse, he was an enemy; and if some of his earliest contacts with colonials were friendly enough, he could never be sure how far he was accepted. Knowing Decaen, few people wished to risk friendship with a 'spy'.

Such, then, were the essentials of Flinders's personal problem at the outset of his captivity. How he survived remains now to be seen.

3

By 1804 there had arisen in the Eastern Seas a fairly sophisticated cartel system by which prisoners of all ranks and stations on both sides could be repatriated. A French privateer, for

[2] Ibid., p. 389.

example, taking an Indiaman such as the *Warren Hastings*, would enter Port Louis with her prize, and place the crew and passengers, if any, in custody ashore. These people were prisoners of war in the accepted sense. As their numbers grew, and further detention became too expensive, certain of them would be shipped out in the next British cartel bringing Frenchmen to Mauritius. Sometimes these prisoners gave their parole not to serve against the enemy for a stated period after their release. In any case, the system was formalised and well known; and if irregular, it still allowed a certain room for hope. To be included in one of these exchanges—always, of course, the next one—became the goal of all these unfortunates.

When, by his letter of 25 December, Decaen had reproved him for rudeness and flatly forbidden him to discuss the justice of his detention further, it being 'useless to commence a debate here between you and me',[3] Flinders began to see that if he were to be released at all, he would need help from outside Mauritius. This realisation generated a *cause célèbre*, the Case of Captain Flinders, which lasted until his liberation in 1810.[4] The Case had two aspects. That is, on the one hand Flinders, determined, but no longer pugnacious, conducted a correspondence with Decaen or his aide-de-camp, Colonel Monistrol, whenever he saw fit, and on a variety of topics, depending on changing circumstances. On the other, he solicited the help of a number of figures on both sides whose influence he thought powerful enough to procure his release. Thus there evolved a dialogue within the confines of Mauritius, and a concomitant conversation across the seas.

By dispatch of 16 January 1804 Decaen reported his action with respect to the prisoner to Decrès, French Minister of Marine and the Colonies, and requested instructions.[5] This placed responsibility for decision elsewhere, and at the same time gave him a valid excuse for punishing Flinders's snub. It appears that Flinders did not immediately appreciate the

---

[3] *Ibid.*, p. 374 sq.

[4] In writing his biography, Professor Scott dealt more fully with the French documents on this matter than the present author has done. In particular, he relied upon the Decaen Papers, esp. vols. 10, 84, 92, and 105, located in the Municipal Library of Caen, Normandy. Cf. Scott, *Life*, chaps. 21–6.

[5] Flinders, *Voyage*, vol. II, p. 460.

significance of the move, for on '16 February he wrote the threefold proposition to Decaen, quoted in the previous chapter. He already regarded his detention as 'protracted'. By 27 February he saw that he might be using his time to profit, and requested more of his books and charts, 'that I may still proceed in completing the account of my observations and discoveries'.[6] Only rarely did Decaen respond to these letters. Rather, he either directed Monistrol to reply, or to take the action indicated, or else he simply ignored the matter altogether. Thus it was with the books and charts which Flinders received in July 1804—all except that third volume of his journal. Thus also the issue over the sword.

For nearly six months Flinders had been permitted to keep his sword; and hence he inferred that he was not technically regarded as a prisoner of war. But on 2 June there appeared a sergeant to demand it. Flinders properly insisted upon protocol, and requested he be waited on by an officer of equal rank, to whom he would consent to hand it over.[7] Again Decaen made no reply, and nothing further happened until September, when an officer, though not one of equal rank, received it, and the matter was closed.

Once again, in November, Flinders found it necessary to write to the General, this time regarding a report that his shipmates were suffering maltreatment. And once again, after some delay, but no letter from Decaen, the fault was corrected.[8]

Evidently the first of his letters to get through to London were those written in March 1804. These letters, one to the Admiralty and one to Banks, arrived together, for both reacted within the same week.[9] At any rate, Flinders had now opened his campaign abroad.

On 16 April, he wrote to Admiral Linois, just arrived at Mauritius from the Battle of Pulo-Aur.[10] Unfortunately, for that and other disagreements with Decaen, Linois had fallen from

---

[6] 'A Narrative of the causes that prevented His Majesty's ship the Investigator from completing the examination and discovery of the Coasts of Australia . . ., July 1806.' P.R.O., Adm. 7/707. Appen. Adm. 7/708 is almost an exact duplicate. Hereafter cited as Adm. 7/707.          [7] *Ibid.*, p. 191.

[8] Flinders to Decaen, 14 November 1804. *Ibid.* Appen. p. xxvi.

[9] See Flinders, *Voyage*, vol. II, p. 388, and Royal Society of London, *Phil. Trans.*, vol. 95 (1805), p. 186.          [10] P.R.O., Adm. 7/707, p. 182 sq.

the General's good graces, and although he expressed sympathy for a fellow naval officer, he could do nothing to intercede. Another, to Captain Pierre-Bernard Milius who, after Baudin's death had taken *Le Géographe* back to France, and then was captured commanding another ship, went to London in April. Still another, addressed to Richard Lord Wellesley, Governor-General of India, went out in May:

'I doubt not that your Excellency will take such measures for the release of my books, papers, and myself as will be best fitted to produce the desired end. Were it demanded what steps would be likely to render me the most effectual relief, I should have much difficulty in giving an answer; since I believe the implacability and haughtiness of general De Caen to be such, that a cartel to demand me would only make him more firmly resolve to keep me, my officer, and people, prisoners; but I can not presume to fathom the depths of your Excellency's arrangements. . . .'[11]

On 22 August Banks, already involved with French savants over other English prisoners, first took up the case of his navigator by writing to the astronomer J. B. J. Delambre. Through Delambre he hoped the Institut National would approach Decrès;[12] and on the following 5 March their unanimous decision to do so was reported back to him.[13]

Two days after Banks's letter the Admiralty took official action by communicating the facts to the Secretary of State for War. On 4 September the War Office returned their advice that all papers relating to the Flinders case should be sent over to the Transport Service for further transmission to the French Marine Ministry.[14] While all this was going on Flinders, of course, sat seething and alone.

That the case had already excited some interest in France appears from the publication on 4 and 11 July of two letters in the *Gazette National ou Le Moniteur Universél*. The first, from

[11] Flinders to Wellesley, 5 May 1804. *Ibid.* Appen. p. xiv. In May, Wellesley did indeed urge Decaen to release him. As predicted, Decaen paid no attention.
[12] Banks to Delambre, 22 August 1804. B.M. (N.H.) D.T.C. 15. 54–7. For an account of Banks's efforts on behalf of Flinders and others see, Sir Gavin de Beer, *The Sciences were never at War* (London, 1960).
[13] Brabourne Collection, 75–6.    [14] P.R.O., Adm. 1/4197.

an unknown writer, argued for the prisoner, charging a mistaken policy on the part of Decaen. The second, presumably official, refuted the first by simply repeating the evidence of that most damaging sentence at the end of the third volume of his journal.[15] Flinders's efforts to break free in 1804 came to an end with a letter to Decaen on the first anniversary of his capture.[16] But this too was ignored.

That the effort and frustration had undermined his health there can be no doubt at all. In April he wrote to the Rev. Mr Tyler, Ann's stepfather, '. . . Add, if you please, that I am recovered from the scorbutic state in which I last wrote.'[17] Again in May to Tyler, 'a conveyance by the French ship of war Berceau, enables me to tell you that I am in good health . . . I am wrung with anguish.'[18]

It is startling to find that all this time he simply could not bring himself to write to Ann. It was, in fact, not until 26 August, about the time his letters to Banks and the Admiralty reached home, that he did so. The letter contained not a word of his health. Perhaps he was trying to spare her.[19] But by the time it left Mauritius on 4 November he had sensibly declined :

October 1804 : 'At this time my health was very bad, and the sight of my right eye almost lost. The great use that I had for many years made of it, in taking astronomical observations, was probably the first cause of this misfortune; but its acceleration, and the derangement of my health, were owing to a want

[15] Flinders, *Voyage*, vol. II, p. 406 sq. Flinders saw these issues of *Le Moniteur* in March 1805.
[16] *Ibid.*, p. 402 sq. Two notable events connected with Flinders occurred in London during the summer of 1804. By letter of 14 August, the Secretary of the Admiralty had written to Princess Saunders & Co., owners of the *Bridgewater*, transmitting Flinders's report of the loss of the *Porpoise*, and requesting further information. The Company replied on 17 August, promising to interview Palmer, and assuring the Secretary that Palmer had always been found an 'intelligent, steady, and humane Commander'. P.R.O., Adm. 1/4979. P 249. Also, on 18 August, Secretary Ramsey, of the H.E.I.C., advised the Board of Admiralty that, in consequence of Lieutenant Fowler's services at the Battle of Pulo-Aur, the Court of Directors had awarded him the sum of 300 guineas 'for the purchase of a piece of plate'. P.R.O., Adm. 1/3915.
[17] Flinders to Tyler, 26 April 1804. N.M.M. 60/017. FLI/25.
[18] Flinders to Tyler, 20 May 1804. *Ibid.*
[19] Flinders to Ann, 26 August 1804. *Ibid.* The letter is endorsed, 'Nov. 4, 1804. No alteration'.

of active employment, and to the oppression of spirits which, in spite of myself, reflexions upon my situation too frequently occasioned.'[20]

With the disability to his sight, even work on his charts was denied him.

On New Year's Eve, 1804, he wrote again to Ann:

'My health is much better here than I could have expected, considering the nature of the climate and my imprisonment; and my appetite is so good that I believe it has an intention of revenging me on the governor by occasioning a famine in the island.'[21]

If this was true, and he was not simply trying to avoid causing alarm, then he quickly fell ill again, for in January 1805 he suffered not only from a bilious disorder, but also from the 'constitutional gravelly complaint' which he had first felt ten years before, and from which he subsequently died.[22]

By May 1805, while he was still in the Garden Prison in Port Louis, he gave her a hint of his condition: 'For some time my health has been neither well nor ill, but such a mawkish kind of health as a prisoner, who was not much oppressed with any particular disease, may be supposed to have.'[23] A hint, but not a word of the kidney trouble.

None of these letters contains significant information about his detention that does not appear in the published narrative. Certainly, letters from prisoners were common enough at this time; and to anyone but himself and Ann they would seem quite ordinary.

In the dialogue with Decaen no occasion for correspondence arose between January and August 1805. On 17 August, being advised that a proper—and temperate—application to move out of the prison into the hills would be favourably received, Flinders wrote to Decaen requesting permission to live at the plantation of one Madame D'Arifat, at Wilhems Plains. Six days later he signed his parole:

[20] P.R.O., Adm. 7/707, p. 207.
[21] Flinders to Ann, 31 December 1804. S.L.V., 'Flinders Papers .
[22] Flinders, *Voyage*, vol. II, p. 403.
[23] Flinders to Ann, 15 May 1805. N.M.M. 60/017. FLI/25.

'His Excellency the captain-general De Caen having given me permission to reside at Wilhems Plains, at the habitation of Madame D'Arifat, I do hereby promise, upon my parole of honour, not to go more than the distance of two leagues from the said habitation, without His Excellency's permission; and to conduct myself with that proper degree of reserve, becoming an officer residing in a country with which his nation is at war. I will also answer for the proper conduct of my two servants.'[24]

Henceforth he would live a life of far greater freedom than he had yet known at Mauritius. Under other circumstances, in point of fact, he might have thought his situation luxurious.

By the time he moved, he considered that he had 'taken every step within my power, that had any prospect of obtaining our liberation and that of my books and papers'.[25] He had, in fact, bombarded both India and Europe. In January he had written to both Admiral Rainier and Lord William Bentinck, the latter to solicit interest in the case of two French prisoners whose home was in Mauritius. In March, Admiral Linois had called upon M. de Fleurieu in his behalf.[26] At the same time, a friend, Thomas Pitot, gentleman and merchant at Port Louis, had sent letters to Joseph Lalande, the astronomer; to the Comte de Bougainville, the navigator, and now a Conseiller d'Etat; to M. Chaptal, French Minister of the Interior; and to M. Dupuis, another Conseiller d'Etat.[27] On 15 April three further letters went out: a second to Fleurieu; one to Secretary Marsden at the Admiralty, and a short memorandum, over Decaen's head, to Decrès.[28] Then, only a few weeks before his transfer to Wilhems Plains, Flinders wrote to Admiral Sir Edward Pellew,

[24] Flinders, *Voyage*, vol. II, p. 418. Flinders, his servant, and one lame seaman from the *Cumberland*, also here regarded as a 'servant', were the only prisoners on the island at this time, all others, including Aken, having been taken off in May.

[25] P.R.O., Adm. 7/707, p. 241.

[26] Charles-Pierre Claret, Comte de Fleurieu, astronomer (1758–1810).

[27] Joseph-Jérome Le François de Lalande, astronomer (1732–1807); Louis-Antoine de Bougainville (1729–1811); Jean-Antoine-Claude Chaptal, Comte de Chantaloup (1756–1832); Charles-François Dupuis, savant (1742–1809). A copy of Pitot's letter to Bougainville may be found in P.R.O., Adm. 7/707, Appen. p. xxxviii.

[28] Flinders, *Voyage*, vol. II, p. 446. It is not clear how or why the letter to Decrès was permitted to go out. Doubtless Decaen felt pretty secure.

who had replaced Rainier as Commander-in-Chief. All these letters carried the same message. Each gave a brief account of the *Investigator*'s voyage, of the disaster at Wreck Reef, of the necessity for putting in at Port Louis. Each retailed the confrontation with Decaen, argued the injustice of the detention, his ill health, and the inhumanity of the captivity.

And what was the effect? It was precisely what both Flinders and Decaen wished. For Flinders, the pressure-group thus formed at Paris carried enough weight to bring the case before the Conseil d'Etat, where the Emperor himself would learn the justice of his cause. For Decaen it meant that Napoleon would see how prudently he was served at the Île de France. On 21 March 1806 Bougainville presented the case, and the Emperor made his decision. Magnanimity would cost him nothing. He would approve the liberation of the Capitaine. On 21 March, Decrès signed the following document in quadruplicate:

Le 11 Termidor an 12 [30 July, 1804], Monsieur, j'ai répondu à votre dépêche du 26 Nivose [16 January, 1804], de la même année, No. 27, relativement à la goelette Anglaise le Cumberland, commandée per le Cap^e Flinders, et aux motifs qui vous ont porté à retenir ce capitaine jusqu'à ce que j'aie pu vous faire connaitre les intentions de S. M. Je vous prévenais à cette époque que le Conseil d'Etat venait, sur mon rapport, d'être saisi de la connoissance de la détention dont il s'agit; et je vous transmets aujourd'huy, ci-joint, l'avis de ce Conseil approuvé par l'Empereur et Roi le 11 de ce mois. Vous y verrez que votre conduite est approuvée et que, par un pur sentiment de générosité, le Gouvernement accorde au Captaine Flinders sa liberté et la remise de son bâtiment.

Recevez, Monsieur, l'assurance de ma considération distinguée.

Le ministre de la marine et des colonies
Signé    Decrès.

Pour copie conforme.
Le chef de l'état-major, commandant d'armes,
[Signed]    Monistrol.'[29]

[29] *Ibid.*, p. 460.

The document was scarcely less interesting for what it omitted than for what it contained. To be sure, it saved everyone's face, and was more or less commendable for that. It did indeed convey the approval of Napoleon for Flinders's release. But it was not an order for it. It did not oblige Decaen to do anything forthwith, or even at all. Moreover, while it sanctioned the return of the *Cumberland* to Flinders, it said nothing about the missing volume of the journal. On balance, and certainly in the event, it was a clear-cut victory for Decaen.

When, late in July 1807, the first of the four copies arrived at Mauritius, Flinders naturally read into the document more than was there; and much of his later behaviour was based upon the false concept that Decaen had been directed to release him. But by then, circumstances had changed in the Eastern Seas. The Cape was in British hands; the *guerre de course* against the Company's ships had begun to decline; and blockade and famine were clearly foreseeable to Decaen.

No one in London had yet learned of Napoleon's gracious favour when, on 14 April 1806, Ann wrote to William Marsden at the Admiralty, inquiring whether it might not be possible again to present her husband's case to the French government. Marsden's disposition of the query read : 'Acquaint her with my compliments that no Cartel has yet been agreed upon, but that when it is, there can be no doubt of Captain Flinders being included.'[30]

Nine thousand miles away, the Captain was just then entering upon the immense task of writing a narrative of his voyage since leaving Port Jackson in the *Porpoise*.[31] This document of 406 pages presents a review—but let Flinders say it. In a covering letter to Marsden, which served as Preface, he wrote :

'Sir,

Since my last letter from this island, dated April 13, 1806, my time has been principally employed in forming into a narrative the more remarkable circumstances of my voyage which have occurred since the condemnation of His Majesty's ship the Investigator, late under my command, and which I intended to

[30] P.R.O., Adm. 1/4578. F131.
[31] Adm. 7/707. See footnote 6 of the present chapter.

complete up to the time of its transmission; but the departure of M<sup>r</sup> Larkins, late commander of the Hon. East-India-Company's ship the Warren Hastings,[32] for America, having furnished me with such a conveyance as rarely occurs, I herewith forward to you a copy of the part finished, for the information of my Lords Commissioners.

'The narrative is put into the form of a publication; and were it placed in the hands of a skilful writer, with his corrections of style and arrangement,—such reflexions as the different situations and circumstances would excite in a well-informed mind, and the addition of appropriate comparisons and facts drawn from naval annals, it would probably be of sufficient interest to be laid before the public of all the nations of Europe; and should its publication be judged inconvenient, the narrative will always remain in the hydrographical office, as so much information relating to the Investigator's voyage. My principal intention in writing it, was to give their Lordships a complete knowledge, as far as I was able, of the various circumstances attending my extraordinary imprisonment in the Isle of France, and the steps I have taken, either to obviate its effects to my voyage, or to obtain justice;—And that they might be able to judge, whether the case merits the interference of His Majesty's ministers,—and if so, what steps are best to be taken, the necessary pieces on both sides of the question, are either interwoven in the narrative or joined in an appendix : the justification of my own conduct, I do not disguise, was also one cause which led to its formation and transmission. . . .'

Neither Ann, nor the Lords Commissioners, nor Flinders himself could now do anything to alter the course of events. The few letters the prisoner wrote to the General during 1808 and 1809 indicate that he then had no clue to Decaen's real motive for detaining him longer. Yet, reading a memorandum from Monistrol, now become the town major of Port Louis, he might have—he must have—guessed. This letter reminded Flinders of his parole not to wander too far from the D'Arifat

---

[32] H.C.S. *Warren Hastings*, having fought at Pulo-Aur, had been recently taken by the newly arrived French frigate, *Piémontaise*.

plantation.[33] With the British squadron closing in, Decaen was
taking no chances with the English officer he had once described
to Decrès as 'dangerous'.[34]

One may suppose that Decaen had other matters to concern
him than the case of a single enemy officer. Yet Flinders persisted in suspecting some sinister design, more than likely
imagining Decaen sitting in his house brooding darkly over
nothing else. Indeed, a later scholar has alleged that in this
whole affair, following Napoleon's approval, there actually
existed a secret conspiracy of silence between Decaen and
Decrès.[35] For, as Flinders saw it in 1810, 'It appears pretty
evident that my detention is prolonged to answer the purpose
of some secret intrigues, or perhaps for the purpose of despoiling
me of my discoveries upon the south coast of Australia
(or Austral-Asia) and appropriating them to the voyage of
Monsieur Baudin.'[36]

Possibly so. And it was not unnatural for him to weave the
unjust behaviour of Péron and his equally unjust treatment at
the hands of Decaen into the same tissue. But the trouble with
the argument, what makes it seem slightly pedantic, is that no
such conspiracy was necessary. Lacking a direct order, Decaen
was left free to use his own judgment. He could hold Flinders
as long as he thought necessary, and he could release him when
he saw fit. In fact, he would let the prisoner go when he had
nothing to lose by it, and not until then. Moreover, from all we
know of Decaen, he was a man of character, whose words and
acts could always be taken at face value.[37]

4

The efforts to regain freedom did the prisoner precious little
good. They had to be tried, but as, time after time, they failed,
they only brought him more heartbreak.

[33] Flinders, *Voyage*, vol. II, p. 472.
[34] A. Auzoux, 'L'Arrestation du capitaine Flinders, 1803–1810', *Revue d'histoire
diplomatique*, An. 26 (1912), p. 510.
[35] *Ibid*.
[36] Flinders to J. Franklin, 5 January 1810. S.L.V., 'Flinders Papers'.
[37] See Scott, *Life*, chap. 21 : an excellent short sketch.

Yet there was another side to the ledger. A handful of colonials undertook, despite the risks, to befriend him. They were a small, tightly knit coterie of cultivated people, merchants and planters mostly, but with a difference. Their interests lay in the direction of literature and music. In an age of science they were as eager as anyone to be informed upon the widest range of subjects. Savants in spirit, they joined hands to form the Société d'Émulation which, in a small way, seems to have been patterned after the Institut National. They held regular meetings, subscribed to European journals, and had no hesitation in corresponding with the great and near-great in Paris. Into this little group Flinders was affectionately received. His work, but even more, the quality of his mind, fascinated them. Here was no rough and hearty old sea-dog, but one who, like themselves, could find pleasure in the things of the mind. The kindnesses he received from Thomas Pitot, Charles Desbassayns, and one or two others, could never, and need never be repaid. Their occasional business trips to Bourbon left him depressed, because these people made life easier for him.

On his side, Flinders contributed a small paper or two for the Société; he tutored their children in mathematics; and he paid them the immense compliment of learning to speak their language. It is indeed doubtful whether Matthew Flinders could have survived these years without them.

In the sense that he hoped someday to return to finish his survey of Australia, these were the consuming years. Yet he could not say they were wholly lost, or even unproductive. These were the years when, by his constant, one might almost say compulsive, writing, he earned the sobriquet, 'scholar-navigator'.

As soon as he recovered his bearing books, astronomical observations, and the journal, he set to work, '. . . and this employment served to divert my chagrin, and the indignation which, however useless it might be, I could not but feel at the author of our imprisonment.'[38]

The first fruit of these intensive studies, written when the effects of the scurvy had begun to abate, was a letter to Sir Joseph for the Royal Society, 'Concerning the Difference in the

[38] Flinders, *Voyage*, vol. II, p. 379.

magnetic Needle on Board the Investigator, arising from an alteration in the Direction of the Ship's Head.'[39]

This paper, twelve pages in length, presented the data from, and some tentative conclusions about, tests he had made, principally on the south coast of New Holland in 1802. It will be recalled that magnetic variation, long known to navigators, depends upon the earth's magnetic field, irrespective of the observer; and that deviation arises from local polarisation, that is, the magnetic field of the ship itself.[40] It was to the deviation function, long known, but never before analysed, that he now gave his attention. As early as the excursion to Bass Strait in the *Francis*, 1798, he had noted that several fixes of the same object on shore produced different bearings, and that these bearings could be correlated with the direction of the ship's heading. His curiosity aroused, he repeated the tests in the *Investigator* and verified his first suspicions. He now drew certain inferences:

'1st I suppose the attractive power of the different bodies in a ship, which are capable of affecting the compass, to be collected into something like a focal point or center of gravity, and that this point is nearly in the center of the ship where the shot are deposited, for here the greatest quantity of iron is collected together.

'2d. I suppose this point to be endued with the same kind of attraction as the pole of the hemisphere where the ship is; consequently, in New Holland the south end of the needle would be attracted by it and the north end repelled.

'3d. That the attractive power of this point is sufficiently strong in a ship of war to interfere with the action of the magnetic poles upon a compass placed upon or in the binnacle.'

These were the hypotheses. With proper diffidence, he went on:

'Constant employment upon practice has not allowed me to become much acquainted with theories, but the little information

[39] Royal Society of London, *Phil. Trans.*, vol. 95 (1805), p. 186 sqq.
[40] See chap. 6, footnote 12, above.

I have upon the subject of magnetism has led me to form some notion concerning the cause of these differences . . . I shall leave it to the learned on the subject of magnetism to compare the observations here given with those made by others in different parts of the earth, and to form from them an hypothesis that may embrace the whole of the phenomena : the opinion I have ventured to offer is merely the vague conjecture of one who does not profess to understand the subject.'

Temporary failure of sight in the right eye precluded work on the charts. Then, despite the 'mawkish kind of health' early in 1805, he went to work once again. Not only was this to his purpose, but it was sufficiently exacting to take his mind away from his troubles.[41] The result was that when, on 7 May, Mr Aken secured permission—not being 'dangerous'—to return home, Flinders had some materials to send along :

'Besides a general chart of Terra Australis, showing the whole of my discoveries, examinations and tracks in abridgment, this packet for the Admiralty contained nine sheets upon a scale of four inches to a degree of longitude, and three sheets of particular parts in a larger size; also five chapters of a memoir explanatory of their construction. . . .'[42]

The title of the memoir amounted to an abstract :

'A Memoir explaining the marks used in the Charts of Australia constructed on board His Majestys ship Investigator; and the manner in which the latitude, longitude, and variation of the compass were obtained, corrected, and applied in their construction; With some new facts and additional observations upon these and other nautical subjects connected with Australia.'[43]

The Preface to this document, dated 14 May 1805, presents the author's explanation for not having completed the survey : the rottenness of the *Investigator*, the disaster at Wreck Reef, and his detention at Mauritius. This much the Admiralty already

[41] Where he obtained the quantities of paper and ink he used for all his letter-writing, monographs, and chartwork is far from clear, but presumably he could buy them.          [42] Flinders, *Voyage*, vol. II, p. 411.
[43] P.R.O., Adm. 55/76, appended to vol. II of his 'Journal'. It is a beautifully written memorandum of 102 pages; a model of its kind.

knew. The five chapters sent off with Aken, to which three others were subsequently added, would be of more interest:

I 'Of the restitution of the name Australia, or Terra Australis, to the extensive country which has lately gone under the name of New Holland.'

'New Holland' was the name given the island continent by the Dutch in the seventeenth century. They never claimed any part of their discovery. Then in 1770, Cook had claimed all the land to the east of 135° E. longitude, approximately half of the continent, and called that half 'New South Wales.' Here, then, was a huge geographical entity, one half of which lay still unclaimed, bearing two names. Flinders, having found no strait dividing the continent, felt compelled as a matter of cartographic necessity to give a single name to the continuous whole. His choice of the term 'Australia' seems to have been dictated by a wish to avoid confusion with the ancient, mythical 'Terra Australis Incognita', as well as being a matter of taste. 'Austral-Asia' also occurred to him, but he rejected it as too extreme. His suggestion of 'Australia' was at first set aside by the chart-makers, but presently caught on amongst, of all people, the politicians.[44]

II 'Of the scales upon which the different sheets forming the chart of Australia are constructed; and of the various marks used in describing the coasts, shoals, soundings, tracks, winds, tides, and currents.'

Flinders has usually been credited with the innovation of distinguishing between the day and night tracks of a survey. But he here disclaimed the invention, giving first credit to M. Beautemps-Beaupré, geographer under Bruni D'Entrecasteaux, whose charts he had examined in London before he sailed.[45]

III 'Of the manner in which the latitudes of places, in the chart of Australia, were usually obtained; with some observations upon meridional altitudes in general.'

---

[44] See *Voyage*, vol. i, p. ii sqq. Also my article, 'The Naming of Australia: a Revised View', *Geographical Journal*, vol. 124, pt. 4 (Dec. 1958), p. 514 sqq.
[45] P.R.O., Adm. 55/76, 'Memoir', p. 4.

IV 'Of the observations by which certain places on the coasts of Australia were fixed in longitude; with the rates of the time-keepers, and the approximations used to obtain the longitudes of the intermediate parts more correctly.'

When we consider that in 1801 the chronometer was thought by many to be still in its infancy, and by one or two to be totally unreliable, if not actually deceptive, the importance of this chapter can scarcely be overvalued. Flinders's understanding of the need for accuracy, and his impeccable standards of performance, resulted in a vast number of fixes that have, since his time, been merely refined, not really corrected.

V 'Of the variation of the compass used in constructing the charts of Australia, and of the means taken to apply it correctly; also, an account of the variation all round the coasts, and of the particular magnetism of Pier Head upon the east coast; with remarks upon the differences usually found in the variations observed on ship board.'

The material presented in this fifth chapter appeared *mutatis mutandis* in the *Philosophical Transactions* of the Royal Society cited above.

Evidently this was as far as Flinders had got when Aken's departure became imminent. The last three chapters, on the navigation of Bass Strait, on Torres Strait, and on the barometer, were added within a year, and sent off to the Admiralty where they were joined, luckily as these things go, to the first five. Actually, the eighth chapter, 'Observations upon the marine barometer, made on board His Majestys ship Investigator during the examination of the coasts of New Holland and New South Wales in 1801, 2, and 3,' appeared verbatim as a letter to Banks, written on 19 August 1805, and read to the Royal Society on 27 March 1806.[46]

He had collected data on the changes of the glass as it was affected by both land and sea breezes close inshore. Not suspecting convection, he assigned the cause to topography. He imagined blocks of air overriding one another in succession as they approached the land as a sea-breeze, thus producing by

[46] Royal Society of London, *Phil. Trans.*, vol. 96 (1806), p. 239 sqq.

compression a pressure gradient high at the surface and lower aloft. In a land breeze the reverse occurred, producing a lower pressure at the surface of the sea. It was ingenious; but it was wrong because he had no simultaneous data from the land. The point to be made, however, is not that it was wrong, but that he did it at all. Here was a sailor, making a contribution to science by using his intellect. A new phenomenon.

With the departure of Captain Larkins early in August 1806, Flinders lapsed into a protracted period of depression evidently so acute that, as he later described it, it 'might have proved fatal, had I not sought by constant occupation to force my mind from a subject so destructive to its repose. . . .' Bitterly he added, 'such an end to my detention would have given too much pleasure to the captain-general, and from a sort of perversity in human nature, this conviction even brought its share of support.'[47]

Such was the depth of his hatred. Yet no man can hate all the time, and Flinders was further from breaking down than even he thought. He resumed work on his charts. The unfinished Memoir, sent off with Aken, he now completed.[48] The smooth copy of the journal, volumes I and II, dates from this period. For amusement he continued his studies of French. 'But what assisted most in dispelling this melancholy, was a packet of letters from England, bringing intelligence of my family and friends; and the satisfactory information that Mr Aken had safely reached London, with all the charts, journals, letters and instruments committed to his charge.'[49]

At least Ann had still been alive and safe a few months ago. But if his work and the letters from home assuaged his bitterness, it was only for a time. 1807 brought him, as we have seen, to the conviction that not even Napoleon had the power to release him. And when, in July 1808, he learned of Péron's *Voyage de Découvertes*, appropriating to France the discoveries he himself had made—'Terre Napoléon,' 'Golfe Bonaparte,' 'Golfe Josephine', etc., etc.—he saw his fate in an even more

[47] Flinders, *Voyage*, vol. II, p. 456.
[48] That is, the chapters on Bass Strait, Torres Strait, and the barometer, referred to above.
[49] Flinders, *Voyage*, vol. II, p. 457.

sinister light.[50] Once again he had to seek ways to protect his sanity.

By 1808 little professional work remained. That mine was nearly exhausted. So, he turned his efforts to applied mathematics. The result was an unpublished text, 'Spheric Trigonometry, followed by Problems of the Sphere, and various other particulars useful to Navigation. Isle of France 1808 and 9.'[51] This is an elegant piece of work of 106 pages, illustrated with diagrams of great beauty and accuracy. The first thirty-six pages are devoted to pure mathematics: Spheric Geometry, and Spheric Trigonometry. Then follows a section on cartographic projection; a chapter on 'Various methods of finding the latitude;' and another on the longitude. The work closes with four short sections: 'Of the dip, or depression of the horizon;' 'To estimate distances at Sea;' 'To estimate distance by the motion of Sound;' and, 'To estimate the course steered by a ship seen at a distance.'

When he began it there is no way of telling. By 27 June 1808, he had written thirty pages; by 5 July, thirty-nine; by 31 August, sixty-five. Whether he then laid it aside, or simply went more slowly, is not clear.[52] The last page bears the date Nov. 2, 1809, perhaps a year and a half after the beginning. It would be a fair guess that Monistrol's admonition to stay within the boundaries of his parole put him back to work.

In the last professional work he did at Mauritius, he returned to the subject of magnetism. The resulting paper, of twenty-seven pages, 'Notes upon the Magnetism of the Earth, and of Ships,' is in two parts, the first dealing with the change of variation which takes place on ship board, on altering the direction of the ship's head; the second with the 'position of the magnetic poles of the earth.' Again and again one is struck in reading Flinders's work with the impeccability of his reasoning, which in turn is reflected in the cleanness of his manuscripts.

[50] See Chapter 6 above. J. H. Rose, writing of Napoleon's determination to crush the British Empire, offers the publication of Péron's claims over the official imprimatur as evidence. 'Napoleon I', *Enc. Brit.* (11th edn.).

[51] N.M.M. 60/017. FLI/7.

[52] His narrative says that in 1809 he occupied some time in constructing a chart of Madagascar, 'reading various French authors', and 'mathematical studies'. *Voyage*, vol. II, p. 469.

In both respects this paper is among the best. As to substance, whereas in 1804 he had disclaimed any competence in the theory of magnetism, he had by now provided himself with enough mathematics to suggest the correct theory. At the conclusion he wrote :

'I purpose, if it shall please God that I may be liberated from this imprisonment in the Isle of France, to take the first opportunity, of making all the necessary experiments for ascertaining the magnetism of ships as far as can be useful to the accuracy of navigation; as also of making such as may enable me to determine the points on the surface of the earth to which the needle of the compass is directed [i.e., the magnetic poles], and also the places of the poles within the earth which affect the dipping needle; what I have done here being only preparatory to what I propose to do hereafter, when I shall have been able to collect proper materials.'[53]

Hence the experiments in the fleet during 1812-13.

But one other bit of writing remains to be noticed : 'A Biographical Tribute to the memory of Trim,' dated Île de France, December 1809.[54] Trim was a tomcat, quite evidently the chief mascot of H.M. Sloop *Investigator*. Not quite pure fancy, this little story is yet so whimsical, so charming, and so uncharacteristic of Flinders's other writings, that it can only be described as a 'sport'.

It begins, 'I can never speak of cats without a sentiment of regret for my poor Trim, the favourite of all our ship's company on the Spyall.' It ends with an epitaph. And in between we learn that Trim was an expert navigator; that he was equally adept at reefing a topsail; and that he was an avid gourmet, not hesitating an instant to snatch a morsel from the fork of an unwary mid at table in the gunroom. He circumnavigated the globe, earning his keep the while guarding the breadroom against unwanted vermin. After a wonderful escape from death at Wreck Reef, he followed his master into captivity at the Île de France. There he had the misfortune, or so his master thought,

[53] N.M.M. 60/017. FLI/7.
[54] N.M.M. 60/017. FLI/11.

of straying into the clutches of some hungry slaves, who stewed him down for their dinner.

No critic would look twice at this contrived little essay; and from his point of view the critic would be right. Yet it shows for the first and only time an unmistakable boyish warmth in the man, a warmth that comes as a pleasant surprise at this stage of Flinders's life.

5

From the mere fact that he wrote about his cat it is obvious enough that by the beginning of 1810, he had exhausted all other avenues for fruitful work. With regard to magnetism he had said as much, though he spent some little time making revisions. Where he might have turned next is anyone's guess. But he never had to decide, because the British squadron now began to close the vice.[55]

A letter to Ann in January shows clearly that he had at that time no idea when, if ever, he would go free. He had not heard from home since 1806, and was now, in fact, suggesting that she apply to the British government for a safe-conduct to go out to Mauritius—Decaen having already said he would have no objection.[56]

Then, on 13 March, the British commissary of prisoners, a Mr Hope, wrote to inform the captain that General Decaen had at last agreed to liberate him. The word was received with scepticism. But on 28 March, Colonel Monistrol wrote briefly:

'His Excellency the captain-general charges me to have the honour of informing you, that he authorises you to return to your country in the cartel Harriet, on condition of not serving in a hostile manner against France or its allies during the course of the present war . . . The cartel is to sail on Saturday next (31st.)'[57]

---

[55] For a recent excellent study of British operations against Mauritius see, C. N. Parkinson, *War in the Eastern Seas, 1793–1815* (London, 1954), chap. 19.
[56] Flinders to Ann, 13 January 1810. N.M.M. 60/017. FLI/25.
[57] Flinders, *Voyage*, vol. II, p. 479.

This was more encouraging. But as he said his farewells at Wilhems Plains, and made his way to M. Pitot's house in Port Louis, he still had dry land under his feet. Moreover, the cartel was not the *Cumberland*, as Decrès had promised in his dispatch of 1806. Nor had anything been said about that third volume of his journal.

He need not have hurried. So long as British cruisers kept close watch, no ships, not even a cartel, would leave Mauritius. April passed.

On 2 May came another commando-type raid, this time on the south coast of Mauritius, where a French packet boat was cut out, and the guns of a fort were spiked.[58] Six days later Decaen ordered all British officers to leave the shore and embark in the cartel. There they would be safely penned up. Still the cartel remained in port, this time at the behest of local merchants who feared that, once at sea, these ex-prisoners would gladly betray expected arrivals from France to the cruisers.

Flinders signed his parole on 7 June.[59] On 13 June he received back his sword, the *Harriet* got under way, and at sunset '. . . after a captivity of six years, five months and twenty-seven days, I at length had the inexpressible pleasure of being out of the reach of general De Caen.'[60]

[58] 'This *sullying of the French territory* [italics F's] produced a fulminating proclamation from general De Caen, nearly similar in terms to that of the emperor Napoléon after the descent at Walcheren.' *Ibid.*, p. 481.
[59] 'I undersigned, captain in His Britannic Majesty's navy, having obtained leave of His Excellency the captain-general to return to my country by the way of Bengal, promise on my word of honour not to act in any service which might be considered as directly or indirectly hostile to France or its allies, during the course of the present war.' *Ibid.*, p. 482, and N.M.M. 60/017. FLI/3.
[60] Flinders, *Voyage*, vol. ii, p. 485. Upon his return to France, and his acquittal of misconduct in the surrender of the Île de France, Decaen received command of the Army of Catalonia. He later commanded the Army of Holland, and the Tenth Division. For his part in the events leading up to the Battle of Waterloo he was committed to prison for a period of five months. In 1814 Decaen was named Chevalier of the Order of St Louis, and received the grand cordon of the Legion of Honour. He died of cholera in 1832.

# PART IV

# The Final Period

## 1810–1814

# CHAPTER FOURTEEN

# Odysseus in London

## 1810–1814

### 1

On 24 September 1810 the Secretary of the Admiralty, Sir John Barrow,[1] thoughtfully dropped a note to Banks:

'In our Bulletin of Intelligence there is one part which I am sure will give you particular satisfaction, the release of poor Flinders. Mr. Yorke[2] however has done very handsomely by sending a Minute that on his arrival in England he is to have a Post Commission; this will make up in some degree for his sufferings & unwarranted confinement. . . .'[3]

Banks, then down at Revesby, wrote immediately to Ann, promising she should see her beloved husband very soon.[4] As these exchanges passed, Flinders himself was out in the Atlantic, only a month away from home.

On the very day the *Harriet* came out of Port Louis, the *Otter*, sloop of war, cruising with the British squadron just outside the harbour, had been ordered to the Cape. Flinders, hoping to avoid going all the way to Bengal in the *Harriet*, requested a passage in the *Otter*, and was forthwith transferred. The sloop took her departure the following morning, and after a run of 2,900 miles in twenty-six days, arrived at False Bay on 10 July.

---

[1] Sir John Barrow, Bart., F.R.S. (1764–1848).
[2] Charles Philip Yorke (1764–1834), First Lord of the Admiralty under Perceval.
[3] B.M., Add. MSS. 32439. 330. Also Yorke's memorandum, 24 September 1810. P.R.O., Adm. 1/1807. F195.
[4] Banks to Ann, 25 September 1810. N.M.M. 60/017. FLI/26.

Flinders promptly reported his presence to Vice-Admiral Bertie,[5] and requested permission to embark in the next ship for England. Bertie, however, had other ideas. Within a few weeks he would be off to Mauritius. He needed all the intelligence about the place he could get, and Flinders was just the man. To his infinite disappointment, Flinders watched a packet from India standing out of the bay for England just as he reached the Admiral's door, and there was nothing he could do about it. Although he was well and frequently received in all the best houses, the next seven weeks were, as he said, 'a tedious time'. At last, having told Bertie all he could within the limits of his parole, he found a berth in the *Olympia* cutter, which left the Cape on 28 August. A fast sailer, the cutter made St Helena in fifteen days, on 11 September, and departed again the same day. Flinders arrived at Spithead on 24 October, exactly four months and ten days after leaving Port Louis.[6]

Next morning the London coach carried him to the Norfolk Hotel where he took temporary lodging. Evidently he went at once to the Admiralty, and there had a talk with both the First Lord and Secretary Barrow. At least so he wrote to Banks that evening after beginning, 'I have the happiness to inform you of my arrival. . . .'[7]

John Elder, Flinders's servant in the *Investigator*, had left Mauritius in July 1807, returning to England by way of Baltimore. On his arrival he wrote to Ann saying, among other things, that the Captain 'does not look so well as he did by a great deal, his read [*sic*] cheeks is certainly gone, and his hair is very white. . . .'[8] With that image fixed in her mind, she was not unprepared for the change. When and where they met is not recorded. She probably came up to London soon after she learned of the release from Sir Joseph, and left her address with her husband's agent, Standert, at Clifford's Inn. Of the

---

[5] Vice-Admiral Sir Albemarle Bertie (1755–1824.)

[6] And 'absent from England nine years and three months, and nearly four years and a half without intelligence from any part of my connexions.' Flinders, *Voyage*, vol. II, p. 494. On the passage the *Olympia* took a prize, the *Atalante*, for which Flinders later received a share of over £40.

[7] Flinders to Banks, 25 October 1810. B.M., Add. MSS. 32439. 332 sq.

[8] Elder to Ann, 11 February 1808. N.M.M. 60/017. FLI/28. She had known Matthew was getting grey from a letter he wrote her early in 1803.

reunion all we can learn—or would wish to know—comes from
Lieutenant John Franklin who was present, at least for a
moment. Writing to Flinders on 1 November, he apologised
for having left him so abruptly several days before : 'I felt so
sensibly the affecting scene of your meeting Mrs Flinders that
I could not have remained any longer in the room under any
consideration; nor could I be persuaded to call a second time
that day.'[9]

It was the First Lord himself who announced to Flinders his
promotion to Post Captain of the *Ramillies*.[10] The appointment
was a great relief and something he had longed for. Naturally
enough he wanted the earliest possible date for his commission;
but he now found it could take effect only from 7 May 1810, the
earliest date compatible with both Flinders's release into the
*Harriet* and Yorke's accession, on 1 May, to the Board of
Admiralty. But had not Spencer promised him the promotion on
his return? Why then could the date not be set for some day in
1804 'when it may be supposed I might have arrived, had not
my unjust detention taken place ?'[11] Such an arrangement would
have placed him well up the list of Post Captains. Had he not,
he argued, done a great deal of work on the voyage while he
lay prisoner at Mauritius? How much more must he suffer on
Decaen's account? But there was nothing further Yorke could
do. Earl Spencer no longer held office; Yorke could not legally
date any documents prior to his own tenure; and only His
Majesty in Council could overcome the difficulty. Unfortunately,
George III was now incurably insane.

Writing to Barrow on 28 October, Banks thought the date
of 7 May 'liberal in the extreme'.[12] In spite of much effort on
Flinders's part, nothing more was done. The Prince Regent
concurred with the First Lord, even if an old friend of *Reliance*
days, Captain Kent, did not, and deplored the fact of 'our

---

[9] J. Franklin to Flinders, 1 November 1810. N.M.M. 60/017. FLI/1.
[10] See N.M.M. 60/017. FLI/3 and FLI/5. The *Ramillies* (74) had been taken
out of commission in 1808. She recommissioned in 1812 and served as a coastguard
vessel stationed in the Downs.
[11] Flinders to Banks, 25 October 1810. B.M., Add. MSS. 32439. 332.
[12] Royal Society of London, 'Miscellaneous MSS.' 6. 71. Having recently lost
his old friend Jonas Dryander, Banks was in low spirits, and in no mood to press
the Admiralty.

devoted Service being in the hands of a set of Borough-Mongers'.[13]

Accordingly, Flinders went on half-pay as commanding officer of a sloop of war, at precisely four shillings per day, from 18 December 1803 forward, and remained so until his death.

The pace of life quickened. There was business to be transacted; threads of old acquaintanceships must be picked up; work on the voyage must begin. By 5 November he had leased rooms at 16 King Street, Soho, and settled down.

The first thing was to get finances into some sort of order. Not that they were in a muddle, but after so long a time away he had some debits and credits to his name. Disappointed in his bid for back-dating the Post Captaincy, he returned to the Admiralty with a request for compensation pay for the servants allowed him in the *Investigator*.[14] At the same time the Navy Board had some questions to ask him about his Purser's accounts. He also wrote to the Court of Directors of the East India Company, reminding them of their undertaking of March 1801; stating that his work on their behalf had been at least partially completed; informing them that the Admiralty now proposed publishing his results; and hoping they would allow him to draw the remainder of his table-money.[15]

The results of these efforts were agreeable enough. Over and above his half-pay, the Admiralty awarded him a lump sum of £500 in lieu of compensation for servants' allowance, payable at once.[16] The Court of Directors, after referring the matter to their Committee of Correspondence, ordered a warrant to be made out for the remaining £600[17]. By letter of 9 December,

[13] W. Kent to Flinders, 17 September 1811. N.M.M. 60/017. FLI/1. As late as 21 May 1811 Flinders was still in correspondence with William Wilberforce on the matter, but Yorke was adamant, refusing to listen to argument. See S.L.V., 'Flinders Papers', and N.M.M. 60/017. FLI/1.

[14] Flinders to Admiralty, 15 November 1810. P.R.O., Adm. 1/1807. F224 sqq.

[15] I.O., East India Company, Court of Directors, 'Miscellaneous Letters Received', No. 121, f. 60–60b.

[16] See subscript to his letter of 15 November 1810.

[17] See I.O., East India Company, Committee of Correspondence, 'Correspondence Reports', No. 35, p. 224 (21 November 1810); Court Minutes, No. 119. p. 1040 (21 November 1810); Committee of Correspondence, Minutes, No. 3, p. 96 (21 November 1810); and Court of Directors, 'Miscellanies', No. 49, p. 658 (22 November 1810).

Flinders notified Brown, Bauer, and Westall that each of them might draw £50 directly and the four gunroom officers that they would each have £37 10. These disbursements left £300 for the Commander.[18]

Here the East India Company behaved on the whole rather more handsomely than the Admiralty. Without conversation they paid up quickly and in full. But with the Admiralty, to his everlasting annoyance, Flinders immediately became enmeshed in a tangle of bureaucratic red-tape. To be sure his case was unique, and the principal problem at Whitehall, top to bottom, seems to have been the fear of creating a precedent, a failing common to all functionaries who lack both authority and imagination (and to some who have authority). Having quarrelled over the date of his promotion, they now haggled over a few pounds' worth of sugar and wine used for the sick during the voyage, and wrote tiresome memoranda regarding the Purser's books which had in fact been lost at Wreck Reef Bank. After that matter died down, Flinders had even to write requesting his full pay as Lieutenant of the *Investigator*—at four shillings a day—for twenty-two days, 16 January to 16 February 1801! And in every instance the time of the First Lord himself was pre-empted by the bookkeepers to attend to these grave questions.

Thus passed the autumn of 1810. On 23 November Matthew and Ann left London for a six-weeks' holiday in Lincolnshire.[19]

2

It is necessary at this juncture to interrupt the day-by-day chronicle in order to deal fully with the writing of *A Voyage to Terra Australis*. The task occupied him from this moment nearly to the day he died.

The fifth article of the Admiralty's engagement with the scientists read in part as follows:

[18] B.M., Add. MSS. 32439. 346.
[19] With all the relatives about him it was an ideal time and place for him to work up the Franklin and Flinders genealogy, which he did in December. S.L.V., 'Flinders Papers'.

'In order, however, to encourage the persons engaged in this undertaking to exert themselves to the utmost in accomplishing the object of their mission, their Lordships hereby declare, that if the information collected during the voyage is deemed of sufficient importance, it is their Lordships intention to cause it to be published in the form of a narrative, drawn up by the Commander, on a plan similar to that pursued in the publication of captain Cooks voyages. . . .[20]

'. . . drawn up by the Commander. . . .'

Going round to the Admiralty rooms on 7 November he was told by Sir Joseph Yorke,[21] one of the Lords of the Admiralty, and therefore reasonably influential, that at one time it was planned that 'some literary man' should write the narrative, but that this idea had now been abandoned in favour of the original.[22] Immediately after the holidays Banks set the project going in a letter to Secretary Barrow. After referring to the 1801 engagement, he begged leave 'to offer to their Lordships, in case they stand in need of it, the same Superintendence in the management of Engravers, Draughtsmen &c. &c. as I had the honour to execute under the direction of the then Board of Admiralty, in the Publication of the third Voyage of Capt. Cook. It will give me great pleasure,' he added, 'if on this occasion I find myself able to be useful to their Lordships.'[23]

In all such matters the Admiralty continued to lean upon the goodwill of an unpaid expert from outside the naval establishment. Acknowledging receipt of the letter, Barrow extended their Lordships' thanks for Banks's offer, 'of the Value of which my Lords are too sensible not to accept of it with pleasure and satisfaction'. Their Lordships did indeed consider the information collected to be 'of sufficient importance to be laid before the Public in the form of a narrative, to be drawn up by Captain Flinders'; and they directed Barrow to turn over all sketches, charts, journals and other necessary manuscripts at the Admiralty, adding that 'the drawings and engravings shall be

[20] Flinders, 'Journal', vol. I, p. 21. See also Chapter 4 above.
[21] Charles Philip Yorke's brother, an Admiral (1768–1831).
[22] S.L.V., 'Flinders Papers'.
[23] Banks to Barrow, 13 January 1811. P.R.O., Adm. 1/4382. B1120.

prepared at the Public expence, and the paper, printing, &c. paid for out of the proceeds of the Work'.[24]

It was, of course, made clear to Flinders that the writing of the volumes was his responsibility, in exchange for which he or his heirs were to own all copies printed, subject to a commission for the bookseller. The profits or losses became Flinders's personal risk.

From this time forward, then, all thought of returning to Australia to complete the survey was laid aside, all other professional activity forgotten, and only the most pressing social engagements accepted.

The materials with which he had to work included, for an Introduction, his own collection of travels and voyages, supplemented as necessary by Banks's extensive library and certain volumes in the British Museum; for the running text, the fair copy of his Journal, volumes I and II, and the several memoirs he had sent to the Admiralty from Mauritius;[25] for numerical data, his logs and bearing books; for embellishment the drawings of Bauer and Westall; and for the botanical matter the work of Robert Brown.

The job of designing the work as a whole fell to Flinders, presumably with Sir Joseph's advice. First in order came a historical introduction, an immense monograph of 80,000 words. The remainder of the first volume dealt exclusively with the journey out to Cape Leeuwin and the first leg of the survey, along the south coast. This section was organised under the heading, Book One, and it closed with an appendix on observations for the longitude along the south coast. Book Two, beginning the second volume, took in the east and north coasts, and the return from Timor to Port Jackson. Up to this point the work comprised a practical guide, a 'coast pilot', so to speak, for the navigator who might come after him. When he decided to include Book Three, dealing chiefly, if not entirely, with his detention at Mauritius, is not easy to determine. Nor is it easy to see why he did so. The tale of his misfortunes, useful at best as propaganda against the French, was quite irrelevant to the survey of New Holland. Adding nothing of practical benefit to

[24] Barrow to Banks, 15 January 1811. P.R.O., Adm. 2/899.
[25] Principally Adm. 7/707 and Adm. 55/76.

mariners, it merely encumbered the book for convenient use. Had he had the third volume of his Journal in hand, he might easily have concluded the narrative with his arrival at Port Louis.[26] But imprisonment had been too desperate an affair. Try as he would he could never expunge the bitterness of it from his mind.

Volume Two would end with three appendices: the first, a discussion of his observations for the longitude along the east and north coasts; the second, a final statement on compass deviation; the last, a study by Brown on the taxonomy and distribution of plants collected during the voyage.

So much for general design. In the execution of it Flinders played two parts, historian and analyst. Arduous as indeed it was, the writing of a running text of 400,000 words cannot have been the most intellectually taxing part of the work. With respect to the Introduction, he was thoroughly familiar with the voyages that had preceded him. Besides, he himself had done a fair share of the original work. As for the part played by the *Investigator*, he had already written that in his daily journal. For the most part he had only to make a polished transcription.

It was the survey data he had collected that offered difficulty; and since the accuracy of his charts depended wholly upon the accuracy of the data, the figures had to be no less than perfect. Unfortunately the data were far from reliable, and in not one,

[26] As for the third volume of the Journal, it was said at the time that Decaen still retained it to provide justification for his detention of Flinders; or to put it another way, to prevent Flinders depriving him of that justification. Decaen certainly carried it back to France, and no amount of effort by the British could retrieve it. On 1 May 1811 the Admiralty Secretary wrote to the Transport Board requesting them to apply to the French government for it. (P.R.O., Adm. 2/665.) Two days later the Secretary sent over to the same Board a copy of a letter from Vice-Admiral Bertie on the subject. Bertie, entirely familiar with the matter through conversations with Flinders at the Cape, had himself searched the Engineer's office at Port Louis for the book, and finding nothing, filed a protest with General Abercrombie against Decaen's being allowed to take it with him. (P.R.O., Adm. 2/665 and Adm. 1/583.) As of 15 July 1811, the Transport Board reported that the volume had not yet arrived in Paris. (See P.R.O., Adm. 12/Ind. 4900.) We next hear of the matter in a letter from Decrès to Rosily, Directeur Général du Depôt de la Marine, transmitting the volume to Rosily, and asking him to examine it and make extracts before sending it away. (Decrès to François-Étienne, Comte de Rosily-Mesros [1748–1832], 10 January 1814 [Service Hydrographique de le Marine, Cn. 102, no. 35].) But 1814 was too late. When it actually arrived at the British Admiralty is not known. The volume was finally accessioned at the Public Record Office on 29 January 1910.

but two respects. In the first place, as a precaution, Flinders's observations for the longitude—the positions of the moon east or west of the sun—were checked against solar observations taken at the same time at Greenwich. To everyone's astonishment, it was soon found that the volumes of the *Nautical Almanac* Flinders had used differed so radically in their predictions with the Greenwich observations as to render Flinders's data useless. To remedy this defect, the Board of Longitude in 1811 set John Crosley, formerly Astronomer to the voyage, and Lieutenant Samuel Flinders to work recomputing the data. Hence a considerable and unexpected delay.

3

This was bad enough. But it was not all. We have seen how much work and thought Flinders had poured into the problem of compass deviation, and how, while he was still at Mauritius, he hoped some day to perform the necessary experiments on the subject. That time had now come.

These experiments must not be thought of as in any way separable from the publication of the *Voyage*. Their effects might well reach far beyond into the future; but the fact is they were undertaken to answer the immediate needs of practical cartography.

Observed differences in compass bearings up to as much as seven degrees had cropped up time and again during the voyage. Flinders's contribution lies chiefly in his discernment first, that they did so according to a pattern—the parameters being the ship's heading and the latitude—and second, of the nature and extent of that pattern. Early in April 1812, therefore, he wrote to the Admiralty suggesting the need for confirming these anomalies by experiment with selected vessels in home waters.[27] His proposals were quickly approved, and by 20 April he was lodged in the Fountain Inn at Sheerness, prepared to proceed. A month later he was at Portsea for further work.[28] And so it

[27] Flinders to Admiralty, 13 April 1812. N.M.M. 60/017. FLI/7.
[28] See his letters to Ann, various dates, N.M.M. 60/017. FLI/25. Also, P.R.O., Adm. 1/1200. A1193.

went until significant data had accumulated from six ships at those yards as well as at Plymouth and out in the Channel. He used the month of June in writing up his findings, which he filed on 27 June in a forty-five-page monograph entitled, 'An Account of some experiments to ascertain the effects produced on the Compass, by the attractive power in ships; with the modes by which they may be obviated. . . .'[29] The Lords Commissioners referred the paper directly to Banks.[30] Sir Joseph, notoriously unschooled in these matters, particularly mathematics, solicited the opinion of his close friend, the geographer, Major Rennell.[31] Rennell reported back that in his experience he had never noted any such anomaly in the compass, and that in any case the experiments were on the whole inconclusive. Flinders's rebuttal[32] was so convincing that Sir Joseph not only adopted his views in spite of Rennell's remarks, but strongly advised the Admiralty to press ahead with the studies. 'There seems,' he wrote, 'to be no question but that Capt. Flinders has made out his case. . . .'[33] By 26 August the new evidence had been reduced to terms suitable for the use of other navigators and set forth in a short memorandum, 'Magnetism of Ships' (see Appendix B).[34] This document was referred to the Admiralty Hydrogapher, Captain Hurd, who, after studying it advised the Board to circularise it throughout the Navy.[35] By 1 October Flinders could write to Banks that the circular had been printed and sent out, and that he had given a copy of it to the East India Company for their information.[36]

Slowly but surely Flinders's correction for the vertical component in the earth's magnetic field became standard equipment on all ships throughout the world. '*Take a strong bar of old iron* [italics mine] *of such length, as that, when one end is let into the deck, the other end will be nearly upon a level with the compass card.* . . .'[37]

---

[29] N.M.M. 60/017. FLI/7; P.R.O., Adm. 1/1809.
[30] Admiralty to Banks, 29 July 1812. B.M., Add. MSS. 32439. 353.
[31] James Rennell, F.R.S. (1742–1830), surveyor of India.
[32] B.M., Add. MSS. 32439. 358.      [33] P.R.O., Adm. 1/4382. B775.
[34] P.R.O., Adm. 1/1809. F178.      [35] *Ibid.*
[36] Flinders to Banks, 1 October 1812. B.M., Add. MSS. 32439. 368.
[37] N.M.M. 60/017. FLI/7, at p. 38 of the 'Account'. Later work by Professor Barlow confirmed Flinders's findings, but added nothing of lasting importance. See Commander W. E. May, 'History of the Magnetic Compass', *Mariner's*

4

These and other minor difficulties were, then, the reasons why the charts could not be turned over to Aaron Arrowsmith for engraving before 1813.

With Robert Brown the case was quite different. In 1810, having severed all connection with the Army, on the death of Jonas Dryander, Brown became Librarian to Sir Joseph Banks. This position allowed, indeed obliged him to devote his full time to botanical scholarship. He was eminently fitted for it. During his four years in Australia he had collected upwards of 3,900 species of plants. Adding to these the number collected by Banks and others before him, the number of known species indigenous to Australia had risen to 4,200. Of these he had described nearly 2,000 in his great unfinished *Prodromus Florae Novae Hollandiae*, published in 1810.[38] Now, as an appendix to Flinders's *Voyage*, he described in detail forty of the 120 orders of plants known to exist there. These forty comprised some 2,500 species, such as 'either contribute largely to form the mass or the striking peculiarities of the Australian vegetation . . .'.[39]

Under Banks's guidance, preparations for illustrating the narrative had begun as early as 1809, when he suggested to Westall that he begin making oil paintings from his sketches. The scenes to be painted had—of course—been selected by Sir Joseph. If he left the execution to Westall, we may at least wonder whether Banks might not occasionally have encouraged the artist to emphasise the flora he always set in his foregrounds. An exhibition of several of these paintings earned Westall election as an Associate of the Royal Academy.[40]

Ferdinand Bauer, too, had already been at his easel by the

*Mirror*, vol. 38, no. 3 (Aug. 1952), p. 218. The Flinders Bar survived even Lord Kelvin's sweeping genius.

[38] Stung by critics for his use of Latin, Brown never published either the general preface, or the first 144 pages of the text. Its merit lies not merely in the addition of so many new species, but also in his adoption of Jussieu's system of plant classification according to natural orders.               [39] Flinders, *Voyage*, vol. II, p. 540.

[40] To those who had the privilege of seeing the Westall paintings and sketches on exhibition at the Qantas Gallery in London, 1962, this honour should come as

time Flinders arrived back home. The combined work of Brown and Bauer, Art in the service of Science, was closest of all to Banks's heart. Not that he knowingly favoured Bauer over Westall, or even Brown over Flinders. It was merely that here his interest flowed most freely and deeply. Bauer's *Illustrationes Florae Novae Hollandiae* appeared in 1813; and ten botanical sketches from his portfolio of over 1,500 were selected by Banks for Flinders's *Voyage*.

By 1 October 1812, the first volume of the narrative, back from his 'literary friends' who had polished it, was nearly ready for the printer; and the second volume had been roughed out. Though far from finished, the work was entering the production stage. Decisions had to be made, and here we see Sir Joseph watching with all that attention and affection of a mother for her child. Engagement of printer and publisher was no problem. The printing would be done by W. Bulmer & Co., Cleveland Row, printers to the Royal Society since 1800. G. and W. Nicol, Booksellers to His Majesty—and to the Royal Society since 1802—would market the work. Banks was not P.R.S. for nothing.

The format would be two volumes, folio, of running text, set in 12-point Baskerville, the same as the *Philosophical Transactions*. Nine of Westall's illustrations would be bound in as appropriate. In addition, there would be an atlas of sixteen charts, two plates of coastal profiles, and the ten botanical drawings. The atlas would be issued in two sizes, 'Imperial' of 69 cm., for the use of navigators at sea, and 'Small', of 48 cm. Binding should be in the usual light blue boards with off-white spine.

The next step was the selection of engravers for Westall's and Bauer's paintings. In the case of Westall's work, seven different artists were employed;[41] for Bauer's at least three.[42] The arrangement was that both artist and engraver should be

no surprise. One is struck by three qualities: the effect of distance, e.g. Entrance of Port Lincoln; the atmospheric luminescence, as in the View of Wreck-Reef Bank; and his attention to detail in the View of Murray Islands, with the natives offering to barter. Professor Bernard Smith's monograph on Westall, in *Drawings by William Westall* (London, 1962), is the best commentary. In fairness to Banks it should be said that Flinders and Westall conferred on the selection of plates for the narrative.
[41] J. Byrne, W. Finden, S. Middiman, I. Pye, J. Pye, L. Scott, and W. Woolnoth.
[42] Elizabeth Byrne, I. Pye, and F. Sansom.

paid a negotiated price for each item selected. Thus, for instance, Westall's twenty-eight coastal profiles brought him thirty guineas, and his sketch of Murray Islands, twenty. Engravings commanded prices ranging from forty to fifty guineas, bringing the cost of each published plate to somewhere between sixty and seventy guineas. Once an engraving was chosen, artist and engraver simply walked down to the Admiralty with a letter from Banks, and collected their money.[43]

With the completion of the last of the sixteen charts, in June 1814, Banks submitted a requisition for £940, payable to Aaron Arrowsmith. At the same time he apologetically explained that the expenses to government, although higher than the sum originally intended, were in his view not unreasonable, the publication being, as he put it, 'rather deficient than otherwise in decoration when compared to similar voyages published under similar protection'. [44]

Flinders's diary for 20 May 1814 records : 'Did a little today in examining for Errata and correcting proof copy of the preface; but it was very little, and ill done.'[45] But also that day he wrote his simple dedication. Instead of obliging Admiral Bligh who had had the brass to ask him for it,[46] Flinders chose to acknowledge the help given him by Earl Spencer, St Vincent, Charles Yorke and Robert Saunders, Viscount Melville, 'Who, as First Lords Commissioners of the Admiralty, Successively Honoured the Investigator's Voyage with their Patronage. . . .'[47]

A month later, on 26 June to be precise, the diary also says that 'Mr. Brown called in the evening to say that he had obtained from Mr. Nicol a copy of the voyage and atlas to be put on Sir Jos. Banks' table this evening.'[48]

[43] See P.R.O., Adm. 1/4382 and 3, various from 1811 to 1814.

[44] Banks to Admiralty, 30 June 1814. P.R.O., Adm. 1/4383. B566. Taking each of the nine landscapes, and each of the ten botanical illustrations at, say, £65, and the charts at the stated £940, the Admiralty spent £2,175 for the 'embellishment' of the narrative, a sum far exceeding what Flinders was paid for the period 1807–10. The Admiralty budget for the work appears to have been £2,000 (S.L.V., 'Flinders Papers'), £1,000 less than for the Vancouver illustrations.

[45] S.L.V., 'Flinders Papers'.

[46] *Ibid.* It should be recalled that he had already recognised Banks in the dedication of his *Observations on the Coasts of Van Diemen's Land* (1801).

[47] Flinders, *Voyage*, vol. i.

[48] S.L.V., 'Flinders Papers'. This, of course, casts serious doubt upon the oft-repeated statement that Flinders never saw a copy of his work. (Scott, *Life*, p. 395.)

It would be nice to believe that the sale of the work was a smashing success. This unfortunately was not the case. The Hydrographer kept Flinders's charts up-to-date, and distributed them to all ships of war bound for the Eastern Seas at least through 1826. But the Admiralty never bought up the remainder from Nicol to give to their captains. From Nicol's rendering of his account with Mrs Flinders in the year 1837, we learn the following:[49]

Of an original press-run of 150 copies of the imperial size, 121 had been sold; and of 1,000 copies, Small, 952 had been sold. As a result:

| | | | |
|---|---:|---:|---:|
| Manufacturing Expenses | £2,451 | 3 | 0 |
| Bookseller's Commission (10%) | 266 | 13 | 3 |
| Total Expenses | £2,717 | 16 | 3 |
| Income from Sales | 2,666 | 13 | 0 |
| Due G. & M. Nicol, 1837 | £  51 | 3 | 3 |

All the labour and all the suffering came only to a loss for the poor widow. Sir Joseph, who might easily have made it good, and would have done so had he known, had been dead these seventeen years.

No moral need be drawn.

But what did succeeding navigators think? A single comment by Robert FitzRoy,[50] Captain of H.M.S. *Beagle*, in which Darwin sailed round the world, will suffice:

'Before quitting King George Sound [sailing westward] I must add my slight testimony to the skill and accuracy with which Flinders laid down and described those parts of New Holland and Van Diemen's Land that I have seen. His accounts also of

---

It is Inconceivable that, if Nicol could give Brown a copy for Banks's library on 26 June, he could not have had one for Flinders ready before 18 July. Actually, whether or not he saw a copy before he died is not a point of overwhelming importance. It has a certain romantic value.

[49] N.M.M. 60/017. FLI/6.

[50] Vice-Admiral Robert Fitzroy (1805–65).

wind, weather, climate, currents, and tides are excellent; and
there are other points of information in his large work, useful to
many, but especially to seamen, which would be well worth
separating from the technicalities among which they are almost
lost in the present cumbersome volumes.'[51]

It is a just observation.

5

Of the three explorers, James Cook, George Vancouver, and
Matthew Flinders, only Cook, at the conclusion of his first
voyage, ever received the applause of the crowd. True,
Vancouver and Flinders arrived during wartime, when the
public attention was absorbed by larger events. But Vancouver
came home under the cloud of the Camelford Affair;[52] and
Flinders, as we have seen, had failed. At least he had not
triumphed. Actually, his treatment fell somewhere between
that of his two predecessors. Untouched by scandal, he was
received with both sympathy and respect. But never with adula-
tion. It was just as well. What he and Ann most longed for
was a quiet life together.

Few activities, very few, diverted him from his work. Among
the earliest to do so was the concern he brought with him from
Mauritius for a group of five Creole prisoners of war in England. Almost immediately on his arrival, he sought them out to
give them letters and money from home. But that was no repay-
ment for the kindness he had received. On 19 February he
wrote to the Admiralty entreating their Lordships to procure
the release of his friends' children, carefully describing them as
worthy and respectable.[53] In June he had the satisfaction of

---

[51] *Narrative of the Surveying Voyages of His Majesty's Ships Adventure and
Beagle, between the Years 1826 and 1836* . . . (London, 1839), vol. II, p. 628.

[52] Vancouver had been involved in the chastisement of three midshipmen on
board H.M.S. *Daedalus*, which for a time formed a part of his expedition. One of
these mids was Thomas Pitt, son of Baron Camelford. In the upshot, Vancouver's
conduct was questioned, after young Pitt had actually assaulted him in the street.
See Bern Anderson, *Surveyor of the Sea* (Seattle, Wash., 1960), p. 217 sqq.

[53] P.R.O., Adm. 1/1808. F274.

learning that the Earl of Liverpool, although 'of opinion that much circumspection should be observed in permitting persons of this description to proceed to the Isles of France and Bourbon [then, be it remembered, in British hands]; he concludes however from the channel through which this application is made, that circumstances of which he is not informed, may entitle the parties in the present instance to the indulgence solicited'.[54]

Doubtless he could have enlarged his social life had he been inclined to do so. Banks pressed him to come each Sunday evening to his 'conversazioni', and noticed it when he failed to appear. He dined out occasionally, and preferably either with a close circle of friends or on business. We find him among those given 'leave to be present' at the meeting of the Royal Society on 21 March 1811, sponsored by Mr Troughton,[55] and again on 6 May 1813, as the guest of Sir Charles Blagden, physician.[56]

This last raises the incidental question, as indeed it must have in Flinders's own mind, why he was never elected F.R.S. It could hardly have been an oversight on Banks's part. Cook had been elected quickly, and was in fact awarded the Copley medal. Bligh had become a Fellow in 1801 'in consideration of his distinguished services in navigation, botany, etc.'[57] Then why not Flinders? Perhaps he was never proposed. But why did Bligh, for one, not place him in nomination? He knew Flinders, knew his work, was pleased to have had a hand in his early training, supported the suggestion of the name 'Australia' against those who opposed it, and now hoped for the dedication. In fact, on 8 February 1812, Bligh, now a Rear-Admiral, took Flinders to the Palace to meet H.R.H. the Duke of Clarence, who had asked to see some of the latest charts.[58] Why not F.R.S.? It is a question without an answer.

The year 1812 opened quietly enough. Work, work, and still

---

[54] Robert Peel to Admiralty, 11 June 1811. P.R.O., Adm. 1/4217. Peel was then serving as Under-secretary for War and the Colonies to the second Earl of Liverpool (1770–1828).

[55] Edward Troughton, instrument maker (1753–1835). Royal Society of London, 'Journal Book', vol. 40, p. 353.

[56] *Ibid.*, p. 631. Blagden (1748–1820) was one of Banks's cronies.

[57] George Mackaness, *Life of Vice-Admiral William Bligh, R.N., F.R.S.* (London, 1951), p. 329.

[58] S.L.V., 'Flinders Papers'.

more work.[59] On 28 February he applied for restitution of the *Cumberland* or its value.[60] On 24 March he received a summons to appear before the Select Committee of the House of Commons, then taking testimony on Transportation. He did so the following day. With the Hon. George Eden in the Chair, Captain Flinder [*sic*] answered some thirty-five questions.[61] The questions dealt exclusively with geography and the capacity of Australia to support colonists. There was nothing at all on social conditions in Port Jackson.

'When was you in New South Wales?'

'Did it appear to you to be in a state of gradual improvement?' (It did.)

'Did you visit the out-settlements?' ('I visited some of them.')

'Were you acquainted with Port Dalrymple?' ('I discovered Port Dalrymple, but I am not acquainted with the colony.')

'Are the harbours good?' ('The harbours are excellent. Port Dalrymple is difficult of access, but it is very good when a ship gets in. The harbours in the neighbourhood of the Derwent River are capable of receiving all the British Navy, and perhaps all the navies of the world.')

'Did you penetrate at all into the interior during your residence in Sydney?' ('I have not been farther than fifty or sixty miles into the interior.')

'Did the colonies at Port Dalrymple and Derwent appear capable of greater extension?' (Flinders had already said he had never seen either of those colonies, and so answered, 'I think the whole of Van Diemen's Land capable of making a very fine colony.')

Worried about being away from Ann for even so short a time as this, Flinders doubtless hurried back across the river. He need not have been exercised, for it was not until six days

---

[59] As a result of which, by the way, he began to have trouble with his eyes. Being nearsighted, he took to wearing spectacles whenever he went out walking *Ibid.*

[60] Flinders to Peel (with a copy to the Admiralty), 28 February 1812. F.R.O., Adm. 1/4220. The request was made, but nothing ever came of it because the *Cumberland* was gone, and the French had no intention of reimbursing the enemy for her loss.

[61] Parliamentary Papers (1812), vol. 2, p. 637 sq.

later, on 1 April, that she gave birth to a daughter, named Anne.[62]

Once both mother and child were out of danger, Matthew felt free to proceed with his compass experiments. Moreover, he could go with his conscience clear on another point. On 13 April he obtained his release from the parole he had signed for Decaen in 1810.

With his out-of-town business over, Flinders turned once again to his family. The birth of a child prompted him to attend to the disposition of his property in the event of death. On 6 July he signed his Last Will and Testament (see Appendix C).

For a will without trusts it is a long document, nearly 2,000 words. It is also completely consistent in its thoroughness with everything else he ever did. If it had a fault, it lay in an excessive generosity to a multitude of relatives beyond his immediate family. He had been the successful one. But more, since his father's death ten years before, he had assumed the mantle of paterfamilias. The consciousness of this seniority within the bloodline led him to a sense of general responsibility for all who bore the name of Flinders. Thus, after specifying that certain tablets be erected to the memory of his direct male forebears for three generations, he left eleven legacies, totalling £420, to collateral relatives or their children(if any), and an annuity to his stepmother. He also left eight mourning rings to friends.[63] To be sure, these were endearing gestures of a generous spirit, nicely balanced one against another. But no one got very much; and in after years Ann could certainly have done with more than she had.[64]

One last professional duty he performed. James Wiles, botanist with Christopher Smith in the old *Providence*, had settled down to the life of planter in Jamaica. For a time he did well, owning a coffee plantation and some seventy slaves. But lately he had, as he said, seen the last of his golden dreams.

[62] In 1851, Anne, who became a competent linguist and studied Egyptology, married William Petrie (1821-1908), chemist and inventor of the self-regulating arc-lamp. Their son was the great Egyptologist, William Matthew Flinders Petrie, F.R.S. (1853–1942).

[63] Including one to Sir Joseph Banks.

[64] The Will may be seen at the Probate Registry: Bridport, fol. 465. Records of legacies paid out appear in N.M.M. 60/017. FLI/6.

Some time in 1811 or 1812 he sent his son off to England to join the Navy. The 'interest' system of naval patronage still flourished; and as Pasley had once taken Flinders under his wing, so now Flinders made his influence available to young Wiles. Actually, he placed him under the eye of Lieutenant Franklin, who schooled the boy and reported to Flinders on his progress.[65]

The years 1812 and 1813 passed too quickly for Matthew and Ann. Working all day, and often into the night, under the relentless pressure of Banks and the others, Flinders took no rest. It was too much. Late in December 1813 he suffered the beginnings of his last illness. His earliest attack of renal colic had struck him in 1795 at Port Jackson. The second bout came at Mauritius in January 1805. In both instances there had been complete remission. Now the pain set in again. By 9 March 1814 his daily distress was such as to bring his work to a stop. By 20 March, following a brief rally, the surgeon was calling in every day. And although he could leave his bed he was 'obliged to move very snail-like'.[66] His last letter to Robert Brown, who was most solicitous, gave the clue to his disease :

'I am very desirous, as is the surgeon who attends me, to see the paper of Sir E. Hume and Mr. Brand on the calculi found in the human bladder and on the effect of calcined magnesia; there is also a paper in the Philosophical Transactions, as I understand, by Dr. Wollaston upon calculi. Might I beg the favour of you to look into the Transactions for these papers; and either to send me the volumes containing them, or send them to Mr. Arrowsmith for me, his nephew or man being in the habit of coming with charts every two or three days.

'Since the day I saw you, my complaint has so much increased as to confine me at home, and during some days caused excessive pain, and it still gives pain though in a less degree and with intermissions. Every day for the last fortnight I have passed a quantity of small crystals, about three grains in weight a day,

---

[65] See various letters : Wiles to Flinders, 20 February 1811 and 14 March 1813. N.M.M. 60/017. FLI/1; and Flinders to Wiles, [Dec. ?] 1812. S.L.V., 'Flinders Papers'.
[66] S.L.V. 'Flinders Papers'.

upon an average. These are undergoing analysis, and therefore it is that I am desirous to see the papers above requested. The discharge of these crystals began three or four days after I commenced taking the calcined magnesia, which, on your recommendation I proposed to my surgeon; distilled water is another remedy to which I have had recourse, but cannot yet say with what advantage.'[67]

In clinical terms, this chronic tendency may have resulted from a lack of vitamin A. While a malignant tumour of the bladder cannot be ruled out, it is most probable that there was a urinary tract infection, that is, an accumulation of calculi. Calcined magnesia was a common medication, but it could, and apparently did, aggravate the condition. By May or June there had probably been severe renal destruction, with death imminent.[68]

It may perhaps seem morbid to dwell upon such matters. But renal diseases were not uncommon among sailors. Moreover, in the present case, not only was a brilliant career cut short, but at the end it very nearly happened that the work of a lifetime went unfinished. Let it be added that there is no evidence whatever for the suggestion that General Decaen must be called to account for Flinders's early death. With a history beginning at the age of twenty-one, and without the techniques of modern surgery, nothing more could have been expected.

Matthew Flinders died on 19 July 1814, aged forty years, four months and three days.

6

In a letter to Madame D'Arifat at Mauritius in mid-1812, he had confessed, 'I am now, indeed, as near to perfect happiness as is usually permitted to man. There is, however, always some *crocodile* [italics F's] lurking at the bottom of the lucid spring;

[67] Flinders to Brown, 1 April 1814. B.M., Add. MSS. 32440. 31 sq. This was little Anne's second birthday.

[68] This is the opinion of Dr J. N. Corriere, corroborated by W. S. Mack, F.R.C.S., Edinburgh, both of whom are urologists of note.

and my crocodile at present is, that my fortune is far from being adequate to my expenses.'[69] He had always been concerned over his finances. Ann had nearly lost him on that account. And if the full pay of an officer was inadequate, how could one possibly manage on half-pay? The answer was simple: one could not. Fortunately, he had a few other resources.

In the first place, he and his brother had each been left a patrimony of £600. Whether Matthew's was now gone is not known. Without children he and Ann may have saved it through the years. But then, in November 1811, he felt compelled to ask the Admiralty for the allowance of a marine surveyor—a guinea a day—to sustain his work on the narrative.[70] Instead, he had been granted an imprest, that is, an advance chargeable against the Admiralty's budget for the publication, to cover his expenses.[71]

Besides this, it appears that Flinders had invested a fair amount of money—actually it was a loan—in a plantation at Mauritius owned by a family named Desbassayns. The exact value of his original outlay is not clear, but from his Will it would appear to have been in the neighbourhood of £500. In any case, the investment did not turn out at all well. To be more exact, Ann was still waiting for a modest return in 1843.[72]

Flinders's personal estate and monies arising out of real estate, as accounted for at the Probate Office on 26 August 1814, were as follows:[73]

[69] S.L.V., 'Flinders Papers'.

[70] Flinders to Admiralty, 14 November 1811. P.R.O., Adm. 1/1808.

[71] Admiralty to Flinders, 18 November 1811. P.R.O., Adm. 2/869. Flinders was irritated that the Board had seen fit to do no more than lend him the £200. (S.L.V., 'Flinders Papers'.) Here again was something the bookkeepers could get their teeth into. On 16 July 1814 the Navy Board asked the Admiralty whether they should call upon Flinders for an accounting of the £200 or charge it off against the narrative. (P.R.O., Adm. 106/2264. 95.) Two days later, on the very day of publication, the Secretary replied that their Lordships had commanded him 'to observe to you that they are not aware that the work in question is ready for publication [!]' (P.R.O., Adm. 2/682.) This day before Flinders died! Finally, on 13 September, Flinders's solicitor, Robert Brine, Esq., requested a clearance of the Imprest, and it was so ordered. (P.R.O., Adm. 1/1811. F137.)

[72] As was pointed out in Chapter 13 above, Flinders had become convinced that a prudent planter might reasonably hope for 20 per cent. All available documents on this venture are contained in N.M.M. 60/017. FLI/29.

[73] N.M.M. 60/017. FI.I/6. It may seem a curious treatment, if not actually in dubious taste, to close the present chapter on this note. Yet the fact seems to be

Monies Received, consisting almost entirely of bank annuities and Consols, sold in settlement :                                      £3,498. 16.   1.

Expenses, including :

| | | | | | | |
|---|---|---|---|---|---|---|
| Cost of Probate | £ 68. | 17. | 0. | | | |
| Funeral | 73. | 17. | 0. | | | |
| Debts | 326. | 10. | 1. | | | |
| Pecuniary legacies | 420. | 0. | 0. | | | |
| Monuments | 101. | 3. | 6. | | | |
| Mourning Rings | 14. | 6. | 0. | | | |
| Annuity payments | 65. | 0. | 0. | 1,069. | 13. | 7. |

Residue                                               £2,429.   2.   6.

Without access to prize-money the professional naval officer was not in a lucrative position.

that in Flinders's eyes money matters were not merely a question of subsistence. They were that indeed; but one has the feeling that he was fascinated by finance, that he wished he could spend more time at it. Else, why his early plans for entering the China trade (see Chapter 3 above)? Why the careful gamble (which was not really a gamble) at Mauritius? Or why the sophisticated, if safe, portfolio of bank annuities and consols?

# CHAPTER FIFTEEN

# Summing Up

Years of revolution and war across the Channel had brought about a universal hardship, with adversity of one kind or another touching nearly every house in England. In the wake had come profound and radical changes in society. The Age of Reason had long ago spent its force; and on the wings of the Romantic Movement the Evangelical Revival had taken its place. Reason alone no longer appeared sufficient to save men's souls. At the same time, in science some fundamental questions began to be asked. The asking was as important as the questions themselves.

Matthew Flinders played his own part in this vast transformation. In a way he was a Romantic, for the spirit that caused him to weep over the distant bones of dead pelicans was not essentially different from that which produced Sir Walter Scott and Lord Byron. On the other hand, Flinders was secularist in the sense that he devoted his life, every breath of it, to the advancement of science, clearly a matter of this world, not of the next. He carried to it a deeply professional purpose, a purpose set alight by his own hope and passion. He asked some of the questions, and his questions were real, not trivial. He sought his own answers with an almost unearthly determination. His successors were able to build upon his work—which is the essence of science.

These successors had high praise for him.

Writing in 1860, Sir Joseph Dalton Hooker gave it as his opinion that, with Robert Brown aboard, the Flinders voyage proved 'as far as botany is concerned, the most important in its result ever undertaken, and hence marks an epoch in the history of that science.' He referred to the results as being 'incomparably greater, not merely than those of any previous voyage, but than those of all other similar voyages put together.'[1]

Brown himself ranked Flinders as high as anyone could: '. . . the amount of discovery and remarkable accuracy of survey has placed him next to Cook among modern navigators.'[2]

Malte-Brun thought that in death, 'the geographical and nautical sciences have lost in the person of Flinders one of their most brilliant ornaments'.[3]

And FitzRoy: '. . . I must add my slight testimony to the skill and accuracy with which Flinders laid down and described those parts of New Holland and Van Diemen's Land that I have seen.'[4]

The fact is it was Matthew Flinders who finally established the existence of the sixth continent as a geographical whole. After him only Antarctica remained unexplored.

To these formal eulogies must be added the mute recognition of all who have sailed Australian waters ever since.

This is high praise. What can we say of the man? He has been called 'that noblest and most attractive of Cook's successors'.[5] Why?

We may wonder, for instance, whether he had a sense of humour. If he did, certainly his letters never showed it. They are sober; they rarely sparkle and never laugh; they contain no wit. Yet it is the case that if shipboard life is rigorous, it is also, and often, hilarious. One may guess that he appreciated humour; but one would never suspect that he generated it.

We admire patience. He had it in his work, but Heaven knows he lost it at Mauritius. For nearly seven years, from the instant of his capture, he never ceased to rail against his fate. In consequence he succeeded only in disfiguring his own personality.

[1] Joseph Dalton Hooker, *The Botany of the Antarctic Voyage of H.M. Discovery Ships Erebus and Terror, in the years 1839–1843 under the Command of Sir James Clark Ross* (London, 1860). Pt. III, 'Flora Tasmaniae', vol. I, Introductory Essay, p. cxiv.

[2] Robert Brown to Admiral Sir Francis Beaufort (1774–1857), 12 March 1847. B.M., Add. MSS. 32441. 431.

[3] *Annales des Voyages*, vol. XXIII, p. 268.

[4] Robert Fitzroy, *Narrative of the Surveying Voyages of His Majesty's Ships Adventure and Beagle, between the Years 1826 and 1836* . . . (London, 1839), vol. II, p. 628.

[5] James Cook, *The Journals of Captain James Cook on his Voyages of Discovery* J. C. Beaglehole, ed. (London, 1955–61), vol. I, p. cclxxiv.

Yet these are surely venial faults. On the other side it is clear that Matthew Flinders was first of all an intellectual. He espoused no doctrine, he preached no creed. He dealt with facts, not with ideas. Ideas without facts made him squirm. It is, for example, a question whether the issues of religion or of politics interested him the least. He at one time got so far as to suppose that Catholicism excited the imagination to a greater extent than Protestantism.[6] It is not known that he ever went further. His sole contact with the world of politics came in trying to procure his own release. Otherwise the noble art never reached his consciousness. His world was almost entirely numerical. If a thing could be measured, he would measure it. If not, he simply ignored it. He chose to measure an entire continent.

But Flinders was more than pure numerical intellect. He was also a man of action. He was indeed capable of most decisive action—as all successful sailors must be. For this facet two ingredients at least are needed. One is courage, which for present purposes we may define simply as the nerve to do what must be done. Of working a ship among the eastern reefs, Flinders wrote:

'The commander who proposes to make the experiment, must not, however, be one who throws his ship's head round in a hurry, so soon as breakers are announced from aloft; if he do not feel his nerves strong enough to thread the needle, as it is called, amongst the reefs, whilst he directs the steerage from the mast head, I would strongly recommend him not to approach this part of New South Wales.'[7]

This same quality led him to continue his dangerous inshore surveying long after he had discovered at Sweer's Island that his crazy ship might never get him home. He was simply doing what he knew had to be done.

The other ingredient necessary to the man of action is professional ability—expertise. It is, of course, born of experience. But some have it, some do not; and some are better than others. Flinders was superb, probably as good a seaman as Cook.

[6] S.L.V., 'Flinders Papers'.          [7] Flinders, *Voyage*, vol. II, p. 104.

'What a ship on discovery may do is not to be given as an example to others, whose sole objects are expedition and safety.'[8]

Perhaps he was referring to nerve. But he also implied that degree of mastery in ship-handling without which nerve is worse than useless. This is the characteristic that gives a ship's company confidence. There is no substitute for it. Thus we see him running in among the rocks at the Archipelago of the Recherche, manoeuvring inside the Barrier Reef, and negotiating Torres Strait. We remember that he saved and then rescued the crew of the *Porpoise* at Wreck Reef. Everywhere he went he knew all the right moves, and made none of the wrong ones.

There remains one other quality which we have not mentioned, and with which Flinders was endowed in the fullest measure : integrity. It was this that gave him his nobility. Two remarkable instances come to mind.

It will be recalled that when, in 1805, General Decaen consented to move Flinders to the healthy upland plantation of Madame D'Arifat, Flinders gave his parole not to stray beyond two leagues from the house. Offered a chance to escape in 1806 by way of an American vessel, he simply refused to move. 'The dread of dishonouring my parole made me, however, contemplate this plan with a fearful eye.'[9] Later on, but only after he had convinced himself that Decaen's word could not be trusted, he did relax his principle.[10] But then it was easy : no opportunity for escape offered.

Again in 1814, with his last illness upon him, Flinders was engaged in finishing his book. It is said that one of the engraved charts submitted for his approval by Arrowsmith was returned with no less than ninety-two corrections.[11] That is integrity of another kind, but it is still integrity.

Flinders once admonished a friend to take Newton and Cook for models rather than Nelson. 'The reputations of the first,' he said, 'are immortal as the light of the sun, whilst that of the last is a flambeau, brilliant indeed for a time, but which in half a century will scarcely be remembered.'[12]

[8] *Ibid.*, vol. 1, p. 248.            [9] S.L.V., 'Flinders Papers'.
[10] Flinders to Ann, 20 January 1808. N.M.M. 60/017. FLI/25.
[11] S.L.V., 'Flinders Papers'.                    [12] *Ibid.*

One sees in all of this the elements of classical tragedy: a good and peaceful man destroyed by forces utterly beyond his own control.

Matthew Flinders gave more to this world than he took back.

# Appendix A

## INSTRUCTIONS FOR THE VOYAGE OF
## H.M. SLOOP *INVESTIGATOR*

By the Commissioners for executing the office of
Lord High Admiral of the United Kingdom of Great
Britain and Ireland, &c.

'Whereas the sloop you command has been fitted and stored for a
voyage to remote parts; And whereas it is our intention that you
should proceed in her to the coast of New Holland for the purpose of
making a complete examination and survey of the said coast, on the
eastern side of which His Majesty's colony of New South Wales is
situated; You are hereby required and directed to put to sea the first
favourable opportunity of wind and weather, and proceed with as little
delay as possible in execution of the service above-mentioned, repairing in the first place to *Madeira* and the *Cape of Good Hope* in order
to take on board such supplies of water and live stock as you may be
in want of.

'Having so done you are to make the best of your way to the coast
of New Holland, running down the said coast from 130 degrees of
east longitude to *Bass's Strait*; (putting if you shall find it necessary,
into *King George the third's Harbour* for refreshments and water
previous to your commencing the survey;) and on your arrival on
the coast, use your best endeavours to discover such harbours as may
be in those parts; and in case you should discover any creek or opening
likely to lead to *an inland sea or strait*, you are at liberty either to
examine it, or not, as you shall judge it most expedient, until a more
favourable opportunity shall enable you so to do.

'When it shall appear to you necessary, you are to repair to *Sydney
Cove* for the purpose of refreshing your people, refitting the sloop
under your command, and consulting with the governor of New South
Wales upon the best means of carrying on the survey of the coast;
and having received from him such information as he may be able to
communicate, and taken under your command the Lady Nelson
tender, which you may expect to find at Sydney Cove, you are to
recommence your survey, by first diligently examining the coast from
Bass's Strait to King George the third's Harbour; which you may

do either by proceeding along shore to the westward, or, in case you should think it more expedient, by proceeding first to King George's Sound, and carrying on your survey from thence to the eastward.

'You are to repair from time to time, when the season will no longer admit of your carrying on the survey, to Sydney Cove; from whence you are to return in the execution of these instructions, so soon as circumstances will enable you so to do.

'You are to be very diligent in your examination of the said coast, and to take particular care to insert in your journal every circumstance that may be useful to a full and complete knowledge thereof, noting the winds and weather which usually prevail there at different seasons of the year, the productions and comparative fertility of the soil, and the manners and customs of the inhabitants of such parts as you may be able to explore; fixing in all cases, when in your power, the true positions both in latitude and longitude of remarkable head lands, bays, and harbours, by astronomical observations, and noting the variation of the needle, and the right direction and course of the tides and currents, as well as the perpendicular height of the tides; and in case, during your survey, any *river* should be discovered, you are either to proceed yourself in the tender, or to direct her commander to enter it, and proceed as far up as circumstances will permit; carefully laying down the course and the banks thereof, and noting the soundings, going on shore as often as it shall appear probable that any considerable variation has taken place either in the productions of the soil or the customs of the inhabitants; examining the country as far inland as shall be thought prudent to venture with the small number of persons who can be spared from the charge of the vessel, wherever there appears to be a probability of discovering any thing useful to the commerce or manufactures of the United Kingdom.

'When you shall have completely examined the whole of the coast from Bass's Strait to King George the third's Harbour, you are, at such times as may be most suitable for the purpose, (which may be seen on a reference to Mr. Dalrymple's memoir, an extract of which accompanies this,) to proceed to and explore the *north-west coast of New Holland*, where, from the extreme height of the tides observed by Dampier, it is probable that valuable harbours may be discovered.

'Having performed this service, you are carefully to examine the *Gulf of Carpentaria*, and the parts to the westward thereof, between the 130th and 139th degrees of east longitude; taking care to seize the earliest opportunity to do so, when the seasons and prevalent winds may be favourable for visiting those seas.

'When you shall have explored the Gulf of Carpentaria and the parts to the westward thereof, you are to proceed to a careful investigation and accurate survey of *Torres' Strait*, and when that shall have

17

been completed, you are to examine and survey the whole of the remainder of the north, the west, and the north-west coasts of New Holland, and especially those parts of the coast most likely to be fallen in with by East-India ships in their outward-bound passages. And you are to examine as particularly as circumstances will allow, the *bank* which extends itself *from the Trial Rocks towards Timor*, in the hope that by ascertaining the depth and nature of the soundings thereon, great advantage may arise to the East-India Company's ships, in case that passage should hereafter be frequented by them.

'So soon as you shall have completed the whole of these surveys and examinations as above directed, you are to proceed to, and examine very carefully the *east coast* of New Holland, seen by captain Cook, *from Cape Flattery to the Bay of Inlets*; and in order to refresh your people, and give the advantage of variety to the painters, you are at liberty to touch at the *Fejees*, or some other of the islands in the *South Seas*.

'During the course of the survey, you are to use the tender under your command as much as possible; moving the Investigator onward from one harbour to another as they shall be discovered, in order that the naturalists may have time to range about and collect the produce of the earth, and the painters allowed time to finish as many of their works as they possibly can on the spot where they may have been begun : And when you shall have completed the whole of the surveys and examinations as above-mentioned, you are to lose no time in returning with the sloop under your command to England for farther orders, touching on your way, if necessary, at the Cape of Good Hope, and repairing with as little delay as possible to Spithead, and transmit to our secretary an account of your arrival.

'During your continuance on the service above-mentioned, you are, by all proper opportunities, to send to our secretary for our information, accounts of your proceedings and copies of the surveys and drawings which you shall have made, and such papers as the Naturalist and the Painters employed on board may think proper to send home; and upon your arrival in England you are immediately to repair to this office in order to lay before us a full account of your proceedings in the whole course of your voyage; taking care before you leave the sloop to demand from the officers and petty officers the log books and journals which they may have kept and such drawings and charts as they may have taken, and to seal them up for our inspection.

'And whereas you have been furnished with a *plant cabin* for the purpose of depositing therein such plants, trees, shrubs, &c., as may be collected during the survey above-mentioned, you are, when you arrive at Sydney Cove, to cause the said plant cabin to be fitted up by the carpenter on the quarter deck of the sloop you command, according to the intention of its construction; and you are to cause boxes for containing earth to be made and placed therein, in the same manner as was done in the plant cabin carried out by the Porpoise store ship, which plant cabin you will find at Sydney Cove.

'You are to place the said plant cabin, with the boxes of earth contained in it, under the charge and care of the naturalist and gardener, and to cause to be planted therein during the survey, such plants, trees, shrubs, &c., as they may think suitable for the *Royal Gardens at Kew*; and you are, as often as you return to Sydney Cove, to cause the said plants to be deposited in the governor's garden and under his charge, there to remain until you sail for Europe : And so soon as you shall be preparing to return home, you are to cause the small plant cabin to be removed from the sloop's quarter deck, and the one brought out by the Porpoise (which is something larger), to be placed there in its stead. In this last mentioned cabin the naturalist and gardener are to place the plants, trees, shrubs, &c., which may have been collected during the survey, in order to their being brought home for His Majesty; and you are, so soon as the sloop shall arrive at any port in England, to give notice of her arrival to His Majesty's botanic gardener at Kew, and to transmit to him a list and state of the said plants &c., which the gardener employed under your orders is to furnish you with for that purpose.

Given under our hands the 22nd of June, 1801.

(Signed),   St. Vincent.
        T. Troubridge.
        J. Markham.

To

  Matthew Flinders, Esq.
Commander of His Majesty's sloop
  Investigator, at Spithead.

    By command of their Lordships,
     (Signed,)   Evan Nepean.'

# Appendix B

## MAGNETISM OF SHIPS

'During the course of my voyage in H.M. sloop Investigator, for completing the discovery of New Holland and New South Wales, I remarked that the variation and the bearings of land taken with an azimuth compass upon the binnacle were very different when the ship's head was in different directions; and, at length, I found that the following circumstances obtained throughout the whole of the observations.

1. When the head was East, the variation differed from the truth; and always on the same side, while the ship remained in the same hemisphere.

2. When the head was West, the differences were equally great; but a contrary way.

3. The head being North or South, made no difference in the variation; and it was then a medium between what was found at East and at West.

4. At the intermediate points, between the magnetic meridian and East or West, the difference from the true variation bore a proportion to the angle made by the ship's head with the meridian. If the head were on the western side, the difference was of the same nature as that when the head was West; if on the East side, as at East.

5. The proportion at the intermediate points obeyed the following law,

> As Radius,
>
> Is to the difference at East or West, (for eight points :)
>
> So is the *sine* of the angle between the ships head and magnetic meridian to the difference for that angle.

Or if the number of points, which the head was to the right or left of the meridian, were taken as a *course*; and the difference for eight points, reduced to minutes, taken as a *distance*; then the difference for the number of points was found in the *departure* column of the traverse table.

6. These differences were of a directly contrary nature in the south, to what they were in the northern hemisphere. In the English Channel, the compass gave *too much* west variation when the head was West; but, in the southern hemisphere, it always gave too little; and the great west variations were found when the head was East.

246

7. The differences did not change suddenly on crossing the Equator; but, all the way from England, they diminished gradually; and, to all appearance, as the dip of the needle diminished. When the south end of the needle began to dip, the differences commenced the other way; and increased gradually as we advanced southward; until, having arrived in Bass' Strait, where the south dip is nearly as great as the north is in England, the differences became almost as great as when we first sailed; but, as I said before, of an opposite nature.

'The experiments lately, made in England, prove that similar differences, obeying the same laws, take place in most, or all ships of war; and perhaps they do in merchant ships also, for I have found them in vessels of 80 and 25 tons. Differences were also found in other parts, often greater than at the binnacles; but these being of less importance, the differences only which were observed at, or above the binnacles, on changing the ships heads *from East to West*, are here inserted.

| | | |
|---|---|---|
| Sheerness, Starling gun brig, difference of variation | 7° 29' | greater |
| Helder frigate, | 13 3 | do. |
| Raisonable 64, armed *en flûte* | 0 42 | do. |
| Portsmouth, Loire frigate | 2 7 | do. |
| Devastation bomb, | 4 2 | do. |
| Plymouth, Orestes brig | Uncertain | |
| Channel, Investigator armed ship | 8 4 | do. |

'In Captain Cook's ships, the Endeavour and Resolution, and also in the Discovery, commanded by Captain Vancouver, the differences appear to have been nearly the same as in the Investigator; and also of a contrary nature in the two hemispheres.

'The cause of all these changes in a compass on shipboard, and the modes by which they may be obviated, I have endeavoured to explain in the account of the experiments drawn up by order of the Admiralty; and, to obtain further proofs, it is desirable that the differences should be observed in as many ships, and as accurately, as possible, in the following manner:

'The azimuth compass to be used, should be a good one; the card traversing freely; and if possible, the needle should be retouched with magnetic bars, before the observations are made. A low stand or stool, must be prepared; so that when the compass is placed upon it, it may be of the same height with that by which the ship is steered. The binnacle being then taken away, substitute the stand and azimuth compass; or if the sun cannot be there seen all round, fix the stand as near to the situation as it can be seen; but *clear of any iron*, and *exactly amidships*. Let azimuths be taken, using both sides of the vane; and this as often as convenient, and with the ship's head in various directions; but more particularly at, and near, East and West; noting the direction of the head to the nearest quarter of a point.

'These observations should always be made with the same instrument, and in the same place; and be entered in a table of ten columns, under the following heads:

*Time*, containing the year, day, and hour.
*Latitude*, of the place of observation.
*Longitude*, of ditto.
*Dip*, of the needle, if an instrument is on board.
*\*Alt. ⊙cent.*, corrected for dip, refraction, and semidiameter.
*Azim. obsd.*, being the mean of three or four sights, with each side of the vane.
   (If Walker's meridional compass be used, the two last are unnecessary.)
*By whom*, mentioning the observer's name against each observation.
*Ship's head*, the mean of what it was at the beginning and end.
*Variation*.
*Circumstances*, specifying if under sail or at anchor: Also, whether the ship was steady, or had motion.

'At the head of the table should be mentioned the number of guns mounted, and whether the place was at the binnacle; or if not, how far before or abaft it. Observations may be made in other parts of the ship; but these should be kept in a separate table.

'A good number of such experiments, carefully made in a variety of ships, and particularly when lying steadily at anchor, would show whether the differences at the binnacle are usually so great as to cause much error; and consequently, how far the discovery of them is of importance to ordinary navigation. With marine surveyors, and all officers who wish to fix the position of places or of their ships, by compass bearings, the subject must necessarily be one of much interest.

MATTHEW FLINDERS,
Captain, R.N.'

*London, Aug.* 26, 1812.

---

  \* The *hour angle* may be substituted, where there is a time keeper, and the altitude cannot be observed.

# Appendix C

## LAST WILL AND TESTAMENT OF MATTHEW FLINDERS

'In the Name of God Amen. I, Matthew Flinders, Esquire, Captain in the Royal Navy, now residing in London, being at this time in sound mind and understanding and in health of body, think it just and necessary to provide against accidents by making this my last will and testament in the form and manner following. I do name and appoint my dear wife, Ann Flinders, my friend, Mr. Charles Hursthouse, farmer of Tydd St. Marys in the County of Lincoln, and my friend John Newbald, Esquire, [?] of Hull, in Yorkshire to be the Guardians, Trustees, and Executors of this my will and testament; and in case of the death or the incapacity or refusal of John Newbald, Esquire, to act as above, I do name and appoint Mr. Robt. Newbald, his Son, to be trustee and executor in the place of his father; and should any of the above circumstances occur to Mr. Charles Hursthouse, I do name and appoint Mr. [blank] to act in his stead. And my Will is that the said three trustees and executors do dispose of my monies, securities for money, real or personal Estate and property of every description, whether in my possession, or that may devolve to me by bequest or otherwise in the form and manner following: first, in the case where I should die without issue lawfully begotten either actually existing, or posthumous, then my will is that the following distribution of my monies ec. do take place: first, I give and bequeath the sum of twelve hundred pounds lawful money of Great Britain to my dear wife Ann Flinders; of, if she refuse that sum, then such part thereof as she may think proper to specify. Second to my dear Sister Susanna, wife of George Pearson, now residing at St [?] in Huntingdonshire, I give the sum of five hundred pounds Sterling, she to enjoy the interest arising therefrom during her life, and the principal at her death to be equally divided amongst her surviving children. Third, to my dear brother, Samuel Ward Flinders, Lieutenant in the Royal Navy, I bequeath all the monies and property belonging to me in the Isles of France and Bourbon, for the obtaining of which he is to be furnished with the necessary papers and authority, but is to do it at his own cost and trouble; and if the said monies and property do not amount to five hundred pounds Sterling, then they are to be made up to that sum from my property in England; and in case his demise takes place

before mine, and he leaves issue lawfully begotten, then I give the
said sum of five hundred pounds from the general mass of my property
to his child, or by equal proportions to his children. Fourth, to
Hannah, wife of Joseph Dodd, of Donington, and to Henrietta
Flinders, my two sisters of the half blood, I bequeath one hundred
pounds Sterling each; but in case of the previous death of one or both
of them, and she or they leave lawful Issue, then the part of the parent
[is] to be given to the children in equal proportions. Fifth, I will that
the sum of one hundred pounds be expended in four marble slabs to
be set up by permission of the Minister and Churchwardens in the
parish church at Donington, in the County of Lincoln, against the
Wall facing the Communion Door of the same Church; and the said
four slabs to have engraved upon them such inscriptions to the
memory of my great grandfather [John Flinders, 1682–1741] grandfather [John Flinders, 1713–1776] father, and myself as the pious
sentiments of my brother Samuel, with the approbation of my wife,
may dictate. Sixth, I give and bequeath the following Legacies : to
my nephew, James Harvey, of Donington, and to his sister, Susannah,
each fifty pounds; to my Uncle, Mr. John Flinders, of Spalding, fifty
pounds; to my Aunt, Mrs. Eliz. Carr, of Louth, fifty pounds; to my
half-Uncle, William Flinders, of Boston, fifty pounds, or in case of his
death, the same sum to his Son, William; to my half-Aunt Mary
Cawthorn, of Spalding, twenty pounds; to my half-Aunt Penelope
Proctor, of London, twenty pounds; to my dear Cousin Henrietta
Newbald, of Hull, twenty pounds; to Mr. Charles Hursthouse, and
to John Newbald, or to their substitutes, on undertaking the trust oath,
twenty p$^d$s. Seventh, I bequeath to the following persons mourning
rings of the value of two Guineas each, and bearing two letters MF as
a motto—the R$^t$ Honble. Sir Joseph Banks B$^t$, Osborn Standert Esq.
[his agent's son $^?$] of London, Captain William [?] of the Royal
Navy Marines, Paul Labauve, of the Isle of France, Mons. Thomas
Pitot, of D$^o$, Mons. Charles Desbassayns, of the I. of Bourbon, Mr.
Thomas Flinders, of Spalding, Lincolnshire, Mrs. Henrietta Newbald,
of Hull, in Yorkshire, and Miss Isabella Tyler, of Beverley, D$^o$.
Eighth, my household goods, plate, clothes, linen, books and papers
I give to my dear wife and Executrix, Ann Flinders, she to give out
of them all manuscript books and papers relating to my voyage (with
the exception of letters) to my brother Samuel Ward Flinders, and to
dispose of the rest as she shall see good. If any of the Legatees mentioned in any of the preceding paragraphs should be deceased before
me, then his, her, or their Legacies, except where the Legacies are
specified to descend to children, shall go to increase the Sums left in
the first, second, third, fourth, and sixth paragraphs, the person therein
mentioned being living; and the respective augmentations shall be

in proportion to the Legacies of each. Also, if the whole of my property as above specified should be more than sufficient to pay Legacies so left as above, then the surplus is to go to the augmentation of them in the same proportionate manner; but with respect to the third paragraph, if the monies therein left exceed the Sum of £500 clear of expense, then the augmentation is not to make it exceed what the sum left in the second paragraph will amount to when so augmented; my instruction being that the Sums left to my brother and sister should be equal if, after the expenses attending on my interment (of which my wife or such person as she may appoint is to have the direction [?] my monies) should be found insufficient to pay and provide for all the above Legacies, then a reduction of those contained in the second, third, fourth, and sixth paragraphs proportionally to the Sums left, is to take place. The sums specified in the first, fifth, and seventh paragraphs are to suffer no reduction. Such is the Disposition I desire to be made of my monies and property of whatever kind in case I should die and leave no lawful issue. But if in the contrary case [which in fact occurred, ed.] I should leave issue one or more children, then my desire is that my said three Executors and trustees dispose of my monies, Securities for money, real and personal property, Estate and property of every description whatever, then belonging to me, or afterwards descending or devolving by bequest or otherwise, in the form and manner following: First, the expenses attending my interment at such place and in such manner as my dear wife Ann Flinders, or a person of her appointment may direct, are to be paid, and the sum of one hundred pounds set aside for the four marble slabs as directed in the fifth article preceding. Second, I bequeath the following annuities and legacies in lawful money of Great Britain: to my dear wife Ann, the clear annuity during her natural life of fifty five pounds; to my mother in law, Mrs. Elizabeth Flinders, one clear life annuity of ten pounds; to my Sister Susanna Pearson, or to her children in equal proportions in case of her death previous to my decease, the sum of One hundred P$^{ds}$.; to my brother, Samuel W. Flinders, or to his lawful children if any in the same case, the sum of one hundred pounds; to each of my half-sisters, Hannah Dodd and Henrietta Flinders, or in the above case to the children (if any) of each, the sum of fifty pounds; to my nephew, James Harvey, of Donington, twenty pounds; to his sister, Susanna Harvey, twenty pounds; to my Aunt, Mrs. Elizabeth Carr, the sum of twenty pounds; to my half-Uncle, William Flinders, or in case of his previous death to his son William, twenty pounds; to my half-Aunt, Mary Cawthorn, ten pounds; to my half-Aunt, Penelope Proctor, ten pounds; to my second and third above-named Executors, or to their substitutes, on undertaking the trust oath, the sum of twenty pounds. Thirdly, the mourning rings to the persons specified in the seventh paragraph preceding are to be given, and to make part of the present disposition of my property. Fourth, my household furniture, plate ec., as specified in the eighth paragraph preceding, are to be disposed of in the way therein directed. Fifth, after all the above bequests and arrangements are satisfied and done so far as the existence of the legatees or of their children before specified will require and allow, then my will is that all my remaining monies ec. of every kind, as well those in actual possession as those that may extend or be devised to me, or that may arise in any way whatever after my decease and including the legacies to such persons as may be deceased with no children, are specified, or being specified, are specified if those are deceased, then the whole of my said remaining monies ec. shall go to my child or children, and if I leave more than one then the said remaining monies are to be divided amongst them in equal proportions, the child or children to receive the whole Sum or division with the interests due thereon, deducting the expenses of bringing up and education as he, she, or they may respectively attain the age of twenty one years. Sixth, in case my said child or children existing at my decease should nevertheless die before the age of twenty one years, and he, she, or they, or any of them should leave no lawful issue, then my will is that all the above-mentioned monies ec. should be divided into four equal parts or portions, of which I give one part to James Harvey and Susanna Harvey, or their survivor, if the deceased leave no children. The second part I give to my brother, Samuel Ward Flinders, or if he be deceased, to his lawful issue, if any is then existing. The third part to my nephew, Matthew Flinders Pearson; and the fourth and last part I give to the remaining children of my Sister, Susanna, in equal proportion. And if any of the persons to whom these four parts are to descend in the case above specified should be deceased, and have left no lawful issue, then the part of such person or persons is to be employed in augmenting the remaining part or parts so bequeathed in equal proportions. Lastly and generally, I do hereby direct and authorize my three Executors and trustees, or my wife Ann Flinders, conjointly with either one of the others, to sell and dispose of any part of my said remaining property in trust during the minority of my child or children, and to replace and invest it in any other way which they may judge advantageous to the interest of the said child or children; also to call in and replace all or any of my said remaining trust monies and Securities for money, when and as often they shall find or suppose it necessary. And I do hereby order and direct that the receipt or receipts of my said three trustees or of my wife, Ann Flinders, with either one of the other two shall be good and sufficient discharge or discharges from time to time for any part of my said remaining trust monies ec. for which the same shall be given. Also, that it shall and may be lawful for my said Executors and trustees to secure and retain to himself, herself, or themselves all such costs, charges, damages, payments and expenses as they may respectively bear, pay, expend or be put unto in the execution of the trust and executorship hereby imposed and confided, or in the defense and protection thereof. Also that my said three executors and trustees shall not be answerable the one for the other or others of them for the acts, receipts, or defaults of the other, but each of them for his or her own acts, deeds, receipts, and defaults only, nor for any loss that may happen to the said trust of monies, property or any part thereof by failure of any Security on which the same may be placed out at interest, unless the same shall happen by their, or out of their willful neglect or default. For witness and confirmation of this my last will and testament and of every part thereof, I the said Matthew Flinders have hereunto set my hand and seal this sixth day of July in the year of our Lord 1812. [Matthew Flinders (s)] This writing was signed and sealed by the said Matthew Flinders, Esquire, Captain in the Royal Navy, by him published and declared as and for his Last Will and Testament in the presence of us who have hereunto subscribed our names as witnesses hereunto in his presence—Witnessed—Isabella Tyler, Spinster, Joseph Hayes, Surgeon.

'Proved at London 26th August 1814 before the Worshipful Samuel [?] Parson LL.D. and surrogate by the oath of Ann Flinders widow, the relict and one of the Executors to whom administration was granted having been first sworn duly to admr power to Charles Hursthouse and John Newbald Esquire, the other Executors.'

Transcribed from the copy deposited in the Probate Registry, London.

# Bibliography

## 1

MANUSCRIPT SOURCES

(*a*) *Matthew Flinders's unpublished writings*

'Observations on places visited when in the Providence.' [1791–3.] 11 pp. N.M.M. 60/017. FLI/8a.

'Narrative of Tom Thumbs cruize to Canoe Rivulet; and of the schooner Francis' expedition to Furneaux's Isles 1796 and 1798.' 44 pp. M.L.

'A Memoir explaining the marks used in the charts of Australia constructed on board His Majesty's ship Investigator; and the manner in which the latitude, longitude, and variation of the compass were obtained, corrected, and applied in their construction; With some new facts and additional observations upon these and other nautical subjects connected with Australia; by Matt$^w$· Flinders,—Late commander of the Investigator : a prisoner in the Isle of France.' 14 May 1805. 102 pp. P.R.O., Adm. 55/76.

'A Narrative of the causes that prevented His Majesty's ship the Investigator from completing the examination and discovery of the Coasts of Australia : The embarkation of the commander and company on board His Majesty's armed vessel Porpoise : The loss of that ship, and of the Cato of London, upon a Coral Reef between New Caledonia and New South Wales; a voyage of 250 leagues to Port Jackson in an Open Boat; and the subsequent embarkation of the commander of the Investigator, with the charts E$^{ca}$ of his discoveries, for England, in the Cumberland—schooner, of 29 tons : Also, an account of his voyage as far as the Isle of France; his reception there by the French captain-general De Cäen; and the treatment he has received during an imprisonment of —— years; interspersed with notices upon the voyage of Monsieur N. Baudin, and various other observations and remarks; with an Appendix, containing various letters &$^{ca}$ referred to in the Narrative. By Matthew Flinders Esquire, Prisoner in the Isle of France, and late commander of His Majesty's ship Investigator July 1806.' 332, lxxiv pp. P.R.O., Adm. 7/707.

'Notes on Grant's History of the Isle of France; Made in the Island.'
1806–7. 18 pp. N.M.M. 60/017. FLI/12.

'Spheric Trigonometry, followed by Problems of the Sphere, and
various other particulars useful to Navigation. Isle of France 1808
and 9.' 102 pp. N.M.M. 60/017. FLI/7.

'A Biographical Tribute to the memory of Trim.' Isle of France,
Dec. 1809. 9 pp. N.M.M. 60/017. FLI/11.

'Notes upon the Magnetism of the Earth, and of ships.' 1810. 30 pp.
N.M.M. 60/017. FLI/7.

'An Account of some experiments to ascertain the effects produced
on the Compass, by the attractive power in ships; with the modes
by which the errors may be obviated. To which is added, Observations on the present state of the compasses used in His Majesty's
Navy, and a proposal for improving the same.' Drawn up by order
of the Lords Commissioners of the Admiralty, by Matthew Flinders,
captain in the Royal Navy. Dated London June 27, 1812. 45 pp.
N.M.M. 60/017. FLI/7.

(b) *Other archival documents*

*Public Record Office, London:* Adm. 1—Papers, (including correspon-
dence): Admirals' Despatches, Cape of Good Hope; Admirals
Unemployed; Admirals' Despatches, East Indies, the Nore and
Sheerness, and Portsmouth; Captains; Lieutenants; Hydrographic
Office; Minute Branch; Transport Board; Doctors Commons; East
India House. Reports, Secret and Domestic; Secretary of State;
and Promiscuous.

> Adm. 2—Secretary's Department, Out-letters.
> Adm. 7—Admiralty Secretary, Miscellanea.
> Adm. 55—Ships' Logs.
> Adm. 106—Navy Board Records.
> Adm. 110—Victualling Board, Out-letters.
> F.O. 27/58—General Correspondence, France.

*National Maritime Museum, Greenwich:* MS. 60/017. FLI/1—Letters
from Sir Joseph Banks to Flinders and Mrs Flinders, 1800–14;
FLI/2—Letters to Flinders from correspondents on Mauritius,
1804–15; FLI/3—Official letters received by Flinders, 1801–12;
FLI/4—Copies of letters written by Flinders, 1795–1808; FLI/5—
Service papers; FLI/6—Personal legal and business papers of
Flinders; FLI/7—Technical memoranda by Flinders; FLI/8a—
Portion of Journal, relating to voyage in *Providence* with Bligh, *c.*
1791; FLI/11—'Biographical Tribute to Trim'; FLI/12—Journal
and letter book of Flinders, 1806–7; FLI/25—Letters from Flinders
to his family, 1799–1812; FLI/26—Letters from Sir Joseph Banks
to Flinders, 1804–10; FLI/27—Letters received from John [later

Sir John] Franklin, 1810–42; FLI/28—Letters received by Mrs Flinders from John Elder, 1808; FLI/29—Letters from M. Pitot, Mauritius, to Mrs Flinders, 1815–43; FLI/30—Letters received by Mrs Flinders from other correspondents, 1814–52.

*British Museum: Add. MSS.* 8100, Sir Joseph Banks, Foreign Correspondence; 31168–70, St Vincent's Letter Books; 32439–41, Correspondence and Papers of Robert Brown.

*British Museum (Natural History):* Robert Brown, Correspondence, vol. III; 'Journal and Diary for the period 1801–4', W.O. 778.

*India Office Library (Commonwealth Relations Office):* Hon. East India Co., Court of Directors. Court Minutes; Miscellaneous Letters Received; Miscellanies; also records of Committee of Correspondence and Committee of Shipping.

*Probate Register.*

*Althorp, Northamptonshire:* Papers of the second Earl Spencer.

*Royal Society of London:* Journal Book, vol. 40 (1809–13); Miscellaneous Manuscripts.

*State Library of Victoria, Melbourne:* Flinders Papers.

*Mitchell Library, Sydney:* Banks Papers, vol. 20, 'Australia and South Sea Islands'; Samuel Smith, Seaman on board H.M.S. Investigator, 'Journal'.

*Municipal Library of Caen, Normandy:* Decaen Papers, vols. 10, 84, 92 and 105.

*Service Hydrographique de la Marine, Paris:* Various documents on the voyages of Baudin and Flinders.

*Archives Nationales, Paris:* AP. iv. pl. 1260, M. 47—Napoleon's approval for Flinders's liberation.

*Sutro Library, San Francisco, Cal., U.S.A.:* Banks Collection.

## 2

PRINTED WORKS

(a) *Matthew Flinders's published writings*

*Observations on the Coasts of Van Diemen's Land, on Bass's Strait and its Islands, and on Part of the Coasts of New South Wales, Intended to Accompany the Charts of the Late Discoveries in Those Countries.* London, 1801.

'Concerning the Difference in the magnetic Needle on Board the Investigator, arising from an Alteration in the Direction of the Ship's Head', Royal Society of London, *Phil. Trans.*, vol. 95 (1805), p. 186 sqq.

'Observations upon the Marine Barometer made during the Examination of the Coasts of New Holland and New South Wales, in the years 1801, 1802, and 1803', Royal Society of London, *Phil. Trans.*, vol. 96 (1806), p. 239 sqq.

[Testimony on Transportation to New South Wales] in, Great Britain. Parliament. *Parliamentary Papers* (1812), vol. II, p. 637 sq.

*Magnetism of Ships* [circular to captains], Admiralty, August 26, 1812.

[Letter on an error in Horsburgh's *Directions for Sailing to and from the East Indies*] *Naval Chronicle*, vol. 28 (1812), p. 318 sq.

*A Voyage to Terra Australis; Undertaken for the Purpose of Completing the Discovery of that Vast Country, and Prosecuted in the Years 1801, 1802, and 1803, in His Majesty's Ship the Investigator, and Subsequently in the Armed Vessel Porpoise and Cumberland Schooner. With an Account of the Shipwreck of the Porpoise, Arrival of the Cumberland at Mauritius, and Imprisonment of the Commander during Six Years and a Half in that Island.* London: Printed by W. Bulmer and Co. Cleveland-Row, and Published by G. and W. Nicol, Booksellers to His Majesty, Pall-Mall. 1814. 2 vols., atlas.

[Same.] Dutch translation, 1815.

[Same.] German edition, 1816.

'Sur le Banc du Naufrage et sur Le Sort de M. De La Pérouse', *Annales des Voyages, de la Géographie et de L'Histoire* (Paris, Gide, 1819–70), vol. 10, p. 88 sqq. [Dated by Flinders, 17 Jan. 1807.]

*Matthew Flinders' Narrative of His Voyage in the Schooner Francis: 1798 Preceded and Followed by Notes on Flinders, Bass, the Wreck of the Sidney [sic] Cove, &C, by Geoffrey Rawson.* [London], 1946.


(*b*) *Other printed works*

Anderson, Bern. *Surveyor of the Sea: The Life and Voyages of Captain George Vancouver.* Seattle, 1960.

*Annual Register.* vol. 56 (1814), 'Chronicle', p. 137.

Auzoux, A. 'L'Arrestation du capitaine Flinders (1803–1810)', *Revue d'Histoire Diplomatique*, An. 26 (1912), p. 481 sqq.

Bain, William. *An Essay on the Variation of the Compass, shewing how far it is influenced by a change in the direction of the ship's head. . . .* Edinburgh, 1817.

Baker, Sidney J. *My Own Destroyer: A Biography of Matthew Flinders, Explorer and Navigator.* Sydney, 1963.

Banks, Sir Joseph. *The Banks Letters: A Calendar of the Manuscript Correspondence of Sir Joseph Banks . . . in Great Britain.* W. R. Dawson, ed., London, 1958.

—— 'Supplementary Letters of Sir Joseph Banks', British Musuem (Natural History) *Hist. Ser.*, vol. 3, No. 2 (1962).

Bassett, Marnie. *The Governor's Lady: Mrs. Philip Gidley King.* London, 1956.

—— *The Hentys: An Australian Colonial Tapestry.* London, 1954.

Bauer, Ferdinand Lucas. *Ferdinandi Bauer Illustrationes Florae Novae Hollandiae, sive icones Generum quae in Prodromo Florae Novae Hollandiae et Insulae Van Diemen descripsit Robertus Brown.* London, 1813.

Beaglehole, J. C. *The Exploration of the Pacific.* (3rd . edn.) London, 1966.

Bertie, Charles H. 'Matthew Flinders: Australia's Navigator', R.A.H.S., *Jour. & Proc.*, vol. III (1914), p. 295 sqq.

*Biographie Universelle Ancienne et Moderne.* (2nd edn.) 'Matthew Flinders', by Walckenaer.

Blackwood, Francis P. *Directions for the Outer Passage from Sydney to Torres Strait.* London, 1847.

Blewitt, Mary. *Surveys of the Seas: A Brief History of British Hydrography.* London, 1957.

Bligh, William. *A Narrative of the Mutiny, on Board His Majesty's Ship 'Bounty'; and the Subsequent Voyage of Part of the Crew, In the Ship's Boat, From Tofoa, one of the Friendly Islands, to Timor, a Dutch Settlement in the East Indies.* London, 1790.

Bougainville, Louis Antoine de. *A Voyage Round the World. . . .* Translated from the French by John Reinhold Forster, F.A.S. London, 1772.

Bowden, Keith Macrae. *George Bass, 1771–1803.* Melbourne, 1952.

Brown, Robert. *Prodromus Florae Novae Hollandiae et Insulae Van-Diemen Exhibens Characteres Plantarum Quas 1802–1805.* London, 1810.

—— *Supplementum Primum. . . .* London, 1830.

Bruny-Dentrecasteaux, Joseph Antoine. *Voyage de Dentrecasteaux, envoyé à la Recherche de La Pérouse . . .* redigé par M. de Rossel. Paris, 1808. 2 vols., atlas (by C. F. Beautemps-Beaupré.)

Bryant, Joseph. *Captain Matthew Flinders, R.N. His Voyages, Discoveries, and Fortunes.* London, 1928.

Collins, David. *An Account of the English Colony in New South Wales. . . .* London, 1798–1802. 2 vols.

Cook, James. *The Journals of Captain James Cook on his Voyages of Discovery.* J. C. Beaglehole, ed. Cambridge, 1955–61. 2 vols., portfolio.

—— *A Voyage to the Pacific Ocean Undertaken by the Command of His Majesty, for Making Discoveries in the Northern Hemisphere. . . .* London, 1784. 3 vols., atlas.

Cooper, H. M. *The Unknown Coast, being the explorations of Captain Matthew Flinders along the shores of South Australia, 1802.* Adelaide, 1953.

—— (A Supplement). Adelaide, 1955.

Cooper, H. M. *French Exploration in South Australia . . . 1802–1803.* [Adelaide,1952.]

Dampier, William. *A New Voyage Round the World. . . .* London, 1697. (See also, *Dampier's Voyages.* Ed. by John Masefield. Edinburgh, 1906. 2 vols.)

de Beer, Sir Gavin. *The Sciences were never at War.* London, 1960.

*Dictionary of Australian Biography*, 'Matthew Flinders'.

*Dictionary of National Biography*, 'Matthew Flinders', by John Knox Laughton.

Elkin, A. P. *The Australian Aborigines.* Sydney, 1956.

Ellis, M. H. *John Macarthur.* Sydney, 1955.

*Encyclopædia Britannica.* (11th edn.) 'Compass', by E. W. Creak; 'Flinders', by J. S. Keltie.

Ferguson, John Alexander. *Bibliography of Australia.* London, 1941–. 5 vols. published to date.

Field, Barron. *Geographical Memoirs on New South Wales. . . .* London, 1825.

*The Flinders Centenary: Discovery of the Port Lincoln District.* Royal Geographical Society of Australasia, South Australian Branch, Adelaide, 1902, vol. 5, p. 45 sqq.

*Gazette Nationale ou Le Moniteur Universêl.* Paris. 7 and 11 July 1804.

Grant, James. *The Narrative of a Voyage of Discovery, performed in His Majesty's Vessel The Lady Nelson, of sixty tons burthen, with sliding keels, in the years 1800, 1801, and 1802, to New South Wales. . . .* London, 1803.

Great Britain. Admiralty. Hydrographic Office. *Australia Pilot.* London, 1948–1956. 5 vols.

—— Selected Charts.

Hannay, David. *Ships and Men.* Edinburgh, 1910.

Hawkesworth, John. *An Account of the Voyages Undertaken by the Order of His Present Majesty for Making Discoveries in the Southern Hemisphere. . . .* London, 1773. 3 vols.

Hewson, J. B. *A History of the Practice of Navigation.* Glasgow, 1951.

Hill, Ernestine. *My Love Must Wait.* Sydney, 1952.

*Historical Records of Australia*, Ser. I, vols. 2–5.

*Historical Records of New South Wales*, vols. 3–7.

Hooker, Joseph Dalton. *The Botany of the Antarctic Voyage of H.M. Discovery Ships Erebus and Terror. . . .* London, 1844–60. (See particularly Part III, 'Flora Tasmaniae', London, 1859.)

Hunter, John. *An Historical Journal of the Transactions at Port Jackson and Norfolk Island, with the Discoveries which have been made in New South Wales and in the Southern Ocean, since the publication of Phillip's Voyage. . . .* London, 1793.

Ingleton, G. C. 'A Brief History of Marine Surveying in Australia', R.A.H.S. *Jour. & Proc.*, vol. 30, pts. 1 & 2 (1945).
—— *Charting a Continent*. Sydney, 1944.
'Kangaroo' [pseud.] *The Spirit of St. George in Action: The Chief Explorer of Australia, Captain Matthew Flinders, R.N. His Life and Times, 1774–1814*. London, [1945?]
King, Philip Gidley. *Remarks on the Passage through Bass's Straits, from the Westward*. Sydney, (April 16) 1803. Broadside.
King, Philip Parker. *Directions for the Inner and Outer Routes from Sydney to Torres Strait*. . . . London, 1849.
—— *Directions for the Inner Route from Sydney to Torres Strait*. London, 1847.
—— *Narrative of a Survey of the Intertropical and Western Coasts of Australia. Performed between the years 1818 and 1822*. London, 1827. 2 vols.
—— Robert Fitz-roy, and Charles Darwin. *Narrative of the Surveying Voyages of His Majesty's Ships Adventure and Beagle, between the Years 1826 and 1836*. . . . London, 1839. 3 vols., appendix.
Labillardière, Jacques Julien Houton de. *Voyage in Search of La Pérouse* . . . *1791, 1792, 1793, and 1794*. London, 1800.
La Pérouse, Jean-François de Galaup, Comte de. *Voyage de La Pérouse Autour du Monde*. . . . Paris, 1798. 4 vols., atlas.
Lee, Ida. *Captain Bligh's Second Voyage to the South Sea*. . . . London, 1920.
—— *The Coming of the British to Australia, 1788–1829*. London, 1906.
—— *Early Explorers in Australia*. London, 1925.
—— *The Logbooks of the 'Lady Nelson,' with the journal of her first Commander, Lieutenant James Grant, R.N.* . . . London, 1915.
Lewis, Michael. *The History of the British Navy*. London, 1957.
—— *A Social History of the Navy, 1793–1815*. London, 1960.
Mack, James D. 'Matthew Flinders and the British Admiralty Orders to H.M.S. *Investigator*', R.A.H.S. *Jour. & Proc.*, vol. 43, pt. 5 (Nov. 1957), p. 205 sqq.
—— 'The Naming of Australia: A Revised View', *Geog. Jour.*, vol. 124, pt. 4 (Dec. 1958), p. 514 sqq.
Mackaness, George. *The Life of Vice-Admiral William Bligh, R.N., F.R.S.* London, 1951.
—— 'Sir Joseph Banks, Bart.', R.A.H.S. *Jour. & Proc.*, vol. 48, pt. 1 (March 1962), p. 44 sqq.
Markham, Sir Clements R. *Major James Rennell and the Rise of Modern English Geography*. London, 1895.
May, W. E. 'History of the Magnetic Compass', *Mariner's Mirror*, vol. 38, No. 3 (Aug. 1952), p. 210 sqq.

May, W. E. 'The Reliance Log-books of Matthew Flinders', R.A.H.S. *Jour. & Proc.*, vol. 39, pt. 5 (1953), p. 267 sqq.

*Monthly Review*, vol. 76 (Feb. 1815), p. 152; vol. 77 (May 1815), p. 35.

Morris, E. E. 'Matthew Flinders'. Library Association of Australia, (Second General Meeting) *Trans. and Proc.* (1900), p. xxiii sqq.

Mountford, Charles P. *Records of the American-Australian Scientific Expedition to Arnhem Land*. Melbourne, 1956–. (See particularly vol. I.)

Mutch, T.D. 'The First Discovery of Australia', R.A.H.S. *Jour. & Proc.*, vol. 28, pt. 5 (1943), p. 303 sqq.

*Nautical Magazine*, vol. 23, No. 1 (Jan. 1854), p. 29 sq.

*Naval Chronicle*, vol. 14 (1805), p. 332 sq.; vol. 28 (1812), p. 318 sqq.; 400 sqq.; vol. 32 (1814), p. 88; p. 177 sqq.

*Orphan* (Calcutta). 3 Feb. 1804.

Parkinson, C. Northcote. *Trade in the Eastern Seas, 1793–1813*. Cambridge, 1937.

—— *War in the Eastern Seas 1793–1815*. London, 1954.

Paterson, George. *The History of New South Wales, from its First Discovery to the Present Time. . . .* Newcastle upon Tyne, 1811.

Péron, François. *Voyage de Découvertes aux Terres Australes, Exécuté par Ordre de Sa Majesté l'Empereur et Roi . . . Pendant les Années 1800, 1801, 1802, 1803, et 1804; Publié par Décret Impérial. . . .* Paris, De L'Imprimerie Impériale, 1807–16. 2 vols. (Tome II, published in 1816, carries the imprimatur: 'De L'Imprimerie Royale, 1816', and omits the reference to the Emperor.)

—— *Voyage de Découvertes aux Terres Australes, Fait par Ordre du Gouvernement . . . pendant les années 1800, 1801, 1802, 1803 et 1804. . . .* Paris, 1824. 2nd edn. 4 vols. & atlas.

Phillip, Arthur. *The Voyage of Governor Phillip to Botany Bay; with an Account of the Establishment of the Colonies of Port Jackson & Norfolk Islands. . . .* London, 1789.

*Quarterly Review*, vol. 4, No. 7 (Aug. & Nov. 1810), p. 42 sqq.; vol. 12, No. 23 (Oct. 1814), p. 1 sqq.

Ralfe, James. *The Naval Chronology of Great Britain. . . .* London, 1820. 3 vols.

Rupert-Jones, J. A. 'Early Australian Surveys: the Story of Matthew Flinders', *Notes and Queries*, vol. 160 (1931), p. 453 sq.; vol. 161 (1931), p. 2 sqq.; p. 25 sq.

Scott, Ernest. *The Life of Captain Matthew Flinders, R.N.*, Sydney, 1914.

—— 'Taking Possession of Australia—The Doctrine of *Terra Nullius*' R.A H.S., *Jour. & Proc.*, vol. 26, pt. 1 (1936), p. 1 sqq.

—— *Terre Napoléon: a History of French Explorations and Projects in Australia*. London, [1910?]

Sharp, Andrew. *The Discovery of Australia*. Oxford, 1963.

Shaw, A. G. L. *The Story of Australia*. London, [1955].

Skelton, R. A. *Explorers' Maps: Chapters in the Cartographic Record of Geographical Discovery*. London, 1958.

Smith, Bernard. *European Vision and the South Pacific, 1768–1850: A Study in the History of Art and Ideas*. Oxford, 1960.

Smith, Edward. *The Life of Sir Joseph Banks*. . . . London, 1911.

Staunton, George. *An Authentic Account of an Embassy from the King of Great Britain to the Emperor of China*. . . . London, 1797. 2 vols.

Stearn, W. T. 'Franz and Ferdinand Bauer, masters of botanical illustration', *Endeavour*, vol. 19, No. 73 (Jan. 1960), p. 27 sqq.

Stevens, John. *The Oriental Navigator*. . . . London, 1816.

Thynne, Robert. *Matthew Flinders or How we have Australia. Being the True Story of Captain Flinders' Explorations and Adventures*. London, 1896.

*The Times*. 27 June, 1801; and 21 October, 1805.

Traill, Henry D. *The Life of Sir John Franklin, R.N.* London, 1896.

Vancouver, George. *A Voyage of Discovery to the North Pacific Ocean and Round the World*. London, 1798.

Walckenaer, C. A. *Vies de Plusieurs Personnages Célèbres des Temps Anciens et Modernes*. Laon, 1830. 2 vols.

Wales, William. *Tables Requisite to be Used with the Nautical Ephemeris*. London, 1802.

Westall, William. *Drawings by William Westall*. London, 1962.

—— *Views of Australian Scenery . . . engraved by Byrne*. [London?], 1814.

Whitington, L. A. *Matthew Flinders and Terra Australis*. Adelaide, 1951.

Williamson, James A. *Cook and the Opening of the Pacific*. New York, 1948.

—— *The English Channel: A History*. London, 1958.

—— *The Ocean in English History*. Oxford, 1941.

# Index